KIBBUTZ
VIRGIN

A BRITISH TEENAGER'S
ACCOUNT OF SIX MONTHS
LIVING ON A KIBBUTZ
IN ISRAEL

JONATHAN NICHOLAS

KIBBUTZ
VIRGIN

A BRITISH TEENAGER'S
ACCOUNT OF SIX MONTHS
LIVING ON A KIBBUTZ
IN ISRAEL

Matador
9 Priory Business Park
Kibworth Beauchamp
Leicestershire LE8 0RX, UK
Tel: (+44) 116 279 2299
Fax: (+44) 116 279 2277
Email: books@troubador.co.uk
Web: www.troubador.co.uk/matador

ISBN 978 1780882 314

British Library Cataloguing in Publication Data.
A catalogue record for this book is available from the British Library.

Typeset in 10.5 pt Stempel Garamond Roman by Troubador Publishing Ltd, Leicester, UK

Matador is an imprint of Troubador Publishing Ltd
Printed and bound in the UK by TJ International, Padstow, Cornwall

To John 'Billy' Sumpton, and Yorkshire.

This is a true story…

Your stay in the Kibbutz

The kibbutz is a communal society in which all
the means of production are owned by the
community as a whole. Private property is
limited to personal possessions. The desire to
establish a just society is the basic principle
guiding kibbutz life, together with a
commitment to undertake tasks important to
the development of Israel and the Jewish
People. It is a classless egalitarian society whose
members do not receive wages or salaries, but
all their needs are supplied regardless of the
kind of work they do.

The kibbutz community is organized through
committees elected for specific periods.
Individual members are elected to act as
managers of the various branches of the
economy and an organizer arranges the day to
day work programme. The kibbutz is not merely
a working community but leads its own cultural
and social life.

Any matters of principle pertaining to the
general running of the Kibbutz are discussed
and decided on in a weekly general meeting of
all the members.

Minimum stay on a kibbutz is one month
We do not consider that a shorter period will
enable you to understand this way of life.

We suggest you take the following clothing

and take into account:

From mid May to mid September the weather is hot and dry. At other times of the year, cold and wet weather may occur and it is well to have clothes suitable for both conditions.

Clothes are laundered in kibbutzim once a week. If more frequent washing is required you will have to do it yourself.

General items
2 towels, toilet requisites, sun hat and sun glasses, anorak or light-weight jacket, sleeping bag (for trips, if you have one).

Girls
Good clothes

2 dresses
3-4 sun tops/short sleeved blouses
1 pair shoes; socks
underwear
1-2 sweaters
2 pairs shorts
1 pair sandals, flip-flops
swimming costume
shower cap
2 pair pyjamas

Working clothes
2 old blouses/shirts
2 pairs shorts
1 pair walking shoes/boots
1 pair working trousers
underwear
1 working sweater
1 hat

Boys
Good clothes

2 pair trousers
1 pair sandals
2 pair pyjamas
socks
4 shirts
2 pairs shorts
1 pair plimsoles
underwear
swimming trunks
1-2 sweaters
flip-flops

Working clothes
2 shirts
4 pairs socks
2 pairs jeans
underwear
1 pair boots
1 hat

Inoculations
It is advisable to be inoculated against tetanus.

CONTENTS

PREFACE

In the summer of 2009 our faithful but rather elderly gas heating boiler finally broke down. I knew it needed replacing because it tried to kill us all one night when we returned from the pub. The carbon monoxide detector was screaming away in the living room as we walked back into the house. A heating engineer subsequently paid us a visit in order to supply a quote for the fitting of a new boiler. He'd been recommended to us by a friend and colleague at my workplace and was a very likeable and reliable chap who lived only a few miles from our house. As I suspected and had feared, in common with the current trend, he decided to locate the new boiler in the attic, or loft as we more usually call the roof space of our house. At that time, our loft was crammed full of household junk accumulated over many years, to the extent that it was very difficult even to get up there, let alone carry up and install a large gas boiler with all the associated pipe work. In fact, there wasn't even a proper ladder to gain access. Anyone wanting to get in, first had to put a chair under the loft hatch at the top of the stairs, balance another article, usually a small waste-paper bin, on top of that, and then haul yourself up like a gymnast practising the parallel bars. So what has all this got to do with Israel and life on a kibbutz? Well, had it not been for this forced necessity to clear the loft in order to make space for the new boiler, this book would not have been written.

In a particularly dark recess of the loft, in a cardboard box, I found a blue plastic folder which had lain undisturbed for, almost, exactly thirty years. In fact, the box was so old and decayed it fell apart in my hands as I tried to drag it towards me. Inside I found a handwritten diary and some photographs. The diary was a Woolworths A4 refill pad and was entitled: *'My visit to Israel'* and dated: *'Sunday 12th*

November 1978 to Monday 7th May 1979'. I could hardly believe I'd found the diary I'd kept of my visit to Kibbutz Dafna when I was a young eighteen-year-old, a diary I'd long since thought had been lost.

I sat cross-legged in happy astonishment in the loft, scanning this old book, holding it gently and reverently in my hands as I struggled to read it by torchlight:

'Day 2. Arrival day. I feel like a lost sheep or someone stranded on Mars – everything is so different – so very far removed from my usual way of life and people I know...'

On my first full day at the kibbutz I was set to work on night shifts in a dark, dirty, and noisy factory. I lived in some rather cramped and Spartan conditions with a group of total strangers. Suddenly, and to my surprise, I remembered the events as vividly as if they'd happened only a few weeks before. I turned the pages and read more:

'Day 22. Sunday December 3rd 1978. Breakfast was great as usual, three fried eggs, some scrambled eggs and two bowls of semolina. At ten o'clock I hitch-hiked into Kiryat Shmona with Chris and Graham...'

The entries continued in great detail and averaged around 400 words for each day, describing everything from the moment I woke up until the time I went to sleep. All the names and events of my time on the kibbutz were recorded, including, written in a rather casual manner, descriptions of the air raids on the kibbutz and on the nearest town, Kiryat Shmona:

'We were woken up at six-thirty this morning by all the windows and walls shaking in our room, and the ground was also shaking... there was some loud thudding and the air raid siren was wailing away...'

I recorded my first Christmas in Israel, then a volunteers' trip to the Sinai Desert, Masada and Jerusalem. There was also a kibbutz romance which blossomed and ended abruptly.

I decided I would use this diary to write a book, detailing my six months living and working at Kibbutz Dafna. I've added some of my own photographs and other items from the diary which may be of interest, including sketches and diagrams I found in the loft with everything else. I have not changed any names, apart from a small minority, so if you stayed on Kibbutz Dafna during this time you may well see your name mentioned. I'm sure anyone who has ever spent any time on a kibbutz may recall similar events from their own stay in Israel. Equally, if you have never been to a kibbutz and wondered what it would be like, then I hope this account may help you to understand the attraction and the lifestyle of a kibbutz 'volunteer'.

I have described my six months in detail, including some of the friendships, the food, drunken parties, the work, and the relentless hot sun and blue sky. Even if you have never even heard of the word 'kibbutz' you may still enjoy the story. I hope so. It all happened exactly as I've written it.

Jonathan Nicholas, February 2012

ARRIVAL

The Interview

I'd heard of Israel, of course, but I knew shamefully little about it. In fact, looking back, I now realise I was as shockingly ignorant as I was hopelessly naïve. I knew only vague details about the conflicts with the surrounding Arab nations, the Palestine Liberation Organisation or PLO, Middle East terrorism and so on. I had some knowledge of and interest in geography, too. I knew the narrow strip of land on the map at the far end of the Mediterranean Sea was where I intended to travel, and where I'd planned to live for at least six months. I could see the region was occasionally in the news and there were some highly contentious political issues concerning the area, but that was about it, really. I'd been to Spain and France on family holidays several times, and so imagined in my rather quaint, old fashioned, middle-class English way, that it would be pretty much the same. The country was as much of a mystery to me as was the reason for my visit, which for the life of me I cannot now remember how it all came about. I vaguely recollect there was some connection to an older cousin of mine, Andy, who apparently suggested with some enthusiasm that we both travel to Israel and spend some time on a 'kibbutz'. Andy went to university instead, and I ended up going without him. I'd never heard of the word 'kibbutz', but I remember thinking it sounded exotic, romantic and strangely familiar, as though I were somehow predestined to be connected to it.

I caught a train to Leeds, from my home city of Sheffield, for an interview. Glancing at the address on the letterhead from 'Kibbutz Representatives', I arrived at the office in good time and rang the doorbell. I was standing at the front door of a large detached house in a prosperous older suburb of Leeds, with tall, mature chestnut trees lining the road on both sides. It was late summer, with just a hint of autumn in the air, and the huge trees shaded the front of the bay window and white-washed walls of the house in a dappled impressionist light. I was quite nervous and unsure of what to expect. I heard someone approach in quick determined steps from inside, on what sounded like a hard stone floor, and the huge, thick door was opened. A tanned, thick-set bearded man in his forties stood with the edge of the door in his hand looking at me briefly, then a great smile beamed out across his face and he ushered me inside:

"Welcome, welcome! You are Jonathan, yes?" he said, pushing the door closed behind me.

"Yes, I am, I have an interview…"

"Yes, come with me," he replied, interrupting me. With a flick of one hand he indicated for me to follow him.

"I am Ori, I am pleased to meet you, Jonathan." He then grabbed my right hand and shook it firmly before dropping it quite abruptly and walking on at a brisk, military pace. He had very thick, curly, fair hair which had as much of a ginger tone to it as it did some encroaching grey. His bushy grey beard fully covered his face, the type with no gaps in growth around the mouth or cheek-bones. He seemed incredibly masculine and physically powerful, and underneath his enviable beard I could see he was most probably a very handsome chap, with quite a square jaw and some chiselled good looks. I immediately imagined he could easily be the type to spend some of his time in Israel, leaping from the back of transport aircraft with an Uzi strapped to his chest.

I was quickly led across the black-and-white chequered tiled floor in the huge churchy entrance hall and up a wide flight of stairs. I was almost running to keep up with Ori, our footsteps clattering, clomping and echoing all around us.

"Jonathan is a Jewish name, you know. You do know this?" he asked, in a strong and distinctive accent I'd never heard before, and which sounded guttural and sloshy, similar to German but with tones of North American English.

"No, I didn't know," I replied, following him from the top of the stairs and into a sparsely furnished and very tidy office, with an astonishingly high ceiling and plain white walls.

A huge desk sat almost in the centre of the room in front of a window. It was laden with books and a small scattering of papers. A large shiny black Olivetti typewriter sat at one side of the desk. The sash window behind was open slightly, and the street was obscured by branches from the chestnut tree closest to the house, some of which I could see were already heavily laden with spiky green conker husks.

"Yes, *Yonatan*, Jewish, you see? It's a Jewish name. Are you Jewish?" he asked, earnestly, as he sat in his chair behind the desk, looking at me and pointing to a nearby chair for me to sit on. I could just see among all the papers my application form sitting plainly on the top.

"No, I'm not, actually. I'm C of E, Church of England. Not that it really means that much, to be honest."

"No, that's okay, it's not a problem! It's good you want to come to Israel, this is *very good,* you know. Have you been before? Do you know what to expect?"

"No. It's my first visit," I replied, a little hesitantly. I could see he was looking at my application form and was nodding and ruminating to himself.

"You will be okay. But you must work, Jonathan, you know this, yes? It can be hard work living on a kibbutz. Everyone *must* work, this is the whole philosophy behind it, yes?"

For the next twenty minutes Ori explained the history of the kibbutz movement, hardly pausing for breath, as though he'd explained the same thing a thousand times before, which he probably had. His pale blue eyes fixed my attention completely as he told me with obvious pride how the many kibbutzim had been instrumental in helping to bring about the State of Israel. His hands flailed and chopped around in front of him as he spoke and I remember thinking I'd never before seen anyone explain anything in quite such an enthusiastic and captivating manner. I managed to extract a few important kibbutz principles from his talk to me that day, such as a strong work ethic, egalitarianism and brotherhood; everyone working together for the greater good of the kibbutz in a communal utopia. It sounded like paradise.

The early afternoon sun flickered through the leaves of the tree immediately outside and danced across the window behind Ori. His voice was beginning to slow, and he seemed to be coming to the end of his talk. He asked me a few questions about my family, and why I wanted to go to a kibbutz. I probably told him something rather silly and vague such as 'for the adventure' or similar. I was young, fit, healthy and willing. It was no real surprise that I passed the interview. I assumed I had passed, as he didn't tell me otherwise.

Ori handed me a form that I was to take home and complete. This was to confirm my intended date of travel to Israel. He then sprang to his feet and grabbed my hand, shaking it vigorously again.

"Jonathan, you will enjoy the kibbutz. Work hard, but have fun too, you know?"

"Yes, thank you," I replied, being more than a little swept along by Ori's highly contagious enthusiasm.

My meeting with him felt right, if you know what I mean; propitious and reassuring. We walked together, slower this time, as though we were now friends, back down the stairs into the cavernous entrance hall. Halfway across the chequered floor, close to the front door, he stopped and shook my hand again, then threw me a warm smile. I heard children's voices from what I assumed was the kitchen of the huge house, and then a woman's voice shouting. It was not an English voice. I'd never heard the language before. I assumed it was Hebrew. Ori paused for a few seconds still gripping my hand warmly, as though he would never let it go. Then, while looking into my eyes very intently, he gave me one final piece of valedictory advice, which I couldn't help thinking sounded a little like a warning:

"You do *know* it will change your life, Jonathan, the

kibbutz I mean. You *do* know this?" We both stood staring at one another for a moment, before Ori suddenly shouted some Hebrew in a clear and commanding voice towards the sound of the children. He turned, and without looking back marched off towards them. He shouted back:

"Goodbye, Jonathan. Enjoy yourself. Shalom!" and disappeared behind the kitchen door. I stood briefly alone in the hallway before stepping over to the huge front door and walking out into the street. I thought about Ori's last remark. I was quite puzzled by this statement at the time. I couldn't possibly have known how prescient his comment would be, and the extent to which my life was about to change.

DEPARTURE

I arrived at Gatwick airport, south of London, in plenty of time. It was Sunday November 12th 1978. I had a small green canvas 'A'-frame rucksack recently purchased from an army surplus store in Sheffield. Inside were two changes of clothing, swimming trunks, a towel, toothbrush, toothpaste, soap, flannel, a sleeping bag and a razor. I also carried a small bag with me as hand luggage, which contained my address book, pens, pencils, a paperback, and my diary. I was a fanatical diary keeper. A little hesitantly, I walked up to the EL AL Israel Airlines check-in desk and was asked numerous security questions by a tall, rather flinty young Israeli woman, with wide hips crammed disproportionately inside a pair of very tight blue trousers, and an equally large chest, which was overhanging heavily in her sharply pressed blouse. She was probably not much older than I was, and had long curly black hair tied down her back with a cheap elastic band, and was actually quite pretty. She spoke with the same distinctive accent as Ori, and chatted briefly in Hebrew to another young woman in uniform, with a huge nose and shiny olive skin, perched authoritatively behind the desk. She checked in my rucksack, weighed it, labelled it, and tossed it casually behind her as though throwing it away.

"You want smoking or non-smoking?" she demanded in a clipped, peremptory manner.

"Non-smoking, please," I replied, handing her my passport and ticket.

"Would you like a window seat?"

"Yes, please," I said, in a rather shy voice, quite surprised I'd even been given a choice.

I thanked them both and took my boarding card and passport. I turned around. They both laughed, a very quick conspiratorial chuckle, which I couldn't help thinking was at my expense. I then walked away in search of Gate Fifteen.

I never tire of flying, any kind of flying. It was particularly in my mind at that time as I'd only just gained a private pilot's licence that summer, following on from quite a lot of flying with the Air Cadets. My head was filled with pre-flight checks, emergency procedures, and endless safety mnemonics. I walked up to the gate and saw a beautiful, huge blue and white EL AL Israel Airlines Boeing 747 parked at right angles to the building, the nose of the aircraft almost touching the windows where I stood. I smiled to myself, my heart leapt, and I could hardly contain my excitement. I had never flown aboard a 747 before. I glanced around and noticed I had an hour before boarding. I wandered over to a row of seats with a view of the runway and sat down. Gradually the seats began to fill up. I took out the only paperback I'd brought with me, *A Postillion Struck by Lightning*, by Dirk Bogarde, and started to read. I heard Hebrew all around me, and the same animated way of talking I saw with Ori, incessant, endless and effusive. I struggled to concentrate on Dirk, so gave up. Then right on time at 1555 the gate was called and there were yet more security checks with passports, a final search of all hand luggage, then down the raised corridor to the plane.

My window seat was above the right wing but slightly closer to the trailing edge. I knew I would be able to see the vast areas of flaps move up and down, and further along the wing the right aileron move almost imperceptibly during flight. Buckled up, safety checks completed, the cabin crew took their seats. The aircraft jolted a little as it was towed backwards a short distance onto the taxiway. Some faint clunking noises from under the fuselage followed as the aircraft tug disengaged, before the engines fired up and the EL AL *Speed Bird* came to life. The massive 300 ton machine eased its way slowly and heavily around the taxiway towards the end of the runway. It had just started to rain. The dark and very dismal black-grey clouds seemed low enough to be almost touching the tops of the buildings as darkness fell suddenly, like a black cloak thrown over the cold, damp, autumnal English afternoon.

The pilot touched his foot brakes and the aircraft stopped.

The engine noise rose for a few moments for the pre-flight check, and the huge wing flaps were lowered ten degrees with a whir and a clunk. The leading edge flaps, which I'd never seen before, popped out of nowhere from the front of the wings. The captain released the brakes and the aircraft taxied onto the threshold area. Before it turned, I saw the full length of the runway through the window to my right. The lights were on and flickering brightly along the tarmac, as the rain now came down hard. I could see it bouncing back up off the tarmac below, and gathering in huge quivering droplets on the outside of my window. Without stopping again, even for a second, once we were lined up the throttles were pushed fully open and the aircraft lurched and roared forwards, gathering speed at an incredible rate.

As though the aircraft was rocket-propelled we thundered down the runway, the tyres thudding faster and faster along the studs on the centre line. The cabin then suddenly rose up at forty degrees and the full weight of the aircraft was briefly and heavily transferred onto the rear main wheels, before the ground left us and we were very smoothly airborne. As soon as we were established into a positive climb the flaps were withdrawn into the wings. In only a few minutes we were through the thick soup of grey and over the top into clear blue sky.

As the cabin levelled out, the crew fussed about and busied themselves in the galley and I could soon smell food cooking. Tea was brought round by tall, slim, dark-haired and shapely stewardesses similar to those at the El Al check-in, and then a meal of chicken, roast potatoes and peas. Everything edible had *Kosher* written on the packaging. The tea was horrible and so was the food. There was no milk in the tea, and there was seemingly none available. The meal was dry and rather tasteless. It wasn't like anything I was used to, but I ate most of it anyway.

I then unbuckled my seat belt and explored the aircraft. It was so huge the toilets were in the middle of the aisle. Near the front I saw the spiral staircase which led up to the flight deck and the First Class cabin area. I walked around the aircraft and sat back down in my seat. Hebrew was being spoken all around me and I soon realised *ken* meant 'yes' and *lo* meant 'no'. I took out my book and settled into some reading. I also made my first diary entry. The flight still had another four hours remaining.

TEL AVIV

The aircraft landed heavily with quite a clumsy bump onto a dark runway at Tel Aviv's *Ben Gurion* airport, and suddenly, as it did so, there was a great human roar from inside the cabin. Everyone around me, in fact everyone onboard the aircraft, started cheering and clapping wildly. I'd never seen anything like it before. It was almost as though some people were having a religious experience. To some it probably was. Before we came to a full stop most people were on their feet gathering their belongings from the overhead lockers, fussing and chattering excitedly, impatiently elbowing their way towards the doors almost as though the aircraft was on fire.

I didn't clear customs until almost eleven o'clock that night. Eventually I stepped outside the air-conditioned arrivals hall into the darkness and felt the heat and humidity for the first time. Despite the fact it was almost the middle of November it was very warm, even so close to midnight. Dark, swarthy men with thick black moustaches and open shirts revealing wide hairy chests were driving large Mercedes taxis, picking people up, apparently arguing about fares, loading their cars with people and luggage, then tearing off into the night towards the city. No-one seemed to be paying me any attention as I stood there, alone, wondering what to do. I could smell car fumes, sweat, and cheap spicy cigarette smoke. Crickets and other insects were loud in the night heat and I started to sweat in the humidity, so decided to retreat back into the airport building.

Utterly clueless as to what I should do at that time of night I decided to find somewhere to sleep, right there on the floor of the airport. I had a rudimentary map of Tel Aviv in my pocket sent to me by 'Kibbutz Representatives' in London, outlining the office in Soutine Street I had to find, but that was all. I thought it would be better to have my first crack at Tel Aviv in the morning, in daylight. I noticed other people were doing the same, young people like me, scattered around in discreet dark corners in their sleeping bags. Part of the check-in area seemed particularly quiet so I opened my rucksack, rolled out my sleeping bag, and nudged myself inside, fully clothed.

At 5 a.m. I was awakened by an airport worker dutifully wandering about with a long and very wide sweeping brush in his hands. The little man in his pressed white uniform indicated for me to move without saying a word, prodding me with his tool as if I was a dead cat he'd found by the road. I stood up and began to roll up my sleeping bag. He frowned a little, then smiled at me and nodded approvingly. I'd actually slept surprisingly well and felt refreshed and ready for the new day. I'd slept on hard ground before when camping, but this was the first time I'd slept rough in a public place, like a homeless vagrant. I packed my belongings into my bag and went into the nearest airport toilets where I had a brief wash and brushed my teeth. I then walked over to a coffee bar area but it was closed. I found an information desk and, though also closed, I discovered I could take an EL AL bus to Tel Aviv Central Bus Station. The first one was at seven o'clock.

I stepped outside into a fine sunny morning. Above me was the deepest and purest azure sky I'd ever seen, vast and flawless as though even the smallest of clouds would never dare to venture across it. It was already very warm and I suddenly felt a surge of well-being, remembering the depressing weather I'd left behind in England. I sat down just outside the building and leant against the wall with my rucksack beside me, and watched the many varieties of people coming and going. When the coffee shop opened at six o'clock, I bought a circular bread bun with sesame seeds sprinkled on it, like a large doughnut, and a very watery coffee. I returned to my vantage point outside and gratefully tucked in. I then caught the EL AL bus to Tel Aviv.

From the window of the bus my initial impressions of Israel were that the countryside appeared dry and dusty, and the streets and buildings seemed cluttered and untidy. It did appear to be not unlike southern Spain, so far. The bus swung into the bus station at break-neck speed, as though the driver was trying his utmost to kill as many pedestrians as possible. To my amazement we didn't hit a single person. Tel Aviv Central Bus Station was legendary, though I didn't know it at the time, of course. There were a dozen rows of long, partly covered bus shelters stretching a hundred yards or more across an area the size of a football pitch. Every few yards there was a standing area with some rather tired looking, dented steel railings where each bus would stop, front end first, at a thirty degree angle. The bus stop signs displayed faded numbers and destinations in Hebrew, with a small English translation underneath, almost as a token gesture. All around the area were shops with stalls which tumbled out into the street right onto the pavement and almost up to the road edge. It appeared these shops sold just about everything from food to cassette tapes, LP records, clothing and cigarettes. There was lots of shouting, car horns blaring, and traffic weaving around a huge preponderance of fast moving buses. The air was thick with the smell of hot spicy food, diesel fumes and cigarette smoke.

Buses continually careered around, recklessly weaving in and out, but no-one seemed to care. My bus pulled up sharply, and the folding door opened with a hiss, a clatter and a bang. We all began to disembark, stepping out while others actually started to try to get on board all at the same time. There were lots of effusive gestures, loud chatter, and shouts of protest from the driver and some of the passengers. It all seemed very chaotic to say the least.

Then there were the guns. There were guns everywhere. Male and female soldiers, most of them young, slim and good-looking in plain green uniforms, and some in pale blue uniforms, were each carrying Uzi submachine guns or M16 assault rifles. Their weapons were slung casually over their shoulders, and they clattered about and occasionally banged on the sides of the buses as they climbed aboard while lugging their hugely cumbersome kit bags.

I managed to find the bus stop which I apparently needed,

a number twelve, and stood waiting. Then I realised I needed a toilet. I scoured the bus station and went in search of a latrine. The legendary status of the place continued once I opened the door of the bus station toilet. I'd never seen anything quite like it before, and hoped never to see anything like it again. The toilet building was a small brick construction with one single WC at the back. The flimsy wooden door didn't appear to have a working lock on it, so I just stood there at the toilet trying to have my pee. I didn't quite know where to aim because there was a pyramid-shaped pile of pooh with a curly bit on top standing defiantly in the toilet bowl, well clear of the water, like an iceberg of excrement. The floor was probably around an inch deep in urine, and the fetid air was thick and buzzing with clouds of the biggest black flies you've ever seen. I padded around slowly, desperately trying to avoid making waves with my shoes, willing and straining my pee to finish as quickly as possible. I was frequently interrupted by others opening the door, seeing me, cursing, and disappearing away. Next to the toilet itself, to my astonishment, I saw a huge pile of *used* toilet paper in the corner which was at least waist high. Pieces of toilet paper were creased into a point where they had clearly been pushed up someone's bottom and were now therefore coated in the resultant brown residue. The flies really loved it. It seemed as though hundreds or even thousands of people had used the toilet and for some reason stacked their many sloppy bottom-wipes next to it, rather than *in* it. Maybe the flush was broken, or wasn't used? Or was the toilet blocked? The smell was as powerful as anything my nose had ever experienced, and formed a fine layer of stench in the back of my throat and in my lungs. It was a kind of raw diarrhoea, sweaty bottom, and nasty stale pee smell, all mixed together. Added to the diesel fumes and cigarette smoke, it was a genuinely unique odour I'd never known before, or since for that matter. Not forgetting, of course, the most important fact that even at that time of the day it was probably ninety degrees Fahrenheit in there…

The number twelve bus took me to Soutine Street, near the town hall. I had to find number twenty-seven, the Kibbutz Office. There were several of these in Tel Aviv, but this was the one on the letter I had been told to report to.

I walked into the office at precisely nine o'clock and introduced myself to a very tall dark- haired woman, probably in her forties, with dark brown leathery skin. She was rakishly thin and had the remains of a white cigarette in her mouth, hanging from some very narrow lips. The smoke from her cigarette smelt spicy and sweet, despite the very pungent toilet smell still lingering in my nose. I immediately recognised this as one of the many smells I remembered from the Central Bus Station. Just as she put it out, she reached for a packet on her desk and took out another cigarette. She offered me one, but I declined. I wasn't a smoker at the time. She then tossed the pack back down on the table. It was the first occasion I'd noticed what was to become one of the most ubiquitous smells quite unique to the country: Israeli *Time* cigarettes.

"So, tell me where you want to go," she said, lighting her cigarette with a match and pointing a finger enthusiastically at one wall of her office. There was a large nicotine-stained map of Israel that was stuck to the wall over each corner, with long strips of once clear sticky tape that had turned yellow with age and the effects of cigarette smoke. I could see hundreds of coloured pins in it, mainly around the edges and borders of the country, clustered in groups with a few dotted singly and in lines. I heard traffic noise outside and the office was becoming quite warm and stuffy.

"These are all our *kibbutzim*," she said proudly, using the plural form of the word 'kibbutz', and looking at the map as though showing me a priceless work of art. "You can go anywhere you want. Which one would you like to go to?" she looked at me, expectantly and yet indifferently at the same time. She took a long pull on her cigarette. Her thin cheeks drew in tightly to her face as she did so. I had no idea which one to choose.

"This looks interesting," I said, feeling obliged to say

something, while moving closer to the huge map. I vaguely aimed a forefinger towards the north, where Israel met Lebanon and Syria.

"Yes, Dafna, that's a *nice* kibbutz," she said, as though relieved I'd made a choice of my own, which clearly I hadn't. I'd just pointed absent-mindedly at the wall.

So that was it, Kibbutz Dafna, about as far north as I could get, and right on the northern border.

נציגות KIBBUTZ
הקיבוץ REPRESENTATIVES

החלוץ באנגליה Hechalutz B'Anglia

College House
Finchley Road, London NW3 5ET
Telephone 01-586 4693/4

LOCATION OF KIBBUTZ OFFICES IN TEL AVIV.

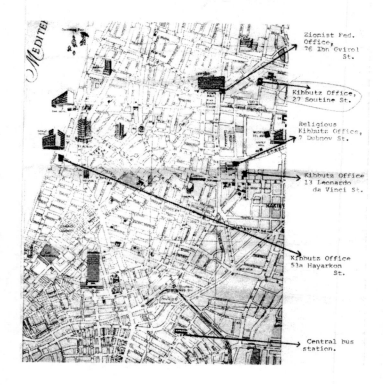

Zionist Fed.
Office,
76 Ibn Gvirol
St.

Kibbutz Office,
27 Soutine St.

Religious
Kibbutz Office,
7 Dubnov St.

Kibbutz Office
13 Leonardo
da Vinci St.

Kibbutz Office
53a Hayarkon
St.

Central bus
station.

16

KIBBUTZ DAFNA

I returned to the Central Bus Station on the number twelve bus and there found the stop to wait for the number 841 bus to Kiryat Shmona. This was apparently the nearest large town in the north closest to Kibbutz Dafna. The blue and white *Egged* (Israeli National Bus Service) bus set off just before ten o'clock. I sat in one of the front seats, near the driver. He had the radio on and it was a relief to hear some familiar pop songs, interspersed with the incessant, gruff chattering of the Israeli disc jockey. The bus was not air-conditioned, so all the windows were wide open. The driver had a small electric fan on the dashboard whirring away next to him, aimed directly at his face. Every time someone clambered aboard the bus they'd say: *Shalom!* When given their change they'd say: *Toda!* back to the driver. Occasionally there was: *Toda roba!* Thank you, then thank you very much, or so I learned.

The flat countryside was extremely pale and arid, as it had been near the airport, with little greenery save for occasional date palms, orange trees, and lemon trees, which filled some fields in haphazard rows. Tall cypress trees, the lower half of which were yellow and brown, discoloured with months of summer dust, lined the roads here and there, particularly at junctions. There were some lush green fields contrasting starkly with the dusty surroundings, with huge automated sprinkler systems in the middle of them, firing powerful thick jets of water a hundred yards or more all around.

The driver of the bus was big and fat, his stomach hanging heavily and uncomfortably over his belt, and his thick hairy arms completely filled the hems of his short-sleeved, pale blue shirt. He gripped the wide steering wheel as though he was wrestling a bear, and seemingly in common with other Israeli bus drivers I'd seen, he drove the vehicle in an almost suicidal manner as if we were being pursued by the police. Heading north we passed a seaside town called Netanya; all the time the beautiful Mediterranean Sea was in the near distance on our left. Then at a place called Hadera the road veered inland and we headed north east, through Afula and then towards Tiberias and the Sea of Galilee. I was in the Holy Land after all, and so some of these place names were vaguely familiar.

Tiberias looked clean, cosmopolitan and fantastic. The Sea of Galilee, or *Kineret* to give it the correct Israeli name, is in reality not a sea at all, but a very large freshwater lake. It looked cool, inviting and wonderful. Boats bobbed around on the clear blue water, and I could see someone water-skiing, cutting wide frothy arcs of brilliant white foam across its surface.

Sadly the bus only stopped for a few minutes before resuming, still further north. A brief moment of panic and regret swept over me for not choosing one of the many *kibbutzim* in this area, before I settled back again in my seat, resigned to my original choice and destination. As we climbed ever higher away from Tiberias, the countryside became greener and more spectacular. My excitement and anticipation began to grow by the mile. I wondered what I would find at the end of the journey. What was going to happen to me? Who would I meet? What would I be doing? Soon I could see the snow-capped peak of Mount Hermon at the very top of the Golan Heights in the distance. It *was* an adventure, and I *was* enjoying every moment of it.

The bus screeched to a halt in Kiryat Shmona Bus Station in typical form, as though it was never going to stop, and I jumped down the steps and out of the door. I tentatively and rather self-consciously muttered my first Hebrew to the driver as I did so, with a very quick *Toda!* when I stepped off the bus. Amidst the noise of everyone else following me out the bus I didn't hear any reply from him. I looked around and soon found the place to wait for bus number twenty-seven to Dafna.

There was a record shop immediately adjacent to and above the area where the buses pulled in, covered from the elements by a seemingly semi-permanent corrugated iron roof. A wire trailed out of the shop and a speaker was hanging untidily high up on the wall outside, from which was emanating some loud and very familiar rock music. I was about to climb the steps to investigate and have a browse, when my bus arrived. Fifteen minutes later, at about three o'clock that afternoon, I was dropped outside the main entrance of Kibbutz Dafna.

No-one else came out of the bus at this stop so the door immediately hissed and banged shut behind me. It was quickly driven off in a cloud of dust and diesel smoke, leaving me standing there alone. I stood briefly with my bag on my shoulder, taking in the sight before me with a mixture of trepidation and nervous excitement. There was a very tall chain link perimeter fence around the kibbutz with a roll of barbed wire on top. A small guard house stood next to the entrance, but it was unoccupied.

Huge wrought-iron gates were wide open and looked as though they were never actually closed, as the ends were partially buried in the dry sandy earth. It looked for all the world like an open prison, or Stalag Luft III – the prisoner of war camp in the movies, or even a weird kind of fortified holiday camp for a weird kind of people.

I walked up the long entrance driveway towards what I perceived was the middle of the kibbutz. I needed to find the kibbutz office, which was the administrative centre and where I was to introduce myself. By this time I was pretty tired, very hungry, and in dire need of a shower. It had been a hot day and I'd been wearing the same clothes for almost forty-eight hours. The main kibbutz office in Tel Aviv had apparently telephoned ahead and prepared Dafna for my imminent arrival. The roads and pathways seemed quite empty as though all the residents were asleep, which on reflection, they probably were. I eventually found a building I assumed correctly was the office, and which resembled a small provincial English Post Office.

I walked in and declared who I was. A diminutive bespectacled woman in late middle age with curly grey hair, barely visible in the semi-dark behind the counter, looked me up and down then abruptly told me to wait a moment, in English and then in Hebrew, shouting at me: *Rega rega!!* She shuffled off and disappeared into the gloom behind a rather ancient looking sprung door which squeaked and flapped around wildly when she pushed her way through it. I heard some chattering then a rather shabby bald-headed little chap with a slight stoop, looking like he'd stepped out the pages of a Dickens novel, emerged from a back room and introduced himself as Yonatan. There was some brief excitement from him at finding out that was also my name, then he led me out of the office and down towards the bottom end of the kibbutz, back in the direction of the main entrance. He didn't speak much, just to say I was being put in a room with some other English lads.

We passed a line of newly-constructed, rather non-descript square block buildings with flat roofs, which seemed to have no windows at all. I was then led to the right and towards a row of very plain looking buildings which were close to, and directly overlooking the main road. Most of the buildings seemed to have an outer skin of pebble-dash under some bright white-washed walls, presumably to assist in keeping them cool inside. Between all the buildings there were grassed areas like well-kept lawns. The sloping roof was covered in overlapping terracotta pan tiles apart from one area on the right which was flat, and similar to some other buildings, apparently windowless. Yonatan nodded occasionally as he walked and pointed at this building and said, 'Here,' a couple of times as we approached it. I was quite relieved, as he seemed to have been leading me in the direction of the main gates. I thought for a moment he was going to send me away.

A few yards in front of the building in which I was to live, there was what appeared to be a large block of concrete about five feet high with several pipes adjacent to it, sticking vertically out the ground. Behind that there was a similar, much larger construction. These were painted in a wavy grey and green camouflage pattern, and the bigger of the two had a steel door at one end. It looked like some sort of air raid shelter, which indeed it was.

THE ACCOMMODATION

Yonatan gave a perfunctory tap on the door of the room closest to the concrete shelter, as though not really wanting anyone inside to hear him. No-one answered, of course, so we both walked in. The room was small, no more than fifteen feet across, cave-like, and despite the windows being fully open, there was a mixed odour of sweat, full ashtrays, stale beer, farts, and bad breath. There were two people lying on beds, apparently fast asleep.

"This is your room," Yonatan told me, in a hushed voice. "That is your bed there," he said,   indicating a very small and saggy steel-framed single bed at the other end of the room, right under the window. It had a mattress that looked as thin as a slice of bread.

"Right, thank you," I said, only half believing him, or perhaps not wanting to believe him. Yonatan then left before I could ask any more questions.

I put my rucksack on the bed and sat down next to it. The mattress and steel bedsprings creaked loudly and worryingly as I applied my weight to the bed and I thought I might fall through it with a crash, so I stood up quickly. I noticed there was what appeared to be a sliding door to my left, which was closed and was probably another room. The walls were plain and rather tatty, as were the blankets on the beds. There were brown stone tiles on the floor, and there was a battered-looking free-standing paraffin heater near the wall on my right. I saw a line of ants crossing the floor from under my bed, heading towards the door. A crowd of them were gathered enthusiastically around what appeared to be a small piece of bread near the heater.

I decided to explore my new home a little more. There was a small, dark, windowless shower room, the floor tiles of which were wet and the drain in the centre of the floor looked

21

as though it was almost completely choked with pubic hair. The shower-head hissed softly and looked as though it dripped constantly, therefore causing a permanently slippery and slimy atmosphere. I was amazed there were no stalactites hanging from the ceiling; the conditions were so damp and perfect. A solitary brown cockroach sat quietly in the corner on the floor of the shower.

Next to this room there was a toilet, the inside of which was streaked and spattered with signs of a great deal of use and very little cleaning. There was dandruff clearly visible on the black plastic toilet seat, so thick in places it looked like drifting snow. Someone had a very poor aim too, as the floor was dotted and discoloured all around with droplets and small pools of a liquid which, judging by the location, could only be urine. There was an even smaller kitchenette area, which merely consisted of a stainless steel sink, a modest area of work surface, an electric kettle, and a wooden chopping board. A small plastic waste bin on the sticky and dirty floor near the sink was overflowing and topped with spent tea bags and cigarette ends, as though it belonged to a house full of first year university students. There was a single cupboard with a few chipped mugs inside, unwashed and stained, and a small fridge. I opened the fridge and found it was mainly full of what looked like beer in brown glass bottles. There was also a carton of milk. I assumed it was milk, as it had a picture of a smiling Friesian cow on it.

In the absence of anything else to do with myself, I decided to make a cup of tea and looked around for a tea pot. It was a hot afternoon, but I didn't think it was yet appropriate for me to help myself to one of the beers, even though they did look very tempting. I plugged the plastic kettle lead into the wall with the flimsy and dangerous two-pin plug, typical of the type foreigners across the world seem to cherish, and it soon started making a low rumbling noise like an oncoming steam train. I then found a very old brown ceramic tea pot, but with no lid. I dropped a couple of tea bags inside and waited. One of the two men on the bed started stirring.

"Are you Jonathan?" said a voice, clearly aimed in my direction, and in an indisputable Birmingham accent.

"Yes, yes, I am," I replied. I obviously wanted to make a decent first impression, so I then asked straight away: "I'm trying to make a cup of tea, if that's alright. Would you like one?"

The figure raised his eyebrows, apparently shocked, but pleased, and said: "Yeah, that'd be great, thanks mate."

I put milk in two mugs, the cleanest two I could find, and mashed the tea. I then filled both mugs and walked over, passing him one.

"I'm Chris," said the blonde-haired chap, now sitting up on his bed, extending a hand. I put my mug in my left hand rather awkwardly in order to shake his right hand with mine, almost spilling my tea, then sat on my bed.

"Where are you from, mate?" Chris said, taking a first slurp of his tea.

"Sheffield," I said. "Do you know it?"

"No I don't. I knew a bird from there once, but I never went myself, you know," he said, smiling at me.

"How did you know my name?" I said, curiously.

"Old Yonatan stuck his shiny little 'ead round the door this mornin' and told us you were on your way. Woke me up he did! He was panicking he was. I've never seen 'im move so fast in all me life! We had to get your bed from the Swedish girl's room next door. There was a Swedish bird sleeping in that until yesterday!" He smiled mischievously and took another loud slurp of his tea. He stood up and walked across to the kitchenette area.

"I need sugar in my tea, Jonathan, I can't drink it without, it tastes like shite otherwise," and Chris dropped two heaped tea-spoons into his mug, and started to give it a slow, deliberate stir. He had shoulder length blonde hair, parted in the middle, and hazel eyes. He was tanned and slim. Not a bad looking bloke really, I suppose.

"How long have you been here?" I asked, conscious of the fact that I seemed to have landed in a very small and already over-crowded room.

"Me and wee Nort have been here since August," he replied, nodding his head towards the chap lying on the other bed. "How long are you thinking of staying?" Chris asked.

"Six months, I think."

The other chap began to stir and groaned a little.

"Have you come here on your own then, Jonathan?" Chris asked, reaching for a pair of brown work boots at the end of his bed.

"Yes I have," I replied, unaware at the time that most 'volunteers', as we were known, came in groups and not usually independently, as I had done.

"Have you been to Israel before?" he asked, now on his feet and buttoning up his shirt.

"No I haven't. This is my first time."

Chris prodded the other chap on the shoulder quite hard with a fist, as only a close friend could, and he then sat up looking as though he'd just come out of a very deep sleep. Without speaking he reached forward and started putting on his work boots.

"We're on the conveyor at four, so we gotta go, Jonathan. We'll be finished at ten, so we'll see you later, eh? This is Graham by the way..." he indicated to the other chap, now also on his feet, and hoisting his trousers up.

I shook Graham's hand, he smiled a little, and then both of them walked out of the room and were gone. I sat sipping the last of my tea, which was truly awful, alone again. There was a small plastic radio on the table next to Chris's bed, so I switched it on. It crackled into life and familiar sounds came from it as I finished my drink. Only a few minutes later the door banged heavily and another chap came stomping in.

"Aye up!" he said as he went straight to the fridge, without even looking in my direction. He took two bottles out and began opening them.

"I'm John. You're Jonathan?" he said, handing me one of the beers. The bottle had *Goldstar* written on the label in English, among some very bright Hebrew writing.

"Yes, I am. Thanks," I said as I took a sip from the bottle. It was fizzy, cool and refreshing.

"From Sheffield aren't you?" John asked. But before I could answer he carried on: "I'm from Menston, near Ilkley, Yorkshire. Best fuckin' place in the world! At least you're from Yorkshire, even if it is Sheffield, not like these other two Brummie wankers!" and he laughed, tipping his beer bottle near vertical and drinking half of it in one go. John told me he had just finished a 10 a.m. – 4 p.m. shift on 'the conveyor' in the kibbutz factory, and had been relieved by Chris and Graham. They would be working their six hour shift together now until 10 p.m. We were only expected to work six hours a day, which seemed perfectly long enough to me! I hadn't known shift working before, so I found this particularly strange. It seemed I was quite likely to be working these round-the-clock shifts too, in the factory. This was something I wasn't prepared for. I thought I'd be asked to pick a few baskets of oranges in the sun every day and that would be it.

John was taller than me, probably six feet two, or thereabouts. He was slim, but not thin like I was at the time. His most noticeable feature was his hair. He had long, shoulder length, mousy-brown hair, which was fine and wispy, and parted in the middle. It wasn't a mess. He clearly looked after it, and I immediately admired him for it. I'd just left school at eighteen but had also just finished five years in the Air Cadets, and so all through my teens I'd been unable to grow my hair beyond it touching the collar. This had been the 1970s too, a time when *everyone* had long hair. I decided at that moment that one of the by-products of my stay would be longer hair.

John strode across the room and pulled open the mysterious sliding door adjacent to the end of my bed. It was his bedroom. I peered inside and could see the walls were obviously smoother and new-looking, and there was one small glass-less window high up on one wall which had thick metal slats over it, controlled from inside. There was a double bed obviously made up of two singles lashed together, and the room was very dark but significantly cleaner and more inviting than the rest of the accommodation. This was actually a relatively new 'blast-proof' room which we were all to rush into in an emergency, apparently, but it wasn't well known as such. In fact, apart from being John's room, he curiously referred to it as 'The Boning Room', while laughing out loud. He didn't elaborate, and I didn't ask. But I had my suspicions. John had a shower and when he emerged a few minutes later with a towel around him he gave me a guided tour of our living quarters, which took all of about five seconds. I showered and changed into my clean clothes.

We talked for a while and then John spent ten minutes drying and combing his hair. I was dressed and ready in five minutes flat. Eventually when we were both dressed, and just as it grew dark, John said:

"Come on, we'll go for dinner."

our Room
NOV '78

THE DINING ROOM

I suppose I latched on to John in those early days, as one would an older brother. You do, when you are thousands of miles from home, and feeling more than a little alone. He seemed to like me and I certainly had no reason to dislike him. He was much older than me at twenty-one, and had a quiet, understated Yorkshire exuberance which appealed to me. He was earthy and amiable, and talked excitedly about his life back home as we walked on the many concrete pathways through the kibbutz. He repeated again how great it was to have another Yorkshire man at Dafna. I was concentrating on trying to remember my way as we walked, so I just nodded appreciatively to everything he said, while keeping very quiet the fact that I was actually born in Norfolk and didn't particularly care a great deal about Yorkshire. He then spoke even more animatedly and enthusiastically about motorbikes and how much he missed his own at home. He told me more than once how he had managed to ride his 750 cc machine from Leeds to his home near Ilkley in ten minutes flat, touching a hundred miles an hour most of the way, or so he said. Of course this was long before the days of all the modern contemptible and ruinous fixed speed cameras spoiling every bit of decent road in Britain. I didn't have a bike myself at the time and I think he could tell I wasn't particularly impressed, though it did occur to me how potentially dangerous it sounded.

As we walked into the dining-room, John's hair flew around his shoulders as he gave it an occasional flick with his left hand to keep it from his face. He was repeatedly accosted by others walking in, mainly Israelis, who would smile and shake his hand with a flurry of Hebrew which John clearly understood and occasionally replied to, also in Hebrew. I quickly learned some of these phrases such as *erevtov,* meaning 'good evening', and *manishma*, meaning 'how are things?' John would confidently throw these words around but then any further past these initial greetings the Israelis or *kibbutzniks* as the members were called, would lapse back into English, probably aware of John's limitations. But I was still hugely impressed.

The dining-room was vast. It could obviously seat hundreds of people. The *kibbutzniks* had their own small houses they could eat in if they wished, but most chose to eat communally in the dining-room. This was, after all, the idea behind the whole thing, the communal lifestyle. There were dozens of yellow Formica-topped tables pushed together in rows, with moulded grey plastic chairs around each one. Large fans, like aircraft propellers turned lazily above our heads in lines along the high suspended ceiling. The majority of the dining-room was occupied by whole families of *kibbutzniks* eating together and talking loudly. In fact the noise was quite deafening, as the entire room was filled with excited chatter, as though all the day's work was being discussed and mulled over, all at once, by a thousand people, which it clearly was.

I followed John and took a tray from a stack at the end of some large free-standing wheeled and heated trolleys arranged in a line across the floor. I walked behind him as we made our way up to the stainless steel containers full of food. I'd never seen so much salad in all my life. Tomatoes, mainly, most of them bigger than tennis balls. Cucumbers, all cut up, hard boiled eggs, soft boiled eggs, some wafer thin slices of processed cheese, and a stainless steel trolley with hundreds of slices of white bread on it. There were large containers full of white liquid and a chunky white mixture which looked similar to cottage cheese. I thought about how many staff it would take to prepare so much food in this fashion on a daily basis and in these quantities. There were a few containers full of what looked like sloppy bits of scrap meat in thick gravy, and several full to the top with large part-baked peeled potatoes, most of them burnt around the edges. Foolishly I declined most if it, despite being very hungry, because of the unfamiliar appearance and the absence of labels telling me exactly what it was. I just took enough salad to make myself a sandwich. It wasn't until years later I realised I'd missed many opportunities to try local food, which I chose not to eat merely on the reserved judgement of its appearance. I've no doubt it could have tasted very reasonable. I noticed people were filling glasses with what looked like lemonade from two taps in the wall. I took a glass tumbler myself and filled it to the top with the clear bubbly liquid and took a sip. It was the worst lemonade I'd ever tasted. It was dry and bitter, similar to an aspirin drink. I was very disappointed. I didn't realise that it was actually soda water. I saw a trolley containing some very promising food that was labelled in Hebrew and English: 'DIET'. This was apparently restricted food for use by diabetics. It looked far superior to everything else on offer.

I sat down with other volunteers and introduced myself. I don't remember who I sat with in the dining-room on that first night, apart from John. I felt quite alone and very apprehensive. There were thirty-one other volunteers at Kibbutz Dafna when I arrived. They all knew each other very well and talked loudly amongst themselves. I felt a complete stranger, excluded from all their conversations, entirely on the periphery of it all, sitting on the outside looking in. It would take some time to get to know them all, if that were possible. As Christmas grew ever closer, quite a few would leave and so I would never get to know them, while yet more would arrive.

That night I lay on my sad little bed wondering what on earth I was doing there. Had I made a huge mistake? The food was awful. The room I was living in was awful. Chris and Graham had described to me their shift on 'the conveyor', which seemed to be a job in a factory where wellington boots were made. The description of the work sounded truly awful, and it included working well into the night, all night on occasions, something I'd never done before. I didn't know how I would cope. It seemed this factory never stopped and was worked twenty-four hours a day.

Someone was continually farting as they lay in their bed a few feet away, and someone, obviously Graham, as Chris didn't smoke, was lying on his bed in the dark smoking cheap foul-smelling Israeli cigarettes. I could hear the shower hissing away in the background and I suddenly felt very hungry, very vulnerable and incredibly alone. It seemed I had little or nothing in common with the people I was sharing the room with, or any of the other volunteers for that matter. The Israelis didn't seem particularly friendly, and there didn't appear to be anything to do other than work in the horrible factory. What on earth *was* I doing there? I was nervous and apprehensive at what might happen to me. I hated it. Then I remembered I'd set myself an arbitrary goal of staying there for six months. Six months! That was 183 days and nights! Why did I do that? I wanted to leave *now*, not in six months!

My diary entry for the end of that day dwelt heavily on this, and was politely understated, in a very British kind of way. The last line for Monday 13th November 1978 was: *The thought of spending 183 days here doesn't seem at all a nice prospect...*

THE WORK

The First Day

I woke up on my first morning to the sound of some very deep snoring from across the room, some more anonymous farting, and what sounded like dozens of chattering house sparrows outside the window next to my bed, so close they seemed to be in the room with me. For a few brief and very surreal moments, I hadn't a clue where I was. I wanted to be at home in the familiar safe surroundings of my own bedroom, my own private, clean and fresh-smelling comfortable bedroom. Lying on my back I looked out the window through the wire mesh fly screen and saw a wonderful clear blue sky. There was a gentle breeze which I could see was teasing the tops of some nearby stone pines, and the idiot sparrows were chasing one another from these trees, back and forth onto the roof of our room. The door to John's room was closed. Chris and Graham lay on their beds in their underpants. Graham's underpants had ridden up on one side and I could see the crack of his spotty white back-side beyond his tan lines. I could see a profusion of pubic hairs, like spiders' legs sticking out around the gathered stretch of Graham's now thong-like and badly stained Y-fronts. I turned my head back to the fly screen window, the blue sky, and thoughts of home.

I had been told I would be allowed to spend my first full day at the kibbutz as a 'free day' as it was known, with no work. I decided I needed to have a good look around in order to keep myself busy, rather than torture myself with further thoughts of home. I dressed and walked disconsolately alone up to the dining-room. I was early, but it was still open for business from seven o'clock, as I walked in.

I was then very pleasantly surprised, not to say relieved, by the food on offer for breakfast: as many fried eggs as I could eat, and a very creamy and thick semolina pudding, which I immediately loved. I had four eggs with bread and margarine, endless cups of tea, and two great bowls of semolina, each spoon of which was nothing less than a spoonful of miracle. I'd been very tired and hungry but now both were gone. My spirits perked up considerably and I chatted briefly to some other volunteers. I then walked over to the huge dishwasher and stacked my plate, bowl and cutlery in a green plastic tray as it moved slowly around on small wheels, before disappearing into the great steaming machine. At eight o'clock I went to the kibbutz office and changed some money for coupons. The kibbutz shop accepted cash, but the kibbutz's own 'coupons' were issued to be used in preference to cash: thin slips of coloured cardboard similar to *Monopoly* money. I handed my passport in for safe-keeping, even though at that moment I could have run for the bus with it like a frightened schoolboy on his first day at boarding school. I knew I had to give the place at least a few days or weeks before I fled. I'd come so far, I didn't want to face the ignominy of running away just yet.

I was told I would earn fifty *lira* a week in coupons, to be spent in the shop. Then at the end of each full month of work on the kibbutz, if I lasted that long, I was to be paid 210 *lira* in cash. Israel was still using the *lira*, divided into a hundred *agorots*, before the *shekel* was introduced in 1980. At the time 210 *lira* was about £7. This was a pittance, but I was surprised we were even given this. I was even more shocked and pleasantly surprised by just how far the English pound would reach when exchanged for Israeli *lira*. I had fifty pounds in my passport. I hoped it would last me my entire stay, however long it would be.

Imbued with some renewed positivity from a wonderful breakfast, I decided to find out how big the kibbutz was. I walked up one of the many paths and within a few minutes I reached a fence where the buildings came to an end, and there was some scrubland like a sterile area fifty yards across. Then there was a very substantial, well-maintained and formidable barbed wire fence. There was also an old metal watchtower, probably fifteen feet high, so I climbed the ladder and looked out from inside. This was the north end of the kibbutz with hills in the near distance, and Mount Hermon standing prominent and very beautiful away to the right. There was snow on the very top of the mountain and it appeared almost three-dimensional and crystal clear, outlined as it was against the deep blue sky. The fresh air was sharp and clean, and I wondered just how far away the border was with Lebanon. I didn't realise at the time that I was actually looking at it, and that this north fence of the kibbutz pretty much *was* the border! I climbed back down the rusted ladder and followed the path back into the kibbutz. There was a river running through Dafna, the Dan, and it added hugely to the tranquil beauty of the place. It seemed more like a wide stream than a river, with trees and bench seats dotted around very much like a picnic park. I imagined I would find it a brilliant place to sit and write my diary.

I returned to the room to find Chris and Graham leaving for breakfast. They were then going straight to work. Yonatan had also brought me some kibbutz clothes, which consisted of a pair of blue cotton trousers and a blue shirt with red buttons. This was standard work attire which everyone seemed to wear, almost like a uniform. I remember that first workless day was very quiet for me. I sat around, alternately reading, sleeping and sitting in the sun.

I loved the warm sunshine. This had to be better than the cold, dark, English November days I'd left behind. I did little else other than perhaps occasionally talk to John, and chat briefly now and then to some other volunteers.

Just after four o'clock that afternoon when they finished their shift on the conveyor, Chris and Graham decided to take a trip into Kiryat Shmona, taking me with them. I was glad of the company, as John had gone to work. Maybe they could also tell that I was feeling more than a little despondent and needed cheering up. We stood on the road outside the kibbutz gates and hitched a lift in the back of a massive truck. We scrambled aboard like fleeing refugees and had a laugh as we were rolled around in the back, unable to hang on to anything. Hitch-hiking was common in Israel at the time, particularly among soldiers. It seemed almost as though drivers had a legal obligation to stop. We didn't have to wait long for a lift anyway. Slightly bruised and battered but aching from laughing all the way in the back of the truck, we jumped down and thanked the driver, who was an Arab. He must have known we'd been thrown around as we were, so he probably also had a laugh to himself about it as much as we did!

Kiryat Shmona is seven kilometres west of Kibbutz Dafna. It sits at the base of some incredibly steep hills and dark vertiginous cliffs, which rise a thousand feet above it on one side. Though not a large town, it is the most northerly in Israel. The majority of the buildings appeared to be quite plain, sectional apartment blocks three or four storeys high and each one seemed to have its own *miklat*, or air raid shelter, similar to the ones at Dafna. In fact there were *miklatim* all over the place; in the main square, on street corners, seemingly everywhere. The border with Lebanon threaded its way around the northern edge of the town and was apparently just over the top of the hill. Kiryat Shmona was therefore a prime target for terrorist attack, though I was unaware of this at the time.

Chris and Graham changed some travellers' cheques in a rather dark and austere bank in the centre of the town called Bank Leumi Le-Israel BM. We crossed a modern looking precinct and into a small café bar. There was a single hand-pumped cask beer sold in chunky pint glasses with handles, just like in most English pubs. The three of us sat at a table near the bar. It was great to sit and drink pints of beer with these two lads. I began to feel at ease for the first time since my arrival. It was good to get to know Graham. They were both twenty-two and from Dudley in the West Midlands, and so Graham also had a strong Birmingham accent, or 'Brummie' as it was known. Despite the fact they hadn't actually lived in Birmingham, people who spoke with such a regional accent were known as 'Brummies'. They'd travelled to Israel together, they were very close friends, and had been on Kibbutz Dafna since the end of August.

Graham was quite a small chap, about five feet seven inches or thereabouts, with collar length fair hair and a thick brown bushy beard. He had bags of energy which in some ways directly balanced and complemented Chris's calm almost phlegmatic approach to life. Graham wore a shiny black leather jacket wherever he went, even to work, which appeared to be at least two sizes too small for him. They were good company.

We finished our first pint of cask Goldstar quite quickly, so immediately decided on another. I remember standing at the bar, perched on the tall bar stool, ordering more beer as dusk fell. A warm breeze was picking up and blowing smells of spicy food into the bar from somewhere close by. I was just starting to feel a very pleasant afternoon beer-buzz following the second pint, when we left the bar and walked towards the bus station. We stopped at a stall selling warm pita breads filled with hot spicy balls of chick-peas and crisp salad, where I ate my first and very delicious *falafel*. The three of us then climbed the steps into the record shop above the bus stop, and began browsing through the LPs. I found some *Genesis* LPs and showed one to Chris. The next moment he took it from me without saying anything and walked over to the counter with it.

"Put this on for us will you, mate?" I heard him ask in his thick Brummie accent. The man took it from him, slid the LP deftly from its cover and dropped it onto the turntable. The three of us stood outside the shop leaning on the rail overlooking the bus stop, finishing the last of our falafels. Just then, *A Trick of the Tail* crackled out from the speaker hanging on the outside wall. This was some of my favourite music. How could I not enjoy this?

Back on the kibbutz we walked up to the dining-room for dinner. Salad again! Later on, to my surprise, there was a movie. The kibbutz had its own cinema, and at nine o'clock we all filed in to see the film, *Rollerball* starring James Caan. I'd seen it before, several times, and loved it. I loved the music: Shostakovich's *Fifth Symphony,* and Albinoni's *Adagio for Strings.* I loved the whole principle behind it too, that of one man standing up alone against 'The System'.

After the film, we called in at the kibbutz office. On the door outside, the daily 'work list' had been published. This was usually written by a *kibbutznik* and a volunteer together and consisted of a list of printed names with the next day's job for each volunteer hand-written against each name. I saw my name at the very bottom, as a new arrival, obviously written quite hurriedly in pencil. My first day at work was to be the 4pm to 10pm shift on 'The Conveyor'.

THE DAFNA WELLY BOOT
SLAVE LABOUR COMPANY

I didn't get out of bed until eight-thirty on my first working day, Wednesday 15th November. I suitably stuffed myself with a large number of wonderful fried eggs and two bowls of lovely thick semolina before returning to the room. I wondered what on earth I was going to do with myself until four o'clock. I couldn't really do much or go anywhere, and couldn't drink any beer or otherwise risk being late for work, certainly not on my first day. I'd never experienced this situation before, where I was just literally waiting around all day in order to go to work. It occurred to me then what a waste of time it was, and that I could be at work now, getting it done, instead of hanging around. But of course, this was the nature of shift work. So I sat around all day again, intermittently sleeping and reading. I was now halfway through *A Postillion Struck by Lightning,* and had found a comfortable spot in the warm sun, sitting on top of our nearest *miklat*, the air raid shelter just outside the door to our room.

At three-thirty in the afternoon I put on my ill-fitting and very baggy kibbutz issue blue work trousers and shirt, and walked up to the factory. I found Chris and Graham inside, standing at the conveyor. They both laughed and cheered when they saw me and eagerly called me over to them. They were keen to show me how the job was done so I stood behind them and tried to take it all in. I could count on one hand how many times I'd ever been inside a factory of any sort before then. When I was young my father had been a manager of a pewter company in Sheffield for a while and I'd seen inside his place of work on a few occasions. Dafna's factory seemed very similar.

The place smelt strongly of burning plastic, sweat and cigarettes. There was a raised wooden platform about a foot high, a yard deep and about eight feet wide. This was the business end of the whole machine, and where we worked. Dozens of steel moulds of wellington boots were fixed about two yards apart to a large oval shaped, chain-driven contraption about thirty yards long, which was powered by numerous electric motors pulling it around at a more or less even pace. It was a very noisy machine, with the constant humming of the motors and occasional hissing and clicking of suction and injection moulding.

The whole thing looked incredibly arcane and dangerous. Every surface was layered in a thick patina of grease and dirt. Even the walls and ceiling were black with some sort of sooty deposit, which caused the place to have a dark cave-like atmosphere. There were open, red-hot heating elements, like those from an electric fire but ten times larger, all along the process in order to keep the metal boot moulds warm. The boots were finally passed into water just before the platform where we stood, in order to cool them prior to extraction. Then the empty moulds were re-heated and injected with plastic and the whole process started again. All this machinery and the heating elements were completely unguarded, as far as I could tell, and as I watched Chris and Graham I wondered what would happen if one of the steel moulds was missed and you therefore had to go clambering about on the machinery, much like Charlie Chaplin in the movie *Modern Times*. Because the platform was only about eight feet wide and the moulds passed at a constant speed, you only had about ten seconds or less to extract the plastic boot from the mould. You can imagine how hot it was in the factory with dozens of these electric elements blazing away so open and exposed.

I stood on the platform and took hold of one of the two strange looking sucker devices for the first time. It was hanging from the machinery above me on a sprung line, with an air hose into it and a power lead. It was a weird instrument, shaped like an enormous, shiny, stainless steel lollipop about a foot long. It was pointing at the ground and had air holes in it, a handle grip on each side, and a small black button on one of the grips. The idea was to ram the device as hard as you could, deep into the steel welly boot mould, then press the button to start the suction. Once a firm seal had been made the boot could then be heaved out from inside the mould, all in one quick movement. That was the idea. At that time I was quite thin and asthenic, with arms like pipe-cleaners, so I wasn't hoping for great results.

On reflection, I think everyone, certainly all the male volunteers, were deliberately started on the conveyor, to see if they could do it. I was immediately and very obviously rubbish at it. I would guess most people find it challenging at first, but it remained a difficulty to me for the whole of that first six-hour shift. I missed so many boots that I found myself clambering all over the damned 'Heath Robinson' contraption numerous times, straddling the moving chains and red-hot elements, trying in vain to recover my pride in a stubborn and dangerous attempt to do what I should be doing. On each such occasion, Arnon, the *kibbutznik* in charge at the time, had to press the large red emergency stop button on the machine. This was quite unheard of, but probably very necessary in order to prevent me from killing myself. The whole process then had to be restarted. I would guess a dead volunteer caught up in the workings would probably cause a huge amount of inconvenience and delay production for some considerable time. I felt like a cross between Charlie Chaplin and Norman Wisdom, completely and utterly inept. But I really did try my best. After failing to pull one boot from a mould I stupidly let the suction device fly from my hands and it swung around wildly in a wide semi-circle and struck me hard on the side of my face, dangerously close to my left eye, as though punishing me for my ineptitude. Blood poured from a quarter-inch gash and Arnon ran off, returning moments later with a first-aid box and some plasters.

I was working with a chap from London called Guy. He was quite well-built and found the conveyor no problem at all. In fact he despatched me off to the factory canteen area to get two coffees several times while he successfully operated it himself, alone, when it was meant for two. At six-thirty I was sent off to have my meal in the dining-room. I was unused to such physically demanding work so I was very hungry. When I came back, Arnon took over from Guy so he could take his meal break. The two of us pulled and dragged the boots out of the moulds; Arnon very quickly, casually and successfully, and me struggling away next to him, a little better than hopeless. I stood to the right of Arnon, so when I missed one, which was often, he could then take over, patiently pushing me to one side with the occasional "*Rega, rega!*" or "Wait, wait!"

Thirty minutes later, Guy returned. After four hours I was exhausted. It was at this point that I smoked my very first cigarette. I was so desperate to impress, and was failing so miserably, Guy offered me an Israeli *Nelson* filter cigarette. Even though I told him I didn't smoke he said:

"Oh go on, it'll keep you going..." and offered me the pack. I eventually took one, and wedged it between my lips. He lit it for me, smiling, just before he lit his own. I sucked in the smoke and coughed quite stereotypically, but carried on. I didn't know *how* to smoke a cigarette. Did you suck the smoke straight down, or fill your mouth up with it first, *then* suck it down, or a combination of both? Without thinking, I drew the smoke into my mouth for an instant before pulling it down deep into my lungs, my lovely, healthy, smoke-free lungs. For a few moments I felt a little light-headed, but otherwise I don't think it had any effect at all, and was a waste of my good health. It may have served some purpose in taking my mind off the work for a while, but it didn't cause any improvement in my abilities.

I remember the last hour of the shift finished reasonably well. There was a dusty speaker hanging from the ceiling right next to us, and the radio played Tchaikovsky's *Sleeping Beauty* all the way through. I walked out of the factory, which was colloquially known as: *The Dafna Welly Boot Slave Labour Company*, at ten o'clock that night. I was truly exhausted. I made my way across to the office to check the work list. My back and head ached and my hands had developed some huge blisters, as though I'd been rowing in a *Ben-Hur* galley ship for the last month. I scanned the bottom of the list for my name. Shit. I was back at the factory in less than six hours, at four in the morning, on something called: 'Zipper'.

THE ZIPPER

The next morning I woke up very early, dressed, and walked into the factory at four o'clock. It was still dark. I could hear the hissing and clattering of the conveyor in the next room as I walked around looking for the *kibbutznik* in charge. Arnon was nowhere to be seen but another *kibbutznik*, Ishi, a thin chap with receding black hair and beard, took me to another miraculous-looking factory contraption, and I was shown 'The Zipper'. This was a circular machine, like a large thick dining-table, with three work-stations around it. All three workers stood at the machine but only one had the controls in front of him. Each person placed a pair of boots onto the machine in line with a series of dots. After this the worker would take a pair of zips from a cardboard box and align them carefully on the boots. The machine would then stamp the zips onto each boot, heat-sealing them permanently in place. I'm pleased to say I quickly grasped this practice and was soon quite proficient at it.

There was a young *kibbutznik* in charge of the machine, who told me his name was 'Eagle', (in actual fact it was *Yigal*) and one other volunteer besides myself at the zipper. Working at our fastest we could each put zips on a pair of boots almost every twenty seconds, and I was very relieved I had found something I could do successfully. The work was much less physically demanding than the conveyor, but it was less challenging, and therefore quite repetitive and boring. But at least I could do it. Just as at the conveyor work-station, there was a loudspeaker close to where we worked, and an Israeli radio station blasted out all the current chart hits which made the time pass much quicker. It wasn't too noisy at the zipper so we could easily chat to one another, which I was soon to learn was the best way to pass the time while working.

Talking to other people about their lives was not only interesting but absorbing and distracting, provided certain subjects were avoided, such as religion and politics. Chris and Graham gave me some advice along these lines soon after my arrival and I often saw them in action. I once observed Chris put an arm around Ishi in the factory and tell him, in his broad Brummie accent:

"Yoh could run this place on your own yoh could, Ishi. Yoh could re-name the blessed thing 'Ishi's Boot Factory', 'cos yoh so bloody good at it, isn't he Graham?" with Ishi staring at Chris and looking rather bewildered. I'm not sure he understood Chris's accent but he no doubt realised there was a compliment in there somewhere. Chris seemed naturally very good at such apparently sincere laudatory banter and could turn on the charm with everyone, including, as I soon learned, the ladies. It was all about breaking the ice and finding some common ground to chat about, such as people's likes and dislikes, certain personal issues, their relationships and even sex. This led to a more light-hearted convivial conversation, particularly between men. I was not a naturally loquacious person and so it took me a while to learn that good 'small-talk' is in fact an art form in itself. If done well, it could really pay dividends. In simplistic terms it starts with picking out something positive from the person you are talking to and perhaps offering them a compliment connected to it, in order to draw their attention. Then there's a listening process involved to make them think you are interested, before you can talk about yourself. But the idea is to let them do most of the talking; no one likes a self-centred, egotistical bore.

I went for breakfast at eight o'clock until eight forty-five. When I finished work at ten I walked back to the room and had a shower. I wrote in my diary, which I kept under my mattress, and read some more. The room was very quiet as John was at work and Chris and Graham were away for a few days on a trip to the south of the country. Volunteers were allowed to collect 'free days' by working overtime and on Saturdays. These could then be taken together, several days at a time, as they frequently were.

At twelve-fifteen I had a lie down on my bed and fell asleep. John woke me up when he came in at one o'clock. I walked up to the dining-room for lunch alone, as John didn't bother. When I returned to the room only fifteen minutes later I had another sleep. I was almost constantly tired from all the physical work, which I was not used to at all, and my entire body ached as though I had the 'flu. I also half expected to be back at the factory that night, so wanted to be fully prepared for either the conveyor or standing at the zipper most of the night. I woke at five o'clock just as it was getting dark. I wrote in my diary and then went for dinner. To my pleasant surprise, I saw from the work list that I was *not* due to work that night in the factory, but to work a split shift in the kitchens the next day.

DAFNA BELLY

John came in at four-fifteen in the morning from working on
the zipper, and other than a slight disturbance from that and
initially wondering who on earth was stomping through our
room in the middle of the night, I slept right through until ten
o'clock. I'd missed the lovely breakfast so entered the dining-
room at eleven-thirty intending to eat lunch. I then realised I
had some quite strong stomach pains, so returned to the room
without eating anything. Walking back from the dining-room
my stomach felt as though someone was dragging it through a
mangle. I needed a latrine, urgently. As the room came into
view I found I had to walk the last few yards in tiny mincing
fairy steps, twiddle-toed, with my buttocks clenched together
as tightly as possible, while still trying to walk.

As soon as the skin of my bottom touched the plastic of
the toilet seat there was an explosion and a massive rush of
liquid pooh which just kept on pouring into the toilet like a
bath tap on full. I had no idea my body could contain so
much liquid! I sat for a few minutes in order to catch my
breath and to be sure the flood had stopped. When I felt brave
enough, and when I felt a little better, I stood up and staggered
into the kitchen. I lay on my bed for a while then staggered
back to the kitchen area and made myself tea without milk. I
sat on the front step of our room sipping it slowly, hoping it
would help, while watching the occasional vehicle pass by on
the main road. I'd obviously acquired some sort of stomach
bug, and decided to starve it to death by just drinking sweet
tea, with no milk. I'd been told this was the best thing to do in
the circumstances.

I started work in the kitchens at twelve-thirty. I felt very
weak. Every movement was a monumental effort. I was
detailed at cutting up gherkins. This sounds easy, but there
were hundreds of the damned things. At least I could stand

still and didn't have to move about. I had continuous waves of wrenching stomach pains and handling the food only seemed to make it worse. I was amazed I didn't throw up everywhere, but I was so hungry there was probably nothing left to come up. Despite being distracted by my condition, I couldn't fail to notice I was one of very few men working in the kitchens. Not only that, I could see a number of female volunteers working there, and managed to speak to a few of them. It was my first real sight of the dishwashing machine too, and how it was operated. It did cross my mind about the possibility of working there all the time. It looked far easier than the conveyor and the working conditions were a great improvement too. It reminded me of the very few 'home economics' cookery lessons I had at school as a teenager; standing at a warm oven baking wonderful pies in the middle of winter, as the rain lashed heavily against the windows, while my other schoolmates outside were soaking wet in the freezing cold, trudging about like idiots in the mud trying to play football.

I finished at two-thirty and returned to the room. I completely emptied my insides again on the toilet and briefly felt a little better. Then it all started brewing and bubbling once more and I had to mince back to the toilet. This process was repeated several times until finally, and thankfully, it came to a stop. The stomach pains were then replaced by chronic hunger pains, which I then satiated a little with endless cups of milk-less tea, as I found I was also extremely thirsty. I read a copy of that day's *Jerusalem Post*, an English language newspaper I'd found in the dining-room. John and I then had a good laugh at my expense, as I read my descriptions and early impressions of the kibbutz and the room from the first few pages of my diary. At six o'clock I returned to the dining-room for three hours more work in the kitchens, mainly sweeping up, hosing down and lifting containers about.

Everyone greeted one another that Friday night affectionately with the words *Shabbat Shalom!* and the dining-room was much busier than usual. People lingered and chatted far longer than the previous nights, and I couldn't finish work until everyone had gone. By nine o'clock I was beginning to feel better. After returning to the room and having a shower, John and I went to another volunteer's room at the other end of our block where it was rumoured there was some sort of party. Indeed there was, and one of the Israeli lads, Motty, brought a huge stereo radio cassette player to the party. Pink Floyd's *Dark Side of the Moon* was promptly selected and set to full volume, and more people crammed into the tiny room, all with bottles of one sort or another in their hands.

I'd been on Dafna all week and this was the first such 'party' I'd been to. They usually started with a rumour among a few volunteers which seemed to spread like a bush telegraph around the whole kibbutz, as indeed did any other type of news or gossip. I soon learned that these 'parties' were most of the time not actually a celebration of anything in particular, but merely an excuse to fill one of the tiny rooms with as many people of both sexes and as much alcoholic drink as possible and see what happened. This one was very well attended.

There was no work the next day, Saturday, so on Friday night it seemed everyone decided to go a little bit mad. The intention was clearly to get as drunk as possible in as short a time as possible. It was also an excuse to grab hold of someone you'd probably been keen to get a grip of all week but had been too busy, shy, or sober to do so. There was a lot of pairing off of one sort or another anyway. Israeli vodka is rather rough to say the least, but the quality of the drink is much improved by the abundance of real oranges freshly squeezed into plastic jugs then thrown away. I don't think my condition prevented me from having a drink that night, and from what I can remember I thoroughly enjoyed it. The stomach bug, if indeed I had one, most probably died a slow death from alcohol poisoning.

SCROT-ROT

I woke up very late at eleven-thirty to the usual bright sunlight and cacophony of chattering sparrows. I was extremely hungry. John was pottering about in his room, having only just woken up himself. We dressed and walked together to the dining-room. I was very thirsty and drank a couple of glasses of soda water. We didn't eat much of the food on offer. The last thing anyone wants to eat after a night's drinking – and a day spent on the toilet – is salad. John winked at me and disappeared into the back of the kitchens and came out moments later with a large uncut loaf of fresh bread. We returned to our room and cut it into thick slices. We then toasted it over the paraffin heater, and ate it with lashings of margarine and strawberry jam. Our room quickly filled with a very satisfying and homely smell of warm toast and paraffin, and in twenty minutes we'd eaten the whole loaf between the two of us! Both my hunger pains and other stomach pains had gone, which I was very relieved about. Following our afternoon feast we cleaned the room. We had an Israeli flag which we fastened to the wall where there used to be a British flag, which we then threw away. We optimistically hung a washing line in the damp shower room, then cleaned out the fridge, swept the floor, and John fixed a curtain over his sliding door. The room was clean and orderly with tidy floors and neatly made beds. It looked much better.

At four o'clock, John took me with him to Guy and Tim's room. I knew Guy quite well, as I'd worked with him that first night on the conveyor, or more accurately, I'd spent the night watching him work. John and I sat down on Tim's bed and settled with our backs against the wall. Tim was lean and tanned, like most people who'd already spent some time on the kibbutz. He had shoulder-length, curly fair hair that was slightly frizzy at the ends, like a young Robert Plant from the band Led Zeppelin. I started browsing through their tape collection, which was quite comprehensive and neatly arranged in a shallow wooden box, which had once carried Israeli tomatoes. Most of the contents were comprised of 'mix tapes' as was the trend at the time. To my great delight, I found a copy of *Seconds Out,* the 1977 live double album by the British progressive rock band Genesis, which was then my favourite music. It had been home-recorded onto a lengthy Agfa 120 cassette tape and was the soundtrack to my previous summer when I'd taken my final exams at school. I knew every single word of the lyrics. I lifted it carefully from the box and Tim discreetly nodded approval, while glancing across at me. He then handed me a beer. I slotted the tape into the machine, and pressed the play button.

The conversation then centred around the current rumours about health issues on the kibbutz, and there was great amusement for all those present when I told them about my recent stomach upset, or 'Dafna belly' as 'the shits' were alternatively known. It seemed almost everyone had a similar experience in the first few days of arrival on the kibbutz, with some suffering more than others. Whether it was actually a bug or merely a complete change of diet, I'll never know. There was a lot of alcohol being consumed along with a great deal of fresh food and fruit, so this could be a factor. It could also be connected to a lamentably low standard of hygiene in the volunteers' rooms, and in particular those solely occupied by male volunteers. The few rooms I'd seen so far that were occupied entirely by females, definitely appeared cleaner and much more tidy, and lacked the defining odours common to most of the lads' rooms.

I was enjoying listening to Genesis, when the conversation inevitably then centred on toilet humour and some recent sexual exploits. John mentioned Guy's health in particular and started laughing to himself. It was a cheeky, conspiratorial, schoolboy kind of laugh, which then caused Tim to throw a knowing smile across the room towards me through Phil Collins' singing. Guy obviously felt the need to say something so he looked straight at John and said rather accusingly, in his north London accent:

"I'm okay now. They reckon I can be back in business any day…"

"Bollocks," John immediately retorted, probably unaware of the irony in what he'd just said. "There's no way! You only went to the clinic two days ago!"

"They fuckin' said it, not me! So tomorrow night, you and me, Billy boy, Tiberias here we come!"

I looked around the room and wondered for a moment who Guy was talking to until I clicked for some reason John had acquired the nick-name 'Billy'. I probably knew I shouldn't have asked Guy what his complaint was, but I did anyway:

"What's been the problem, Guy?" I said, as he then turned and looked blankly at me, as if deciding whether nor not to tell me, or to pick me up and throw me out the room. He took a quick swig of beer from his bottle, and looked at John and Tim, who both seemed to be trying very hard not to laugh. He then stood up, and positioned himself bodily in the centre of the room. He gripped his crotch tightly with his left hand and raised his head as though about to make a proud announcement to the whole world. He then shouted very loudly:

"Fuckin' scrot-rot, that's what! A touch of the old 'ball-bag crumble'!"

There was a brief deafening and embarrassing silence, during which I deeply regretted asking the question in the first place, then the whole room burst out into uncontrollable hysterics.

We drank more beer, and then the four of us were joined by two other lads who I didn't know. As the six of us left the room and walked across the lawn slowly, we were joined by a seventh who walked in front with a cross and rather stern expression on his face, as though keen to show us the way. We then went out of the gates of the kibbutz, most of us laughing and talking loudly. We walked a few hundred yards up the road to a place called She'ar Yashuv. This was not a kibbutz, but a *Moshav*. It was similar in every way to a kibbutz but the residents apparently lived less of a communal lifestyle and were allowed to keep more profits for themselves. It looked exactly the same as a kibbutz. There was a very slight trace of an autumnal coolness in the air as the afternoon sun fell quickly behind the nearby hills above Kiryat Shmona, while we noisily stomped our way along the tarmac. We paid five *lira* each to get into their cinema, and watched a very poor US film about an Englishman in the Wild West who had become a gunslinger. I don't even remember what it was called.

We returned to Dafna after the film and drank a few more beers. At nine o'clock, to my surprise, not to mention disappointment, the work list stated I was to work on the conveyor again at four o'clock the next morning.

THE PLAY

The P-51

The alarm clock rudely snapped me out of a very pleasant deep sleep at ten minutes to four. I'd been having some very strange dreams. I dreamt I was working the conveyor with my sister Sally, and together we were both making a complete mess of it, despite some very attentive supervision from my brother-in-law, Malcolm. Again I wondered where on earth I was for a moment, as I lay there wide-eyed in the darkness. Just for an instant I thought I was at home in my own bed. Then the awful thought of another shift in the factory swept over me and I reluctantly rolled out of bed. I realised I was a little hung over and I dressed like an automaton in the dark and trudged straight up to the factory.

Arnon was clearly wearing his feelings on his face that morning, as his expression seemed to drop visibly when he saw me. He sent me straight into the open area between the zipper and the conveyor. There were racks of boots slotted onto long wooden pegs with the bottom of the boots facing up at a slight angle. Boots which had been pulled from the moulds needed to be hung up to cool completely before being sprayed black, in order to make them look like leather. This was just the next part of the process. There were hundreds of them. They needed to be hung quickly to preserve their shape in readiness for spraying, and at this point some quality control checks could also be conducted on them.

So it was that I spent my first shift 'hanging boots'. It was obviously a great deal easier than 'pulling' boots but a lot less demanding and so the time passed quite a bit slower. The worst boots were the long ones, as the tops flopped about and so were not as easy to drop down onto the hangers. Sometimes there would be shorter, ankle-length boots which were quicker and easier to hang. In order to help pass the time I often set targets for myself to beat the machine; I'd work frantically as fast as I could to hang the batches of boots as soon as they came from the conveyor. I managed occasionally to achieve a short break as the gap in production at one point was up to twenty-five boots. This meant there would be no boots to hang for a while and so it allowed me three minutes in which I could quickly run to the small factory canteen and make myself a coffee and return with it before the process started again.

Other volunteers were pulling the boots and I was asked to relieve them for breakfast. Luckily the line was then producing smaller boots, and I found these easier to pull as well as hang. I was still rubbish at it though, and struggled frequently. I don't remember anyone ever formally showing me around the factory but it *was* interesting how gallons of hot, ochre-coloured liquid plastic at one end was turned into smart looking, faux-fur-lined, zip-up boots at the other, all in less than an hour or so. They were not actually wellington boots, in the true sense of course, but I suppose up to where the bottom of the zip started they would be waterproof, due to them being moulded in one piece. Further along the line there was a paint spray area where one person usually stood with a spray gun in hand, wearing gloves and a face mask. This job was usually only trusted to a *kibbutznik,* and the only chap I ever saw doing it in those early days was an athletically-built and very convivial black man called 'Ethiopian Paul', a man who seemed to be constantly smiling and laughing, even while at work. Finally, the fake fur lining was fixed into the boots using some very thick strong-smelling glue, a process which I was never involved in. They were then put into pairs and boxed up for onward sale. There was a small circular trademark on the sole, which said *Dafna Boots* in English and Hebrew. I quite enjoyed the 'hanging boots' process but found this the slowest of the jobs I'd done so far. At least there was more freedom to wander into the factory canteen, drink coffee, and eat some of the seemingly endless quantities of biscuits that were always around. I could also smoke a cigarette or two, obviously. I was content with working the zipper and hanging boots, but still felt I hadn't found my niche job I was entirely happy with.

After breakfast that day, John and Guy left in a car for Tiberias, with a *kibbutznik*, as they'd planned. Chris and Graham were due back from their trip down south later that evening, so I was to spend the whole day on my own. Because the work list wasn't published until nine o'clock it felt like I had a day off. I was tired and slept for a while before I again decided to have an exploratory wander around the kibbutz.

To my astonishment, I found a very interesting machine plonked incongruously in a bit of land amongst the children's swings, right in the middle of the kibbutz. I was amazed I'd not seen it before. At first sight I could hardly believe my eyes, or my luck at finding such a thing. It was a late model P-51 Mustang, just standing there on its own wheels, a once fearsome fighting machine now looking sad and very neglected among the trees and children's toys. I didn't see anyone around so I clambered onto the wing and peered into the cockpit. There was no canopy covering it, so I lifted my leg then slowly and reverently lowered myself inside. The seat was quite high and I had an excellent view around me, as I was not at all sunken inside. There would therefore have been brilliant all-round visibility from the cockpit, no doubt a huge advantage for a fighter aircraft. The first thing that amazed me about it was that it appeared to be made entirely from sheet metal. Not a bit of wood or stretched canvas anywhere. It must have been immensely strong as a result.

Sadly, there were no controls inside the cockpit, only remains of where they had once been. The gun sight mount was in front of me. I felt the sheer presence the machine must once have had, and the raw power of the huge engine in front, accompanied by a massive four-bladed propeller. The guns had been taken from the wings, as had the access panels and those for the ammunition, but most of the engine was still there. The cowling which should have covered the engine was also missing, and I felt a, not insignificant, surge of pride as I read the bold lettering on the side of the engine: ROLLS-ROYCE. There were some miscellaneous pieces of the aircraft lying in the dirt underneath it, and so I foraged around to find a small tin plate about four inches by three inches with PACKARD BUILT ROLLS-ROYCE written along the top. There were figures underneath such as 'Firing Order' followed by a string of numbers and letters, and 'AAE Serial No. V-324735'. Across the bottom of the plate were written the words: PACKARD MOTOR CAR COMPANY DETROIT MICHIGAN U.S.A. The aircraft camouflage pattern was faded, as were the Israeli Air Force markings, which consisted of a blue 'Star of David' in a white roundel background. I wanted to take it home. It was such a shame it was sitting there, and I hoped one day someone would find it and restore it to its former glory. I slipped the small plate into my pocket as though it was long lost treasure and left the P-51, occasionally looking back over my shoulder as though frightened it would suddenly disappear.

I breezed into the kibbutz office with a *Boker-tov!* which meant 'good morning' to the lady behind the counter, despite the fact it was probably well into the afternoon by that time. I withdrew three hundred *lira*, which was about ten pounds, from my own money supply. I needed to visit Kiryat Shmona to see if I could have my watch strap fixed, which had broken when I tried to attach a brown leather face cover to it the day before. A lot of Israelis had these on their watches at the time, and I'd bought one in the kibbutz shop. Guy and John found it highly amusing when I broke my strap attempting to put it on my watch.

KIRYAT SHMONA

I hadn't yet been hitch-hiking alone in Israel. In fact, I don't think I'd *ever* hitch-hiked alone before, anywhere. I paused for a moment in the dry earth by the main road, near the gates of the kibbutz, before selecting a place to stand. There's obviously an art to hitch-hiking. It's very important to find the right spot. You need to be prominent and visible, but not so far into the road that you risk getting flattened. A white Peugeot van came trundling towards me heading towards town, and I stuck my right arm out in front of me. My index finger pointed ambitiously across the road, in the same manner as the Israeli soldiers. No-one would have known it was my first solo attempt. The driver passed me, but then pulled over, screeching and juddering to a stop in a cloud of dust, twenty yards ahead. I ran up to the side and opened the door.

"Kiryat Shmona?" the driver shouted loudly and impatiently at me, before I could say anything, without actually looking me in the eye. I climbed in and we set off.

"*Ken,*" I said, catching my breath, strapping myself in and nodding. I then said "Thank you," in English, not wanting to be too ambitious with my fledgling Hebrew linguistics. This brief exchange was the sum total of our conversation in the ten minute journey. There was a CB radio in the cab, covered in a thick layer of yellow dust, along with most of the interior, and every few minutes my driver would chatter away to someone at the other end of the radio, obviously in a heated dispute over a very important issue. He held the radio microphone in his right hand and didn't put it down. He used the gear stick with the same hand, just managing to avoid the coiled black wire from becoming wrapped awkwardly around it. He spoke animatedly into the microphone. Occasionally there was a distant and crackled reply from the CB speaker, bolted untidily to the dashboard. A lot of the conversations between Israelis, particularly those between men, seemed to contain a very serious intensity, as though they were resolving issues of earth-shattering importance. This conversation was typical. It seemed incredibly urgent and of huge importance. I would occasionally pick up a few words I recognised here and there, but I had no idea what he was talking about.

We pulled up in Kiryat Shmona, and he said to me in perfect English: "Here, you can get out now, okay?" as I opened my door.

He quickly drove away, still talking on the CB radio, before I could properly thank him. It was as though thanks were not actually expected.

It was becoming cooler as the late afternoon sun began to disappear behind the hills. The town was bathed in a soft, red-orange twilight glow across the tops of buildings and the smooth concrete *miklatim*. I wandered into the centre where I'd been before with Chris and Graham, only to find most of the shops were closed. They would re-open at four o'clock. It was three-thirty in the afternoon, so I needed something to do for a while. What better than to have a beer and a cigarette in the café bar in the precinct?

I strode towards the bar feeling quite contented. Thankfully, it was open and there were a few customers inside talking loudly at the back. The front of the premises was shuttered when closed, so there was no door as such, it was completely open. The man behind the bar asked me if I wanted a pint, in English, and so he poured the dark brown beer into a jug and handed it to me across the bar. I paid him twenty-one *lira* and sat at a table nearest the outside. After taking a sip I lit a Nelson, and then sat back in my chair. I gazed around, giving some thought to my new home town.

I realised where I'd seen and heard the words *Kiryat* and *Shmona* before. There were quite a few place names with the prefix *Kiryat*, meaning 'settlement', and discovered the word *shmona* was the Hebrew number eight. I assumed the name therefore meant 'the eighth town' but in actual fact it meant 'the town of the eight' and was named after a corresponding number of prominent citizens who helped to establish and defend the settlement in the early twentieth century, and who were killed in the process. It was finally declared a town in its own right in 1949 after Israel's success in the war of the previous year. I was not concerned with the politics at the time. Maybe I should have been. I wasn't aware then that Kiryat Shmona was built on the site of a former Bedouin village, the occupants of which apparently fled rather than remain to face the advancing Israelis. If I'd known these details I would probably have better understood why the town was frequently targeted by terrorists from just over the border. I wasn't even aware, as I sat there calmly sipping my beer, that the town and all the surrounding settlements were frequently subject to attack. The ubiquitous *miklat* air raid shelters should perhaps have been an indication.

I caught a glimpse of myself smoking, in a mirror next to the bar. A freshly-lit cigarette was hanging down casually from my mouth, the blue-grey smoke spiralling quickly and evenly upwards. I remember this image of myself which looked to me, at that moment, as being very cool and adult. Like so many photographs of James Dean or Lee Marvin, and other Hollywood greats. It *did* look cool. I watched myself blow the smoke from my mouth and I tapped the end of the cigarette into the ashtray as though I'd been smoking for years, while playing with a matchbox in my left hand. It never occurred to me that I was damaging my health. Such thoughts just don't spring to mind when a teenager.

I finished my beer and walked across to the shops, now open, and found a jeweller's. The old man behind the counter fixed my watch strap quickly and easily, and for only five and a half *lira*. He handed it back to me with just the hint of a very delicate smile rippling very slowly across his heavily lined face. Yet at the same time there seemed to be a strangely distant, almost pained look in his eyes. I thanked him and he answered not in Hebrew, but in what I took to be German, but later realised was Yiddish.

I stepped out of the shop and back into the street. I then

saw a tobacconist's which sold a vast array of cigarettes from all over the world. I'd not paid tobacco products much attention before, so was amazed at the sheer variety on offer. Obviously there was not merely the handful of Israeli brands usually available in the kibbutz shop, but dozens of other varieties. As a new smoker I was a blank canvas for the tobacco industry and open to any suggestions regarding brand loyalty. I selected a soft pack of US *Camel* cigarettes and paid thirty *lira* for them. I chose these cigarettes from all the others mainly because one of my favourite rock bands at the time was the British band, Camel. I had seen them perform live the year before in Sheffield. One of their albums, *Mirage*, had the same logo on the front of the LP cover as these cigarettes. That's how thin and tenuous brand loyalty can be! I lit one of the Camels and inhaled. A few seconds later I almost passed out. Compared to Israeli cigarettes these were so incredibly strong. There was also a very rich and distinctive flavour to it which I could actually taste on my tongue, something the Israeli cigarettes obviously lacked, and which I found quite remarkable.

I returned to the bar and drank another pint. I sat smoking a Camel, drinking my beer quite contentedly as the sun finally disappeared. I was really enjoying myself, and was slightly overcome by a very warm and satisfying sense of well-being. I was also becoming a little intoxicated.

As darkness fully descended over Kiryat Shmona, I noticed the lights high up above the town for the first time. As I stepped into the precinct and walked in the direction of the bus station, I could see numerous lights from roads and settlements unfeasibly high up on the tops of the hills immediately behind the town. These cliffs and steep slopes were in complete darkness and so there appeared to be nothing supporting the flickering lights at the top, as though someone had stretched a line of them across the very sky itself. It was an incredible sight. I was also becoming increasingly curious to find out what was up there.

As I walked into the bus station I was pleasantly surprised

to see Chris and Graham were there too, waiting for a bus, having returned from their trip. I was pleased to see them. They looked tanned and their hair was slightly matted and bleached by the sun and the dry desert air. They were with a Canadian guy called Norman, who was apparently planning to visit Dafna and stay for a while before moving on. My head was spinning a little from the Camels and the beer, so I walked straight into the record shop and to the Genesis LPs. I selected *Selling England by the Pound* and handed it to the chap behind the counter. I joined the others on the balcony area leaning against the railings, just as the music started. Graham took one of my Camels with little or no persuasion, as did Norman, which I was a bit angry about as I didn't even know him, and they were so very expensive. Chris and Graham said they'd had a fantastic time in Eilat on the Red Sea coast, and further down in the Sinai at a small Bedouin settlement called Dahab. It was much hotter down there, apparently, and they'd met some really interesting people. They'd also been snorkelling in the Red Sea and said it was warm, clear, packed with fish, and generally an unbelievable experience.

As our bus pulled away from the bus station in the dark, I could see to the right all the many flickering lights of the various settlements further down the Hula Valley from Kiryat Shmona. The lights twinkled like fallen stars scattered across the ground, as did the surreal ones on the hills high above the town.

We arrived back on Dafna at five thirty and walked up to the dining-room. We ate a leisurely meal while Chris and Graham relived their trip for anyone willing to listen. We then made our way to the volunteers' club where we drank coffee with Ezra, one of the young kibbutz soldiers. The club consisted of a single huge room with a high ceiling inside a separate old building, similar to a church hall or barn. It was known as the *moadon*, which was the Hebrew word for 'club'. We were allowed exclusive use of the place in order to play music and drink beer, usually on Friday nights. Ezra had grown up on the kibbutz and had started his National Service, as everyone did in Israel. He was a very amiable chap, about our age, and obviously enjoyed socialising with the volunteers, probably in order to improve his English. He was far more sensible than most of us, but then he had to be I suppose, he was in the army.

At nine o'clock I checked the work list. I had a four o'clock start in the morning on 'conveyor' and 'hanging boots'.

THE OLD BRIDGE

I was now into my second week at Dafna. I finished work in the factory at nine o'clock in the morning and strolled across to the dining-room for breakfast. I ate two bowls of thick semolina in quick succession, and sat with a tall lad from the North East of England called John. He spoke with a strong 'Geordie' accent and so he was therefore, not surprisingly, known as 'Geordie John'. After breakfast, Graham instructed me to put on some swimming trunks under my shorts. We were going fishing. I wondered what sort of fishing required us to strip off in this manner, but went along with it anyway. I wasn't a huge fan of the sport, having only been fishing a handful of times with my grandfather and father on the River Trent when I was much younger. But I was interested in finding out where we were going.

We went out of the north entrance of the kibbutz and walked for about ten minutes along a track towards a rough line of cypress and willow trees among some densely growing bushes. I could hear flowing water as we grew nearer, and we came to a slight gap in the undergrowth, which you probably would never know was there until right upon it. We were now about half a mile further upstream of the same river, the Dan, which flowed through the kibbutz. Graham was carrying a six-foot length of bamboo pole and had some fishing line wrapped around another stick, plus one small fish hook. Eventually he led the way by pushing through the trees along a very overgrown path, and we emerged onto the river bank at a point where it was about twenty yards wide. I saw some strange wild creatures floating about in the water, then I realised they were actually three or four huge blue dragonflies, skimming around and occasionally hovering very still just over the surface. They all fled immediately upstream once we disturbed them, and from then on they only occasionally ventured closer before darting away again.

In front of us was what could only very loosely be described as a footbridge. There was a steel pipe about ten inches thick, which crossed the river just above the water, and a very rusty iron frame attached to the side of it. There were some long planks of wood sitting on this flat, ramshackle construction, along with quite a few random pieces of scrap board, making it about six feet wide in places. The whole thing really looked as though it would collapse or get washed away at any moment. Even though it certainly didn't look appealing at first sight, it was in fact a quiet, secluded paradise.

Graham set up his line and baited it with a small piece of meat he'd brought with him from the dining-room. He dipped his fishing rod into the water, and the baited hook disappeared in the current. He spoke optimistically to me about how many fish we would catch, while carefully and methodically removing his boots and socks. I took mine off and we both dipped our very moist and sweaty bare feet into the gently flowing river. There was a wonderful sensation as the cool water covered our feet almost up to our knees, while we sat on the boards facing downstream, the bridge only a few inches above the gently rippling surface. By midday it was very warm and it seemed as though I could feel my body slowly melt like soft ice-cream in the strong sunshine. Maybe it was the first delicate nascence of unexpected contentment that was beginning to wash over me.

I looked around and reached into the pocket of my shorts for my Camels. Graham and I then sat on the old bridge, smoking and chatting about everything and anything that came into our heads. There was no wind of any sort, and the smoke from our cigarettes rose slowly and gently, hanging in the calm air. Graham was staring intently into the water for signs of any fish near his baited hook.

I lay back on the boards and folded my left arm behind my head as a pillow against the hard wood. A small amount of ash from my cigarette dropped onto my face and I sat up briefly to brush it away. A deep red and brown spotted butterfly fluttered across the bridge around us. There was nothing but a vast, cloudless azure sky above, and all I could hear was the cool crystal water flicking, swirling and babbling about underneath me, around some of the partially submerged structure of the old bridge. Save for this gentle mesmeric trickling sound and a few sparrows in the nearby trees, there was absolute silence. It was as though the earth had otherwise come to a complete stop, and Graham and I were the only two people left alive. The rich, spicy scent of our cigarettes mixed with the cool dampness of the river. I could almost taste the old wood of the boards on which we were lying, inches from my face, which were now, like us, baking in the hot sun.

Graham stood up very suddenly in characteristic abruptness and started to remove his shorts. His trunks were underneath, and he threw his shorts down hard onto the boards. There was a section of the bridge overgrown with reeds and shrubs, an area which seemed to have been partially reclaimed by the bank. It was adjacent to the deepest part of the river nearest the bridge. Graham pushed his way through to the edge and looked down. The water was so clear, the pebbly bottom was easily visible probably four or five feet down. He jumped in with a huge, clumsy splash. He surfaced and shook his head, water droplets clinging to his beard. I was very hot and sweaty in the sun and my legs felt as though they had grown quite accustomed to the cool water, so I was happy to follow Graham. I plunged in with an equally untidy splash.

We both laughed and huffed and puffed, as the cold water gripped our bodies tightly and seemed to suck all the air from our lungs. It felt *extremely* cold. It probably wasn't, but it *was* incredibly refreshing and I was cooled in an instant.

We both clambered out of the river after only a few minutes and sank back into our positions on the bridge, dripping cool drops of water onto the dry planks. I lay back again, spreading the drips further across the faded and cracked surface of the wood. I shivered a little, but then the afternoon sun started to warm my skin again and I could feel the moisture evaporating quickly. Graham picked up his home-made fishing rod and I saw there had still not been a bite or even a nibble of any kind on the bait. I doubt there would have been any fish anywhere near us for quite some time after the disturbance we'd just caused. He lay back on the boards and I offered him another cigarette.

The two of us lay side by side on the old bridge, trying to blow smoke-rings into the clear emptiness above. Graham was lean and tanned, the result of many such long afternoons spent at the old bridge. My skin was pale by comparison, and I was thin, almost insipid. Graham blew fantastic, powerful hoops of smoke one after the other, which danced and climbed high into the air, holding their shape for what seemed hours but was probably only a few moments. We both laughed when I tried, and great cloudy balls of untidy smoke blew about like scruffy chuffs from an old steam train. All was warm sunshine, peace and calmness. I fell in love with the old bridge.

We didn't catch anything all day, but this didn't seem to matter in the least. We walked back to the kibbutz, happy and relaxed after a brilliant afternoon. We called in at the factory canteen for coffee and biscuits on the way back to the room. It was just after five o'clock and almost dark by the time we arrived home. It was nearing the end of November and yet that day had been very hot and sunny. No doubt back in England there would have been fog, rain, and freezing cold weather.

Chris, Graham, John and I made toast on the paraffin heater in our room again that night. Despite the day being so very warm, and the skin on my face feeling very tight from being in the sun, for the first time I noticed a perceptible chill in the air outside. The evenings were getting cooler, but once again our room smelt of warm toast and hot tea.

The days began to merge into one continuous stream of increasingly enjoyable partying, punctuated by a few hours work here and there. Any desire I once had to run for home to England began to fade away, and was almost lost in the recesses of my mind amidst the hard work and increased socialising. In fact, any thoughts of England at all, and even anywhere else in the world for that matter, had almost completely vanished.

There was a very definite mind-set on the kibbutz. It was one of calm and happy isolation, of a willingly subsumed abandonment of the outside world and all its problems. There was a gradual descent into a very slow and linear existence, where the days and weeks began to melt away into one single beguiling experience. There was no need for money and so it rarely, if ever, changed hands. The only currency necessary were the coupons used at the kibbutz shop. For us volunteers there were no bills to pay, no shopping to do, and no errands to run. There was no need for Social Security payments, and there was no hunger. Everything was provided. There were few real worries or concerns of any kind. We were almost living a life which was comparable to that of the delicate and ineffectual Eloi in H.G. Wells' *The Time Machine*. Where were our Morlocks to create a balance in the order of things and spoil this paradise?

Time certainly did seem to pass at a slower rate on the kibbutz. In fact, everything slowed down. The work was often boring and unchallenging, but is this not frequently true of any job anywhere in the world? Six hours did not make for a long working day, and with breaks in between, it was barely five hours in total.

But I had still not found a job on the kibbutz I was entirely happy with, and the next few days I continued to work the conveyor and hanging boots on the night shifts, as dictated by the daily work list. I was still hopeless at pulling boots, but continued trying my best. I spent more time hanging them rather than pulling them. I was becoming tired of eating salad, and although not a huge fan of red meat, I would have relished a decent meal of steak and chips. I'd not even seen chips or anything like them for nearly two weeks.

One Wednesday afternoon, the four of us in our room decided to travel into Kiryat Shmona to celebrate Graham's twenty-third birthday. It was rare for us all to be together due to the various shifts we all worked, but on this particular day we'd all finished work by four o'clock so descended on the town at about five o'clock, just as it was dark. We went to our usual bar, which was probably the only one at the time selling pints of beer. I don't think we ever bothered looking around for another. Not surprisingly, silver-tongued Chris managed to obtain the first name of the proprietor, a man by the name of Yuval, a corpulent but very friendly chap with masses of black curly hair on all his exposed skin as well as his head. And so, from then on, he was our best friend in all of Kiryat Shmona, even more so than the chap in the record shop at the bus station. John told me about his new job at the kibbutz 'fish ponds', catching and sorting the fish. It sounded much more interesting than pulling or hanging boots. We saw some other customers in the bar sharing a large plate of chips. We had no idea these were available so ordered a large plate each. Every time Yuval and the other bar staff disappeared out of sight we craned our necks to see if they were bringing our food. When our order finally arrived we tucked in like a bunch of rapacious schoolboys playing truant, and ate every delicious little scrap.

We each bought Graham a beer and forced him to drink them down in one. It was Graham's evening and it was clear he was thoroughly enjoying himself. He smoked the rest of my Camels. His Brummie accent became much more pronounced the more he drank. He spent some time telling me what a wonderful place his home town of Dudley was, and asked me if I'd ever been there. He told me I would have to visit when we all returned to England. On each occasion when he wanted to make himself heard, Graham would shout "*Whoa!*" at the top of his voice in order to attract everyone's attention, like the command given to a wayward horse. This was a habit which seemed to work well, even if it was a little rude. I sometimes use it to this day myself, after having consumed a lot of beer, while behaving a little too loud for my own good.

This was a very different Graham to the quiet and contemplative one who had sat with me all afternoon on the old bridge. I remember thinking he was now quite old, at twenty-three. As an eighteen-year-old I could tell he was a lot older. It's strange how you can almost inevitably become a very good judge of a person's age when they are relatively close to your own, but much less so of people who are decades away from yourself. At the age I was then, a year or two seemed an eternity, so five years was almost a lifetime. There is real age snobbery involved in youth, where we all have automatic membership of an exclusive club made up of our own peer age group. Trespassers are treated with suspicion until they can prove themselves. Eventually you may earn a little respect as a person from another generation, and even some quiet admiration or acceptance, but you will *never* truly be one of them. I was the youngest in the group, so to a certain extent I had to just listen and learn. In this case, the oldies were in full control.

As Graham downed his last pint we met some other English lads from Kibbutz HaGoshrim, which was quite close to Dafna. We discussed parties and other social events, and compared the work at each kibbutz. We told them about our volunteers' club in the *moadon*, and they invited us over to their club one Friday night for the disco. The main topic of conversation however was how poor we all thought the quality of the female volunteers was at that time, on both Dafna and HaGoshrim. We all laughed as we described our female volunteer colleagues in an extremely derogatory manner, as variously resembling farm animals and the back ends of buses. I chatted to one of the lads who told me his name was Stuart. He was a tall, slim, and good-looking chap with collar length black hair and thin steel-framed glasses. He spoke with a degree of calm, self-assured, pragmatism in a North Midlands accent I was unfamiliar with. He used the word 'shocking' constantly as a synonym for the word 'fuck' and referred to most of the female volunteers he'd met so far in Israel as: 'shockin' ugly bods'. I nodded in agreement, even though at first I had no idea what a 'bod' was, until he pointed towards two female Israeli soldiers walking by, stating:

"Look at them two shockin' bods over there, they'd be rayt," or similar. In fact many of the Israeli women came in for high praise, particularly those in uniform, even though they were notoriously difficult to catch, like the fish at the old bridge. Then I realised how John's room had acquired its name, 'The Boning Room'. It was one of very few volunteers' rooms with a double bed. It was very private and the door had a lock on the inside. It was therefore one of the places where romantic encounters could flourish in some civilised privacy.

We parted company from the HaGoshrim contingent, and trudged up to the bus station. I'd drunk four pints and so was pretty happy and quite drunk, having only had the usual salad for lunch. Bus twenty-seven was already at the bus station, so we jumped straight on board, with no time for a *falafel* or a browse around the record shop. John sat with a very pretty Israeli girl called Denis, who, we all realised, he was very keen on. When the bus stopped at Dafna they both walked into the kibbutz together, ahead of us. We very childishly giggled and prodded one another as we saw them walk away into the darkness, obviously very deep in conversation. Chris and Graham whistled at them as they disappeared up the road. John rightly ignored us except for an occasional one-finger salute from his right hand behind his back.

THE KITCHENS

My next working day started at six o'clock in the morning in the huge dining-room kitchens. I spent all morning until eleven o'clock gutting, cleaning, and cutting up 170 recently thawed frozen chickens. We separated the various parts of each carcass, dropping the main sections into one container, and the wings in another. There were three of us volunteers employed at this task. The other two were Phil, a very posh and phlegmatic Home Counties Englishman in his early twenties, and Karl, who was extremely old and Danish. He had a long grey beard and straggly grey hair on a balding head, and was very thin. His teeth cluttered his mouth like ancient grave-stones, now toppling and falling around one another. His English was brilliant of course. I also heard him converse in German with a rather ebullient and untidy girl from West Germany called Marianne, who chain-smoked roll-up cigarettes. She was very friendly and always seemed to wear baggy jumpers. I was envious of anyone who could lapse into other languages, with such apparent ease.

Marianne came in to see us occasionally from another part of the kitchens to collect our finished pieces of chicken, and told me she was from the Southern Ruhr area of Germany. She also stated she was very conscious of her country's past, particularly in relation to the recent tragic history of European Jewry. Karl spoke about the war too. He stated he was a child during the Second World War and carried feelings of guilt that he had survived when so many had perished. I just wondered how such an old person was even allowed to be a volunteer on a kibbutz. He must have been at least fifty.

After lunch, John and I sat quietly in our room writing letters and postcards home. I sent a brief card to my parents: *Mum and Dad: I arrived safely. The food and work are okay, there's good and bad, but I'm okay so far.*

I'd agreed to send them something on arrival and so I was very late in doing so. In fact I'd taken an anxious phone call from them a few days before in the kibbutz office because they'd not heard anything from me at all. They must have been worried sick. It's not until you have children yourself that you realise what you must have put your own parents through. But in those first few days while I was in a state of shock and despondency, I didn't feel inclined to contact them. By the time I did speak to them I was just beginning to reconcile myself to my surroundings and told them: 'Oh yes, it's great, don't worry...' and similar. It was strange to hear their voices from so far away. It seemed as though they were much further away from me than a few thousand miles. It felt like we were now on entirely different planets.

I then read some more, and wrote another entry in my diary. I drew a Genesis logo on the wall above my bed, and at Chris's request a Bob Marley one above his bed. That night after dinner, John, Chris, Graham, Guy and I had a lengthy discussion about British regional accents. Guy was the only Londoner and felt a little out of place. John found it highly amusing that Chris and Graham described a bus as a 'buzz' in their Birmingham accents. Eventually, having not even had a single beer, or alcoholic beverage of any kind, at about ten-thirty everyone decided to get an early night.

I started work in the kitchens the following day at twelve-thirty. I was chopping gherkins again. I finished at two o'clock and was told to return at five-thirty. Back at the room, Yonatan came to see me and gave me an old, pale green army coat. The cuffs were frayed and it was clearly well past its best, but I loved it. I had a pair of cloth RAF-style wings with me which looked very similar, minus the 'RAF' letters. These were my brand new Private Pilot wings of which I was very proud, and so I decided to sew them onto my new kibbutz coat. I must have known that from then on they would attract some attention. Maybe that was why I did it. John came in with some blancmange mixture he'd bought from the shop for seven *lira* and some cartons of milk with the smiling

Friesians on the side. After whisking it together in a jug, the mixture was left to set in the fridge for about forty-five minutes. We made toast in our room and had blancmange pudding for dessert.

Back in the kitchens at five-thirty I seemed to be a general skivvy all evening, and scullion to the biggest and busiest kitchen in the world. I was tasked at cleaning out seven large stainless steel vats, like huge witches' cauldrons. Some were caked in rice and had to be zapped with a high pressure hose and scalding hot water. Like an idiot, I accidentally emptied one of these straight onto my feet and drenched myself. I decided then that I needed to get hold of some waterproof boots. I was given thirty minutes for a meal break and I thoroughly enjoyed dinner. Not surprisingly it was chicken, as much of it as you could eat! I didn't finish work until close to nine o'clock and was wet through by the end of it. But I enjoyed working in the kitchens that night, probably because I had a long chat with Gary for the first time. He said he was an ex-Royal Air Force Aircraft Technician, but no-one would have guessed. He had long black hair which fell far below his shoulders, a moustache and goatee beard. He was slim, almost wiry, and looked a lot like how people imagine Jesus to have looked, though I'm sure this was not Gary's intention. He worked in a part of the kitchens where the huge stainless steel cooking containers were washed out by hand, dozens of them, and so therefore the job was known as 'the containers'. He was soaked through to the skin and was also sweating profusely, his arms submerged deep in a huge stainless steel sink full of hot soapy water. Gary seemed to be blessed with huge quantities of aphoristic knowingness and I liked him almost immediately.

"The world's in a right mess, Jonathan. It's like a boil on someone's arse. It needs squeezing so all the bad can come out and be disposed of..." he said to me, also in quite a strong Birmingham accent, if a little less obvious than Chris and Graham's. Such a comment seems very simplistic now. But to a naïve and impressionable eighteen-year-old, this thirty-year-old, aeroplane-loving, ex-RAF chap who looked like Jesus, and who also loved the rock group Genesis, as I did, was virtually a deity. Gary was proud of the fact he was from the West Midlands and reminded me that some of the greatest rock bands in the world had originated from Birmingham; Black Sabbath led by the charismatic front man Ozzy Osbourne, and of course Robert Plant and the rest of Led Zeppelin. Then there was Slade and the ELO, the Electric Light Orchestra led by Jeff Lynne, who had written the musical version of *The War of the Worlds*. He told me how much he loved *The War of the Worlds* album, largely for the narration by Richard Burton. Gary also recounted an occasion when he was in an ordinary pub in Birmingham one night, when most of Led Zeppelin appeared and gave an impromptu performance in between drinks and watching another band.

While we were talking Gary came up close to me, a large container in hand, soap suds falling everywhere, and pointed towards the huge dishwashing machine nearby. He then said in his Brummie accent, sounding very similar to Ozzy Osbourne:

"It's *Welcome to the Machine* that thing, eh Jonathan? Just look at it, look at the size of it! What a machine. You know, the Floyd..." and he laughed out loud before turning and going back to his sink. I hadn't a clue what he was talking about. Gary was also very high in my estimation because he was sharing a room on the kibbutz with his girlfriend, a gorgeous young French woman called Claudie, who was very pretty, curvy and slim, and looked a lot like a young Ingrid Bergman. She was lovely in every way.

After work, Chris, Graham, Phil and I walked three kilometres up the road to Kibbutz Dan. We took a bottle of Israeli vodka I'd bought in the shop for twenty-six coupons. We arrived in some volunteers' room, some people Phil apparently knew. They were two Americans who were both from Michigan, and who were entertaining a pair of demure and quite plain-looking German girls. One of them declared she was from Bavaria as though there was some great significance to this, and seemed incapable of smiling. They looked like twins and both had masses of white-blonde hair and huge bosoms, which were hanging in a rather heavy and pendulous manner, flopping about loose like water balloons inside their t-shirts. We drank the vodka mixed with freshly-squeezed orange juice, and chatted in a rather subdued and surprisingly civilised manner, until it was all gone. We returned to Dafna at about one in the morning. Just before we left Dan, I noticed in the near distance, parked close to the centre of the kibbutz, another aircraft wreck. This time I recognised a more modern shape, sitting on its own tripod undercarriage. It was an early twin-engined British jet-fighter, a Gloster Meteor, in old Israeli Air Force markings. I had no time to explore it in the dark, so I promised myself I would return again sometime in daylight.

THE PEOPLE

Sick Mick

Another Saturday and no work, as it was the Sabbath, (or *Shabbat*) and was our one and only day off a week. It was also yet another hot day with a clear, cloudless blue sky. Four of us walked up to the old bridge in the afternoon to try some fishing. We only stayed an hour or so, having not caught anything, again. All the Israeli fish of the Upper Galilee clearly hated us. We walked back to the room via the factory, and took some ice-cream from the factory fridge which I'm not sure we were entitled to, and carried it back to the room. At four o'clock we walked to She'ar Yashuv to their cinema and each paid our five *lira*, without actually knowing in advance what the film was going to be. Luckily it was *Exodus* starring Paul Newman. It was in English with some very scratchy home-made Hebrew sub-titles, which looked as though they'd been etched onto the celluloid with a sharpened stick by someone with sight problems. The awful Hebrew writing obliterated a huge proportion of the screen, and after half an hour we left. The sound quality was rubbish too, and was deteriorating further as the film progressed.

By this time the sun was a huge, glowing orange ball, dipping down very quickly over the Naftali hills above Kiryat Shmona. Chris suggested we visit 'Sick Mick'. Mick apparently had an excellent radio which could pick up anything from anywhere in the world. I imagined it to be similar to the huge radio set in the *Schloss Adler* castle in the movie *Where Eagles Dare,* and so was keen to meet Mick and see his brilliant radio. All Chris and Graham were interested in was hearing the Saturday afternoon football results from Blighty. So we left She'ar Yashuv and made our way back to see Sick Mick.

I'd not met Mick formally yet. I'd seen him on numerous occasions driving a tractor around the kibbutz, often with a dog on his lap. At meal times he almost always sat with *kibbutzniks* in the dining room. I assumed therefore that he was Israeli, and was shocked when I was told he was a volunteer like the rest of us, even though it seemed he'd lived there for years. We arrived in his room at about five o'clock. It was warm and cosy, if a little musty, in an unclean masculine sort of way. His room was quite poorly lit with a single sixty-watt bulb hanging from the ceiling, shrouded almost completely in a very dusty fabric shade. It smelt of burning paraffin, *Old Holborn* tobacco smoke, and his dog, a black and brown mongrel called Blackie. Mick seemed happy to see us, as did Blackie, even though the four of us made his tiny room appear much smaller. He was sitting propped up on his bed against the wall, smoking, and ushered us inside. He swept bits of tobacco from his bed and in a loud voice shouted:

"Come in, lads, sit down..!" as we all spread out on his bed. It was clear there wouldn't be enough room so John sat on a stool near the door. I then heard Mick shout in a loud, bellowing and peremptory voice:

"Sit down, SIT, go on, sit, there's a good lad!" and thought for an anxious moment he was talking to me. Then I noticed his dog had stood up when we walked in the room, and was looking up at us intently, his short stubby little tail wagging frantically before settling again on the floor. Mick's paraffin heater was lit and was bubbling and hissing away on low. The semi-circular wire mesh element, just a little bigger than half a tennis ball, glowed a faint orangey-red, completing the cosy atmosphere. It reminded me of my late maternal grandmother's house on a Saturday afternoon when I visited with my parents as a child. She would be seated in a dining chair in her dark and diminutive living room while busily knitting, a cigarette constantly hanging from one corner of her mouth. She always watched the wrestling on her tiny old black-and-white television in front of her, the room almost completely filled with cigarette smoke.

Graham reached over to Mick's bedside table, which was in fact a pile of rough wooden pallets, and picked up his tobacco.

"Can I have one of these, Mick?" he said, already taking out the *Rizla* cigarette papers from inside.

"Sure, yeah, go for it!" he replied. "Anyone else want one?"

I declined and padded my coat pockets for my Nelsons. As I did so, Mick noticed the wings I'd sewn onto the left breast of my coat.

"Pilot then are you? RAF or what?" he said, rather accusingly at first and with a hint of sarcasm. He looked at the others and then started laughing. He took his tobacco from Graham and began rolling himself another cigarette. I'd already told the others about my flying experiences but Mick seemed particularly interested. I told him briefly how I'd recently obtained my licence and he seemed genuinely impressed:

"We've got a *real Biggles* living amongst us then, eh?" and laughed again. He had to tap his glasses in the middle with a forefinger to stop them falling down his nose. Mick was old too. He looked at least thirty and had a round, ruddy kind of face, pock-marked and dominated by a thick bushy moustache. He reminded me of 'Popeye' Doyle, Gene Hackman's irascible, uncompromising character in the *French Connection* films. The lenses in his silver-framed glasses looked quite thick and he had what appeared to be grey flecks in his collar-length, curly reddish hair, so maybe he was even older. He was lively and engaging and from that moment on kept calling me *Biggles* at every opportunity; this was the First World War pilot character from the Captain W.E. Johns books, so much so that John started referring to me as such too.

Mick's radio was chattering in the background as he reached forward and tuned it to the BBC World Service, and turned up the volume. Sadly it looked rather disappointing and very much like an ordinary radio. But I did notice there were several wires from the back of it that reached, like thin tentacles, all around the room and split up into the top corners.

This was clearly the reason why he could achieve such good reception.

Blackie stood up, jumped onto the bed and sat close to me. After throwing me a quick glance, as though checking for my approval, he edged himself even closer and sat curled up next to my legs. He then placed his head on my lap.

"Blackie!" Mick shouted, and he lifted his head up, looking across at Mick, ears raised, head slightly tilted to one side.

"He's alright, Mick, I don't mind…" I replied, and started stroking the top of Blackie's head with the fingers of my right hand. My grandfather once had a mongrel, Penny, and Blackie reminded me of her. The chap from the BBC proudly announced in a very serious and plummy English accent: "This is London," followed by the music of *The Lilliburlero*. We all sat around in the hushed silence of Mick's room, listening intently to the BBC voice passing the vitally important messages from home. Graham's team, West Bromwich Albion, or 'West Brom' as it was better known, had won, one-nil.

"They're still in with a chance then eh?" Chris said to Graham, in a reassuring tone.

"Yeah, they just need a couple more wins to be safe," Graham replied, looking very serious indeed. Apparently his team were in some danger of relegation to a lower division in the league, which would really upset Graham if it happened. They both then went on to discuss the fortunes and prospects of West Brom, like two seasoned football pundits. I gleaned a few snippets of invaluable and re-usable football advice from the conversation such as: you need a very good goal record to climb higher in the league, you must have some excellent players, and you also need to keep on winning as many games as possible if your team is to do well. It all sounded rather obvious to me…

The BBC was crystal clear, as though broadcast from the next room. We heard all the day's football results, and the horse racing results, and then the news.

Just for a few seconds I felt a very slight twinge of what I could only describe as home-sickness. I'd not really thought much about home for a while, having successfully managed to keep it at the very back of my mind. Hearing the BBC that afternoon caused me to feel a strange and uncomfortable emptiness inside.

We didn't leave Mick's room until seven o'clock, when we went to dinner. I had acquired a new nick-name which stuck with me for the rest of my stay, to the extent that very soon I was even using the name myself. I hadn't the courage to ask what was wrong with Mick, and why he was known as 'Sick Mick'. He looked perfectly alright to me.

ALL CHANGE!

For the next few days I worked in the factory hanging boots, pulling boots, and the zipper. I also worked on a small piece of equipment called the 'tear-drop machine'. This was closely associated to the zipper and punched holes in the boots near the zips. It was very tedious and repetitive, as was the majority of the factory work, so I shall spare you any further descriptions. Occasionally, the conveyor would be stopped for an hour or so to change the size of the steel boot moulds, which then obviously had the knock-on effect of causing everyone else down the line to stand idle for a while. We could either go into the factory canteen to eat handfuls of 'rich tea' type biscuits, dunked in sludgy milk-free Turkish coffee, or stroll down to the dining-room, if it was open. One of the very few good points about the factory work was finishing at ten o'clock in the morning after the four o'clock start. The day was then your own, and I frequently made trips into Kiryat Shmona, either alone or with anyone who would go with me. I had a small Kodak Instamatic camera, redolent of the time, and took some film to be developed, at great expense, and bought more Camels. Evenings were then spent in the volunteer's club, the *moadon*, drinking yet more coffee and playing backgammon with Marianne. I did like Marianne and could see she must have had the most fabulous pair of breasts under her woolly jumper, and therefore showed great promise. But unbeknown to her, she sadly followed the great British comedian Ken Dodd for her hair style, or lack of it, so she was otherwise not particularly feminine at the time. She was good company though, and was clearly a very kind and generous person. Not that I was actively on the lookout for any romantic entanglements, though I suspected there may be an increasing inevitability in something of that sort.

I also discovered the television room which seated about fifty, and was near the *moadon*. A large black-and-white television on four legs was placed against the back wall, facing around half a dozen short rows of plastic chairs. The room was dimly lit and very plain. It was far from salubrious and had an atmosphere akin to that of a very dull and unsatisfactory bereavement office. Once a week, usually on Mondays, at eleven o'clock at night, Israeli TV showed *The Sweeney*, the classic British cop drama, and it usually drew a full house. Thankfully the sound and dialogue had not been tampered with and the Hebrew subtitles were small and professionally made, rather than the usual huge scratchy ones at the She'ar Yashuv cinema, so it was always very watchable. Back home I watched far too much television, so I quickly learned the value of selective viewing. This was the only show we watched. Probably because of this it seemed absolutely fantastic. It was then that I developed an inclination to perhaps become a police officer myself one day, charging around the streets of London with a gun sorting out all the bad guys. How incredibly exciting! Those were the days before remote controls, so the television was usually left on the one channel. If there was a *kibbutznik* already in the room, sitting at the front brooding and alone, no-one would dare ask for a change.

Breakfasts continued to be by far the greatest meal of the day and I rarely missed them. All the other meals consisted mainly of salad and some very foreign-looking food I would foolishly stay away from. John and I frequently made trips to the kibbutz shop in order to buy butter so we could make toast and jam in the room.

I was almost three weeks into my stay in Israel before the weather broke, at the beginning of December. I remember getting out of bed at four o'clock in the morning for a shift on the zipper, running up to the factory in the rain. Rain! I could hardly believe it! There was an overwhelming damp smell of fresh rain on long-dry earth, the sounds of splashing in puddles from my own hurried feet, and water pouring from the roofs and guttering, such as I'd not seen before in Israel. The whole day was dull, overcast and seemed very unpleasant and incongruous, with a strong cool wind and occasional very heavy rain.

John and Graham each caught a nasty cold. Chris had apparently caught a mild dose of 'ball-bag crumble', so yet more dustings of fresh dandruff appeared on our toilet seat. He told me in all sincerity he must have caught it from some other toilet seat, so for a while I was quite paranoid about my own precious little bottom sitting on the same seat he was using. I wiped it diligently before using it, on the occasions when I was sober and could remember why I was doing it. Our room then resembled some sort of cool, damp, sick room, with two patients coughing and spluttering all over the place, and another scratching his parts, frequently cursing under his breath, bemoaning his condition.

It was now almost completely dark at four-thirty in the afternoon. Every day we had the paraffin heaters on for warmth and not just to make toast. Doors were shut, and windows closed. More blankets were now on the beds and the wind rattled and pulled at the roof and guttering, whistling eerily through the stone pines outside my window, as though we were living in some *Wald* in the Austrian Alps. I hand-washed some clothes in the sink and had to hang them on our washing line in the shower to dry. It was all very different from the hot and dry atmosphere of only a few days before, when wet clothes would dry on the line outside in less than an hour.

We ran from room to room in the rain socialising, and after dinner we called in to see Phil in his room. No-one had any booze, so as a rather disappointing alternative we ran across to the factory canteen and stuffed ourselves with biscuits and coffee. The film at the cinema was *The Wind and the Lion* starring Sean Connery and Candice Bergen. It became one of my favourite films. It was full of action, romance and unrequited love. After the film we returned to the factory canteen for yet more coffee and biscuits. We managed to dodge the rain and puddles and made it to the office where we checked the work list. I saw I was due to work 'kitchens' the next day at six in the morning, and imagined I'd be slicing gherkins again. John, Chris, Graham and I went back to our room on one of the rare occasions when we were all together. Such occasions began to develop a distinctive quality, like when members of a close family are reunited at home, which is exactly what we began to feel like. We drank more tea and spoke about work the next day. John stood brushing his hair, which he did with dutiful regularity, and Chris stood at the kitchen sink brushing his teeth. With the heavy rain outside, and the cosy atmosphere inside, thick with the pungent smell of paraffin and tea, our room seemed more like a large but very scruffy seaside caravan on a wet summer night.

There was a barely audible and very tentative knock on the door to our room. A diminutive figure of a man with curly black hair and bushy moustache stepped inside slowly and asked for me. I looked across the room at him, volunteering my name. The windswept and rain-soaked stranger then said to me, in the broadest New York accent I'd ever heard:

"Jonathan? Hi there! You are working with me tomorrow morning on the dishwasher, I'll see you at six o'clock, okay?" and then left. I shut the door after I watched him disappear quickly into the night. It was Perry, 'The King of the Dishwashing Machine'.

THE DISHWASHER

I arrived on time in the kitchens at six o'clock, but was instructed to make myself a coffee until Perry was ready for me. At six-twenty we began work together on the dishwashing machine. He was to show me how it worked while I shadowed him for a few days in order to get the hang of it, as though it was a complex *NASA* space programme. The machine was probably around twenty feet in length and was, in essence, a long, stainless steel box, three feet square, standing at waist height, into which dirty plates and cutlery were placed at one end and taken away clean at the other. Electric motors pulled the plastic trays around through the machine, and out into the working area where the clean items were removed and stacked.

Inside the machine the items were blasted with very hot water, steam, and a detergent mixture, before a final rinse process. It was a huge and very noisy monster version of the one you probably have sitting very quietly and discreetly in your own kitchen.

Most people came in for breakfast from around seven o'clock, so Perry and I worked at removing the clean cutlery and dishes as they came off the machine, still very hot and steaming. Rubber gloves were needed, as most of the items were far too hot to handle immediately, at least until you became used to it. He showed me how to stack everything in the various trolleys and compartments; forks in one container, knives and spoons in the others, glasses and cups in their own trays and so on. The glasses, French-made *Duralex* glass tumblers, were placed upside down individually in the plastic trays for people to select. There were some cups and saucers but these amazing little glasses were the main drinking receptacle used on the kibbutz, particularly by us volunteers. They were incredibly strong and used for hot drinks as well as cold. Sometimes if one of them dropped onto the hard tiled floor it would explode into a thousand tiny pieces, like car window glass. On another occasion it would hit the ground and bounce around the room without sustaining any damage at all. They were chip resistant but similar to well-used beer glasses in a busy pub, older ones bore thousands of tiny scratches on them, causing a slight opaqueness, clearly indicative of their age and length of service.

Stacking the clean items was only a small part of the duties surrounding the dishwashing machine. Once the plates had stopped coming around and the meal had obviously finished, the whole machine needed to be shut down and cleaned. This involved removing and emptying the three bucket-sized stainless steel drain baskets underneath the machine, where bits of food and even items of cutlery had fallen. Several of the large panels on the side of the machine were removed and hosed down, where, again, particles of food would regularly gather. There was a green 'start' button and a large red 'stop' button. There were also individual controls for turning on the steam, hot water and detergent. When the machine was working at full capacity it was hard work removing all the clean items while trying to keep pace with it. It was also extremely noisy. Even though it was a brilliant machine it couldn't cope with anything larger than a dinner plate, due to the twists and turns in the cycle, hence the need for Gary in another part of the kitchens working on his 'containers'.

Perry was eccentrically and irritatingly thorough in his explanations and instructions. He made punctiliousness an art form. It took him fifteen minutes just to explain how to turn the machine on and off. This was not because he was slow, but quite the opposite. He had boundless enthusiasm for his subject and real affection for the dishwashing machine, occasionally anthropomorphising it by tapping and stroking it down its full length and referring to it as 'she' and 'her'.

He bounded up and down around the machine in his unique and peculiar skipping kind of gait, giving me instructions in his New York drawl, like a curly-haired and slimmed-down version of Danny DeVito. A huge bunch of keys rattled and flew about as they hung from his belt, in common with a lot of *kibbutzniks*. Keys were obviously a status symbol; the more keys you had, the more responsibility you were entrusted with by the kibbutz. There was no other way to visibly display your own importance in such an egalitarian paradise. Perry also reminded me of Woody Allen, of whom I am a huge fan. He was incredibly agile and worked with astonishing alacrity. He would disappear underneath the machine and be part way into demonstrating how to remove the drain baskets even before I could bend myself in half to see what he was doing. The most enjoyable part of the whole process was when the panels had been removed and you had to walk around the whole thing with the high pressure hose. There was a pistol grip on the hose with a trigger, and it could be adjusted to fire a fine spray or a concentrated jet of high pressure water quite some considerable distance. I suspected I might have some fun with this. In fact, I felt relaxed and happy with the prospect of working this machine, at that time.

Another plus with the dishwashing machine was the regular morning coffee breaks at around ten o'clock, when all the kitchen staff would gather for a drink and the inevitable biscuits. The warm soapy atmosphere of the huge kitchen, which was already filling with the early smells of the day's cooking, was then mixed with the aromatic and sweet smell of Time cigarettes and coffee. It was windy and raining outside and quite cool compared to recent weeks. I was glad to be in there. I thought of my cooking days at school in home economics. I felt quite liberated and it seemed noticeably more civilised than the dark and gloomy welly-boot factory.

A TYPICAL FRIDAY NIGHT!

The next day I had a long lie in while I wrote a couple of letters to friends of mine who had been with me in the Air Cadets. Mike had just started at Leeds University, and Tony was still living at home, wondering what to do with his life. My small clique of close friends I knew from school and Cadets had broken up that autumn, and we'd all headed off our very separate ways. The centre of our little world had been the local pub, *The Hare and Hounds* in Sheffield. We spent as much time as we possibly could in the pub, probably in order to escape the increasingly pressing realisation that we were now adults and could no longer delay the inevitable search for job and career. Some friends, like Glen, had successfully joined the Air Force. Others like Dave, one of my best friends, also continued to live at home and frequent *The Hare* as we called it, several times a week. In my ever persistent naivety, I imagined I'd perhaps follow some of them onto further education or the Air Force when I returned home to England. I was still unaware of just how much the kibbutz experience would change my life.

I started work on the dishwasher at one o'clock after lunch. I had to take two paracetamol tablets due to a headache generated from a late night party the night before. Two volunteers, Sheila and Elva, were leaving the kibbutz. I didn't really know them but it was rude not to attend and have a few drinks.

Perry showed me yet again what needed doing with his beloved machine, but this time I did most of the work myself. It was not as boring as in the factory, and there was much more autonomy involved, with greater control of your own working day, which I enjoyed. The peak times were very busy but rarely lasted for more than a couple of hours before you could turn on the hose and have some fun. One of the ubiquitous, plastic and cheap (but effective) kibbutz radios sat on a shelf right next to where I stood unloading and stacking the clean dishes, so this also helped pass the time. Perry left me to work the machine on my own. Probably as some sort of graduation ceremony he disappeared off into the kitchens, soon returning and presenting me with a piece of cake and cup of tea. The cake was awful, but I was glad of the tea. Any significance in the gesture was lost on me at the time, as was the obviously sincere and sadly unreciprocated kindness that Perry showed towards me. But it did mark a certain point when he formally handed over sole responsibility of his noisy, steamy machine.

Richard Harris's version of *Macarthur Park* blasted away loudly in my ears only a few feet away as I turned off the machine at the end of my midday shift, stripped it, and hosed it down. I cleaned the floors, emptied the drains, dried the floor with the squeegee mop, set everything up for the evening, and at three o'clock turned off the radio and left. It was raining heavily again and the sky was cool, dark and threatening. A north wind was picking up and was ripping leaves and small branches down from the trees lining the roads and paths, scattering them around on the ground. I ran straight through the kibbutz where I found John and Guy in our warm room, sitting on Chris and Graham's beds, both quietly writing letters and listening to the radio. Guy said he was returning to England the following week, so I took the opportunity of asking him to write a message and sign his autograph in the back of my diary. He wrote:

'To Jonathan. With all my love (and I've still got a sore arse darling) Much Love, Guy. X.' He also signed his name in Hebrew, which was impressive. I decided I must find out how to write my own. I wasn't asked about the dishwasher, I never was, at least not by them. It wasn't really seen as being much of a man's job, unlike the conveyor or the fish ponds. It seemed only Ian and I from the volunteers worked Perry's wonderful machine.

I had a shower and when Chris and Graham finished work we decided to go into Kiryat Shmona if the rain stopped, until Donald, a grey-haired and grey-bearded English volunteer, popped his head around the door and reminded us it was Friday afternoon and the start of *Shabbat,* so most of the shops would be closed. Graham gave me twenty *lira,* apparently for all the cigarettes of mine he'd recently smoked, and we turned up the heater so we could make toast. Just as we were tucking into some lovely buttered toast, Chrome Dome walked through the door, as though he'd been passing and could smell it. 'Chrome Dome' was the rather cruel, but not necessarily inaccurate, nick-name given to an English volunteer in his thirties called Nick, who happened to be completely bald. But his head was *shiny* bald, not just free of hair and stubble, so it glistened and shone like a sweaty convex mirror, even in poor light. Hence the name, I suppose. He was a polite, very well-spoken and obviously a mature and intelligent man, unlike most of the rest of us. He paused briefly in the doorway. The shining silver head of wisdom stood there quietly, looking at me, so I indicated for him to step inside the room, as though he had been waiting for some formal permission to enter. He'd brought with him a full bottle of cherry brandy, which immediately made him extremely popular. Any hint of indifference at his arrival in our room therefore quickly evaporated, even though the brandy was quite nasty and cheap and had probably been bought at the kibbutz shop. Genghis Khan himself could walk in our room at any time unannounced and uninvited, but if he brought with him a full bottle of booze we would all make him feel very welcome.

We helped Chrome Dome drink it all anyway, and at seven o'clock we weaved our way up to the dining-room where we had a leisurely meal of bread, hard boiled eggs, cold salad, copious glasses of tea and quite a few after dinner cigarettes. At nine o'clock we walked across to the *moadon.* There was a disco, of sorts, which usually consisted of a small group of well-meaning but rather inept young *kibbutzniks* messing around with a large stereo system. Several crates of free beer were provided by the kibbutz, of which half was the quite decent Israeli Goldstar beer. The other bottles contained a dark, alcohol-free root beer, and I soon found out why very few people drank any of it.

I was quite well inebriated when I walked into the *moadon*, but helped myself to a couple of beers anyway. The *moadon* was dark and church-like inside, and was very popular with the teenage Israelis of the kibbutz as well as the volunteers. Everyone drank to excess, some far more than others. As far as I can recall, the *moadon* toilets consisted of the nearest wall outside, adjacent to some bushes. At busy times of the evening there could be up to half a dozen men standing against this wall taking a pee and chatting together, often with one hand pressed firmly against the bricks just in case the building fell down. There were examples of some very poor dancing, not least from me, and it was probably the first time I had ever tried dancing in a public place. Thank goodness for subdued lighting. There was much general silliness, but there was also a lot of laughter and fun; it was an excellent way to unwind at the end of the week.

Some of the volunteer girls from the kitchens were present and I sat for a while talking to one in particular, Chrissie, a recent new arrival from the USA. I doubt I made much sense and probably made a terrible fool of myself. She was blonde, gorgeous, lovely, and from what I could remember I thoroughly enjoyed talking to her. I was too drunk to know if anything had been reciprocated in the conversation. I returned to our room at midnight and promptly threw up in the kitchen sink and went to bed. This became a typical Friday night.

COFFEE BREAK

Saturdays were spent mostly in recovery from the previous night. On this particular *Shabbat*, we sat around on our beds in the room listening to the rain falling heavily on the roof, our paraffin heater on full. It was warm and cosy and I finally finished reading Bogarde's *A Postillion Struck by Lightning*. I dreamt of being a writer and of writing something, *anything,* even remotely as good as Bogarde's first volume of autobiography. We lazed around all day, very gradually recovering from the excesses of Friday night. Graham defied the elements and ran from our room in order to visit Sick Mick. When he returned half an hour later he told us most of the football matches in England that day had been cancelled due to the grass pitches being frozen over.

We made toast, drank tea, and slept on and off until dinner time. After dinner we checked the work list for the next day. I was 'dishes' again, as working the dishwasher was called, starting at one in the afternoon. We all had an additional written instruction with the work list too. If we wanted to go swimming at a nearby kibbutz, in their indoor heated pool, we each needed to provide a passport photo. If we didn't have one, then we had to travel into town to obtain one. This was for reasons of security. Chris, Graham and I decided to do this the following morning.

We hitched into town with no problem and found a photographer's called Martins, just off the precinct. For a very costly forty *lira* each, we obtained the necessary photographs a little quicker than we'd planned, so with time to spare we decided to go for a beer. One beer inevitably led to two and consequently we missed the twelve-thirty bus back to the kibbutz. I was due to start work at one o'clock so I was getting desperate to return to Dafna. We ran together in the torrential and near-horizontal rain to the usual hitching place on the eastern edge of town. Luckily Graham and I were picked up very quickly, but with only room for two we had to leave Chris behind. I walked into the dining-room at exactly one o'clock, already tired and very wet.

I took over from 'Ian Anarchist', an English lad from Peterborough, who had some bizarre political ideas, and who was the only other volunteer the same age as me. At two o'clock, disaster struck when the machine broke down. It hadn't occurred to me what would happen in this situation, so I was now to find out. Several febrile but vain attempts were made to fix the monster machine by a succession of *kibbutzniks* scrambling about underneath it with spanners and a lot of shouting. In the meantime the dirty pots were quickly piling up. Perry thankfully appeared from nowhere and together we filled six large plastic bins full of hot soapy water. We then started washing the dishes by hand. This process continued all afternoon.

There was no proper break in the shift, other than a few minutes to grab a quick drink and a smoke. Wandering in the chaos with a moist cigarette in my hot, soapy hands, I began to doubt whether we would ever return the area to any normality. At six o'clock, just as we'd managed to clear most of the lunchtime backlog, the whole process started again. Another *kibbutznik* then helped Perry and me hand-wash all the evening's dishes, as we'd done at lunchtime, while engineers continued to come and go underneath the machine. Eventually I saw a large electric motor arrive in a cardboard box which was then hastily unpacked. It quickly disappeared in a scrum of overall-clad men fussing around on the floor, amidst a cacophony of very serious Hebrew chattering and loud cursing. Perry reluctantly translated some of the most common curses for me, and he clearly resented his machine being referred to as a *Benzona*, which apparently means 'son of a bitch' or similar. At nine o'clock it was finally fixed, and a quick test run proved it was running okay. At ten o'clock the shift was over. Before I left, the dining-room was partially cleared and some Israeli folk-dancing started. I sat for a while and watched it, a little dazed and exhausted, with a cup of sweet tea and my Nelson cigarettes. I was to learn later in the week that I'd earned myself an extra day off, a 'free day' in gratitude for this episode.

The next morning, Perry and I worked together to clean the machine and clear the final remnants of the previous evening. At ten o'clock we all had a break for coffee. I was the last to sit down at the long table and reached forward to take a large handful of biscuits. I began dunking them four and five at a time in my coffee. I noticed the girl across the table was looking at me, probably disgusted at seeing me dunking my biscuits, and then lighting a cigarette at the same time. I probably belched and broke wind simultaneously too, as Perry rattled on in my ear next to me, expounding the benefits of a clean dishwasher. I then realised, to my horror, the gorgeous girl sitting opposite me who I'd noticed occasionally looking at my biscuit dunking, was Chrissie from Seattle. She was the poor soul who had been subjected to some of my drunken ramblings two nights before in the *moadon,* after I'd helped Chrome Dome drink all his cherry brandy. I'd almost forgotten the incident, but not how stupid I must have seemed. I felt terribly self-conscious, extremely sober and very exposed.

I remembered her name, reached across the table, and offered her a Nelson. I don't know why I did this, other than perhaps that I knew she smoked, and I felt an overwhelming desire to do *something.* She took one with a 'Thanks' in her West Coast American accent then promptly stood up with the others and returned to work. She didn't even light it. What did she do with it?

Perry and I went back to work and at three o'clock the machine was turned off for the afternoon. I looked around, but all the other kitchen staff had gone.

OLD HOLBORN

On Wednesday 6th December, no fewer than fifteen of the thirty-one volunteers were taken on a five day kibbutz trip to the south of the country. I didn't qualify for a place as I'd apparently not been there long enough. Despite my desperate pleas I was not allowed on the bus. John, Chris and Graham, amongst others shouted:

"See you next week then Biggles!" laughing as the bus pulled out of the kibbutz gates. I was more than a little upset at being left behind. The next few days were going to be very quiet. I continued working the dishwasher, and I began to find the work quite enjoyable. I also had our room to myself too, apart from one night when Ian slept in John's bed so Guy could use Ian's double bed in his room in order to 'bone' a new volunteer. I don't remember ever changing the sheets on my bed, or anyone else changing their sheets. One morning, Phil and Donald burst into the room with a huge, filthy, long-haired red-setter dog which leapt and bounded around on all the beds with dirty wet paws, before they took it away, much to their amusement. The room was reduced to a scruffy mess in ten seconds flat.

The rain continued and the weather became very much like an English autumn. Though cool, it was never actually 'cold' by Northern European standards. I hitched into town with Guy and Donald, mainly for something to do, but I was also in possession of a shopping list of cigarettes to buy for Karl and Marianne. The kibbutz shop had run out of Nelsons and the closest alternative was a brand of cigarettes called *Royals*, which were cheap but rather tasteless, and which no-one really liked, including me. Time cigarettes were another choice, but I didn't particularly like them either, and neither did Karl or Marianne. They certainly had a distinctive and unique smell but were an acquired taste and actually a little weak.

Friday night came around again. Everyone wished one another *Shabbat Shalom!* in the dining-room and lingered much longer over their meals than usual. Consequently, I finished work late on the dishwasher, at ten o'clock. I returned to the room, showered and changed. With no-one in the room I went next door to see if anything was happening, as was the custom, and talked to Christine, a German girl, and Wolfie, also German. Christine told me a story of when she was learning English, she thought 'let it be' meant 'leave me alone'. It wasn't long after the final Beatles album of the same name had been released, and this simple misunderstanding had caused her a lot of embarrassment. There weren't that many Germans on the kibbutz, and I think they appreciated being able to relax and converse among themselves without having to constantly speak English. When all the different nationalities were together, it was usually English spoken between them as the common method of communication. This was brilliant for the English speakers, but it meant there was very little incentive for people like myself to learn another language.

I wandered up to the *moadon* but found there was no-one there who I was particularly enthused about spending any time with. I then walked across to the kibbutz cinema and saw a movie called *The Front* starring Woody Allen. It was quite good and I watched it to the end before returning alone to our empty room. It became one of the quietest Friday nights I'd ever had since I'd arrived on the kibbutz, and I went to bed completely sober.

In the morning I slept undisturbed almost until midday. This was probably due to the absence of shift workers coming and going in the room. I dressed and walked up to the dining-room. I sat with the few volunteers who remained on the kibbutz. Lunch was quite a nice meaty goulash and baked beans concoction which I really enjoyed. I then took a jug of milk and some bread from the kitchens and returned to the room. I hand-washed some of my best clothes, which had all been pretty dirty, then turned the fire on. There was a laundry on the kibbutz but some of the better items of volunteer clothing had a tendency to disappear in the wash, or so I had heard. Washing powder was available at the shop and was very cheap so most of us did this instead. My wet clothes were hung around the room to dry as I needed them all the next day. I hoped they would be wonderfully clean in the morning.

At four o'clock I decided I would pay Mick a visit. I'd not been to see him on my own before and wondered what sort of reception I'd get. I needn't have worried, as when I stuck my head around the door, tapping on it with due deference, he saw me and bellowed:

"Biggles old chap! Come in and shut the door will you, it's bloody freezing!" and laughed a sort of grunting noise as he reached down to light his paraffin heater. I had no idea what he'd been doing before I'd arrived. Sleeping probably, as this was one of the most common kibbutz pastimes. His dog, Blackie, was curled up asleep at the end of his bed. He stirred and looked up at me. He then resumed his position, head resting on his front paws, completely disinterested, apart from a very slight and almost imperceptible couple of tail wags, which padded about on the bed, as though he could be only half bothered to say hello. Blackie was a small dog, with mainly black fur; hence the name, but he had a light brown head and legs, with flecks of grey on his back, shoulders and chest. He was a very brave little hound who wouldn't think twice about taking on other dogs more than twice his size, according to Mick. He was also a brilliant hunter, able to wriggle and force his way down the smallest holes in the ground with great alacrity, in the hope of catching rabbits and other similar vermin. All this despite the fact that his favourite food was fish!

"Are you alright, Mick?" I said, pulling up his wooden stool nearer the bottom end of the bed.

"Yeah, fine Bigsy, are you? What have you been up to today? Not very much I shouldn't wonder, eh? Not on a Saturday, and everyone away on the trip!" and he laughed again, having successfully lit the heater and replaced the guard around the element. It began to glow a warm red as the flames filled the wire mesh semi-circle. The ceiling light then dimmed very slightly when he reached up and dropped the switch on his electric kettle.

"Tea?" he said, peering across at me over the top of his thick glasses. His ruddy complexion and bushy moustache, together with his crisp south of England accent, gave him the appearance and demeanour of a late Victorian British Army officer.

"Yes, thanks Mick," I replied. I moved off the stool and sat next to Blackie on the bed. I touched his head and he stretched his legs out in front of him in response, and yawned at me. He nudged himself a little closer towards me so he could feel the full benefit of my attentions. I reached inside my pockets for my Nelsons, but Mick handed me a small packet of English Old Holborn rolling tobacco.

"Go on, have one of these..." he said, handing it to me rather insistently.

I'd never rolled my own cigarette before so this was to be yet another new experience. I pulled out a cigarette paper from the packet and loaded it with a few stringy bits of tobacco. My first attempt was predictably a dismal failure as I hadn't put nearly enough tobacco in it. Not only that, in my ignorance I didn't even know there was a gummed edge to one side of the paper, so it promptly fell to bits all over the floor. Mick laughed a deep, slightly haughty chuckle and took the Rizlas from me.

"Here, look, one edge, there. You see? You need more than that, but not *too* much eh; it's not bloody cheap you know! Try it again..."

I dabbed some of the tangled dark brown tobacco onto another cigarette paper, the right way around this time, licked the gummed edge, and successfully rolled it, though it had a slightly conical shape at one end.

"That's alright," Mick boomed. "Here," he said, as he lit a match and thrust it towards me.

I drew on the cigarette and the smoke was very strong,

similar in strength to the first Camel I'd smoked. I felt light-headed for a moment, as though I might pass out. I took a few deep breaths of air in between puffs, and waited until my body caught up with the nicotine rush from the stronger tobacco. I looked across at Mick and asked him about the tractor I'd seen him driving with Blackie, and he spoke about his work and life on Dafna:

"You *can* feel like you've been here all the time," Mick said as he passed me an ashtray. "I've been here quite a long time and so they trust me with it. You have to find some work that suits, Bigsy, then like it or not you have to settle for it. You *have* to like what you've got, it's not easy at first, getting used to it I mean. But then none of the work is *difficult* is it? I love driving the tractor. I'm like a farmer looking after a farm! I'd never done anything like this before until I came here. I really feel like I've set roots down in this place, under the soil, deep in the soil."

My first ever home-made cigarette broke apart slightly in the middle and red hot chunks of burning ash dropped onto my jeans briefly before I swept it all onto the floor. I was nodding at Mick, and he continued:

"Where are you working now, the dishwasher? You didn't like the factory, did you?" and he laughed before I could answer, and he carried on: "You see all of us fit in our places, eh?" and he looked at me and winked, "If you know what I mean?" then he laughed. I continued nodding in serious agreement but I wasn't at all sure of what he was talking about.

He handed me my tea, and just as I started sipping it, Ian Anarchist stomped in, brushing the rain from his coat. He came straight in without knocking, as though it was his right to enter unannounced. He seemed surprised to see me sitting on the end of Mick's bed, Blackie now curled up almost entirely in my lap. Whether this surprise entrance was Ian's anarchistic political views demonstrating that deference didn't matter, or that he was just such a good friend of Mick's, I wasn't at all sure. In fact I wasn't at all sure of Ian in any respect. He was my age but this seemed to be the only thing we had in common. He was very thin, probably even thinner than I was, with collar length curly brown hair, a fairly big nose, pale skin and freckles. I've no doubt he was an intelligent lad but I had little to talk to him about. He often spoke about 'the proletariat' and 'the ruling classes' and that 'property is theft' and so on. He constantly enthused about how great it was to be living in a socialist commune based on Marxist principles. I suppose I didn't gel with him very much initially because most of the time I hadn't the first clue what he was talking about! His favourite band was The Clash, who I then thought were just awful, and he loathed progressive rock bands such as Genesis in favour of the new, more political, screaming and spitting 'punk' bands of the time. But I met Ian halfway I suppose, as I'd seen The Stranglers at the Top Rank club in Sheffield, and The Jam headlined one night at the Reading Rock '78 music festival when I was there with Dave in the summer. So we were not *that* far apart, musically at least. Mick looked on in quiet amusement at all this and claimed to have very catholic musical tastes. He assured us that he enjoyed the music of both Genesis *and* The Clash. Ian and I were the two youngest volunteers on the kibbutz and Mick clearly relished his unofficial position as occasional surrogate father to us both.

As Ian sat on the bed next to me, Mick immediately made another tea without asking or being asked, and handed it to Ian. We then had a discussion about music and politics which was notable in the sheer breadth and depth of the subject matter. Most of it went over my head. My politics were quite simple at the time. I thought of myself as something of a democratic constitutional monarchist, if there is such a thing. This did not sit well with Ian at all. But I enjoyed our discussions and his company. There was a very civilised atmosphere in the room that afternoon; the three of us sipping tea, smoking and chatting, as though we were sitting in some old gentlemen's club.

Then all stopped for the football results when Mick tuned

his radio in to London. Ian was visibly distraught when he heard Walsall Football Club had lost again. I didn't really support any team in particular, though if pressed I would almost always say 'Sheffield Wednesday'.

At six o'clock I made my way to the dining-room. I was still there at eight o'clock when the kibbutz trip returned. I was happy and relieved to see them all back. Chris and Graham were angry about the state of their beds from the dog jumping about on them and generally seemed quite unhappy to be back on Dafna.

THE CONFLICT

Katyushas!

Coffee breaks were a great occasion in the mornings, and I looked forward to them immensely. As the days and weeks passed I was able to settle into the warm, comfortable and familiar routine that became my first real niche job on the kibbutz, that of operating the dishwashing machine. My initial drunken evening spent talking to Chrissie had not been repeated, at least not with her. I wanted to speak to her again but I'd been unable to find an appropriate moment. Morning coffee breaks in the dining-room could have been an ideal opportunity. In the middle of preparing the dishwashing machine for the day, I would turn it off and casually try to arrange it so I could sit opposite her as often as possible. I found myself frequently peering into the hubbub of the busy kitchen area while operating the machine and stacking the dishes, perhaps in the hope of seeing her, even just for a moment.

I'd usually sit with Gary or Perry at the coffee breaks and always hoped we would perhaps by chance be seated close to Chrissie so I could make some attempts at small talk with her. I was incredibly shy and diffident when it came to exchanges with the opposite sex, and contented myself with just catching the occasional glance and few brief words every now and again, not daring to think that Chrissie would be interested in reciprocating any conversation. She must have thought I was extremely generous with my cigarettes. The brief fifteen minutes at the table during these relaxed and convivial morning coffee breaks facilitated a great opportunity to gossip and tactfully explore common ground between us. I was too naïve at the time to realise that whenever I did speak to Chrissie she was always friendly and happy to provide a warm response. She was apparently sending me some positive signals but I was too stupid to catch them, and they floated by me like butterflies on a warm summer breeze.

I couldn't remember what I'd spoken to her about on that drunken Friday night in the *moadon*, and was perplexed and frustrated by this. I was resentful of my own shyness and craven inability, which brought about my idiot clumsiness and persistent reticence. Maybe it was because Chrissie was a grown woman, and not a girl; I was certainly attracted to her, but she frightened me at the same time. She was about five feet six, slim, with shoulder-length, curly blonde hair which tumbled delicately over her shoulders, and deep sky blue eyes. And pretty. Very pretty. Despite wearing floppy over-sized wellington boots, ridiculously baggy kibbutz trousers, and a tatty and baggy kibbutz shirt, she definitely had something, and I was captivated by her. She had a strong American accent which gave me the impression she'd just stepped from a Hollywood film set. I was an eighteen-year-old teenager from England, thousands of miles from home, talking to a gorgeous American woman. How could I dare assume she would even be bothered with the likes of me? Even though I didn't always pick up the positive signals fired in my direction, I was at least aware I was not being sent any negative ones. I was beginning to acquire a slight, but real sense of anticipation and excitement at what may happen. I knew she was older than me but I wasn't sure just how much. But then everyone seemed to be older than me, apart from Ian Anarchist. In addition to this, I often saw other male volunteers and *kibbutzniks* talking to her. I'd even seen Sick Mick dance with her in the *moadon* on more than one occasion. Who could blame them though, she was lovely.

Coffee break was over after twenty minutes and I was back at my machine. I managed a few minutes' chat to Gary in amongst his containers, during which time Chrissie would occasionally bring over a dirty, food-encrusted container while I was there, and leave it on the side close to us. She didn't really need to do this, and sadly I didn't click that she may have had ulterior motives for doing so. She would sweep in and out and I knew my eyes were following her every move constantly, but I couldn't help it. I smiled at her and tried a casual: 'Hi!' to which she replied with the same, but also with a sweet, knowing smile, as though she knew I felt that I was window shopping without any money in my pocket. She then returned to stand working with the other female volunteers in the kitchen, preparing the food.

To my horror Gary suddenly said to me: "Jonathan, why don't you do something about that?" smiling at me, while emptying one of the containers down a drain in the floor in front of me.

"About what?" I said, feigning disinterest, astonished and terrified in equal measure that he may have noticed the way I always looked at Chrissie.

"Just go up to her and give her a big kiss, Jonathan…" he said, laughing, turning back to the sink, his thin white arms submerged almost up to the shoulders in masses of frothy bubbles. He started scrubbing away furiously at the food-encrusted stainless steel, singing to himself very loudly: "Dum de dum diddley dum diddley…" while washing up, as bubbles and foam flew about everywhere. Then, without looking at me, he shouted:

"You can't hide that look you know, it's obvious! I think she likes you too. As sure as eggs is eggs all you'd have to do is ask her. What have you got to lose?!"

Ian took over the machine at one o'clock and I went back to the room for a shower. I was surprised to find a middle-aged *kibbutznik* in our shower room with a tool box, screwdriver in hand and huge bunch of keys dangling from his belt. The hissing leak was finally fixed! I walked at a brisk pace across the grass towards Gary and Claudie's room. I couldn't stop thinking about what he'd said.

I tapped on their door and walked in. Gary was alone in the room, sitting on their make-shift double bed reading a paperback copy of Len Deighton's *Bomber*. I sat on the edge of the bed, and we talked about the armed forces, world politics and the future of civilization. I wanted to talk to him about Chrissie of course. Gary postulated the ridiculous notion that some currently impoverished countries such as China would eventually emerge in years to come as the world's most powerful nations, economically, politically and militarily. This seemed very unlikely at the time as everyone in China rode about on pedal cycles because they were so poor. Prophetic words indeed. He then reverted to a topic much closer to home and to the real reason for my visit. He told me again that I should speak to Chrissie, and to grasp any opportunity I could in order to become better acquainted with her. What had I got to lose?

Claudie came into the room and sat on the bed next to Gary. She looked happy and bubbly as usual.

"Hi Jonathan," she said in her soft French accent, effortlessly sweet and sexy. "Chrissie is very nice you know, Jonathan..." she said, smiling at me then at Gary, as though she'd been listening at the door.

"I've told him, Clauds. He's just got to go for it, eh?" Gary stood up and reached for his coat. He kissed Claudie gently on the cheek, and I then accompanied him around the corner to Tim's room. We stayed there all evening drinking vodka, wine, brandy, and some awful Israeli aniseed liquor known as *Arak*. I felt reassured and pleased with myself after my conversation with Gary and was determined to make an impact when I next spoke to Chrissie. I drank far too much and I remember staggering back to our room at around three o'clock in the morning. I must have fallen over a few times as I discovered my coat was covered in thick mud the next day.

I slept until seven o'clock and was over an hour late for work at the dishwasher. When I finally arrived I took over from a *kibbutznik* who didn't seem particularly upset at my being so late. I thought I was in for a roasting, or at least some sarcastic mumblings in Hebrew, but my tardiness was not even mentioned. Work dragged for me that morning, I was so very tired and hungover. I soon felt quite a lot better after some very welcome eggs and semolina.

I missed my seat across from Chrissie at the coffee break and only managed a few bleary-eyed minutes seated at the end of the table, before it seemed I was back on the machine as the lunch-time plates started to come through. I still felt a little drunk and took pot-shots at the flies on the walls and ceiling with the hose. Eventually there were dead flies everywhere and the floor was inches deep in water. Suddenly an Israeli shouted at me rather abruptly through the narrow gap from the dining-room, pointing angrily at the kitchen area as he did so. He shouted again and looked very cross. I didn't understand what he'd said. I think I'd accidentally wet him with the hose. I assumed that was why he'd shouted at me. I ignored him and carried on working, occasionally shooting at flies again with the hose. I started singing away loudly to myself when The Eagles' *Hotel California* came on the radio. I cranked up the volume as loud as it would go. This was a new song to me and I'd heard it a lot while working at the zipper in the factory. I half expected to be told off for being so loud, as I sometimes was, but curiously, no-one bothered. My corner of the kitchens echoed loudly to the resolute din of the dishwashing machine, my singing, and the distorted radio at full volume. There was very little that could be heard above this cacophony.

It should have been the height of lunch-time when I was usually at my busiest. Plates and cutlery would have been emerging from the hot steamy darkness of the machine at such a pace that I would find it a real struggle to keep up. But on this particular day, Monday 11th December 1978, the lunch-time plates suddenly stopped coming through. The machine was still dragging the plastic trays through the process as usual, but there was nothing clean coming out for me to remove and stack. Why had people stopped putting their dishes to wash? Had they all stopped eating? Had I upset them so much with my singing?

I tried to stick my head out into the dining-room but couldn't see anyone. Rather stupidly I finished singing along to The Eagles, and spent about ten minutes stacking the items I'd just taken off the dishwasher. I couldn't resist taking advantage of the rare opportunity to get ahead of the machine, and so I cleared some plates and cutlery trays before finally deciding to stop the dishwasher. I thumped the big red 'stop' button on the side of the machine and the huge stainless steel beast fell silent with some hissing and spluttering, and water briefly pouring noisily into the drains underneath. I reached up onto the shelf and turned off the radio.

There was absolute silence. What on earth was going on? I stood for a moment, rigid to the spot, not really knowing what to do. I saw all the dead flies on the floor and then curiously thought what an idiot I'd been. I was suddenly extremely sober. I knew there should be hundreds of people eating, chattering and laughing. I walked around the machine and stood at the opening into the dining-room in my wellies, wet trousers, baggy blue shirt, and a quizzical look on my face. Hundreds of meals had been abandoned. I could see steam rising from some of the hot food on the plates closest to me, and the cutlery was just left sticking in the food. There was no-one walking around outside the dining-room either. There was just no-one about at all. Everyone had gone.

I walked slowly through the kitchens. I looked for the *kibbutzniks*, and wondered if Gary was among his containers, or if Chrissie was still there, but everything had been abandoned. A tap was running at Gary's sink so I turned it off. This was like a dream, or a nightmare. I soon began to realise just what might be happening. The main back doors to the kitchens had been flung open and light was streaming in from outside. I pushed my way through the thick heavy strips of plastic at the door and stepped into the back yard. I jumped down off the loading ramp and walked the few yards towards the *miklat*. Though I wasn't entirely sure why, I looked around me all the time, and in particular up at the sky.

When I reached the heavy steel door of the huge kitchen *miklat* I took hold of it with both hands and eased it open. It was much heavier than I'd anticipated and it made a loud creaking sound as I pulled at it. I leaned my head inside slowly and looked down into the darkness. Twenty feet down the steps in the quiet gloom of the bunker, I saw a dozen anxious faces, their wide eyes staring up at me with a mixture of anger and relief on seeing who it was staring back down at them. Before anyone had chance to say anything, at that moment a loud siren started wailing nearby and all those in the *miklat* suddenly started to climb the stairs amid some typically effusive hand gestures and loud talking. I stood there, near the door, as dozens of people emerged from the shelter, chattering away and paying me no attention at all. Then the volunteers emerged, including Gary and Chrissie.

"That's the first time I've ever been caught in an air raid Jonathan!" Gary remarked to me in his Brummie accent. He took out his cigarettes and offered me one.

"Where were you, Jonathan?" Chrissie asked, taking one of Gary's Nelsons.

"No-one told me anything about it!" I exclaimed, a little upset but not particularly angry. Gary laughed as he lit our cigarettes, passing a match around.

"That's bloody typical that is. Didn't anyone tell you?" and he laughed again. I was unsure, but maybe the chap who was shouting at me had been warning me about it? I was also unaware, as we all were at that moment, whether anything had actually happened. Gary said he'd sensed some thuds in the ground, but I hadn't heard any explosions or banging of any kind. *Kibbutzniks* hurried away in all directions with very serious and concerned expressions on their faces. As calm began to descend once again, Gary, Chrissie and I just stood for a few minutes at the rear of the kitchens, smoking.

Gary suddenly said: "Are you going to the *moadon* tonight, Chrissie?" and he winked at me before taking another drag on his cigarette.

"Yeah, I guess. Unless we have to spend all night down *there*..." and she threw a scathing glance toward the open door of the *miklat*.

"I bloody hope not!" exclaimed Gary.

We all laughed and then I said: "I'll probably be there tonight. I might see you there..?" trying my utmost to sound casual while flicking some cigarette ash behind me, and seeing just a hint of a smile forming on Gary's face.

"Sure, why not. See you there later." Chrissie stood on her cigarette and twisted her foot very slightly to make sure it was completely extinguished. She then turned and drifted slowly away, her long blonde hair catching the sunlight as she moved, causing it to shine golden yellow. Even though I could see her over-sized wellington boots flopped about awkwardly around her ankles as she walked, she looked lovely.

"There you go, Biggles. You'll probably end up giving her one tonight, thanks to me!" and Gary walked off, laughing, back to his containers. I returned to my machine, switched it all back on and started stacking plates again. I was thrilled at the prospect of meeting Chrissie later and had completely forgotten we'd all just been in an air raid.

Ian took over again at about one-thirty. He brought some news about the air raid. To my astonishment, several *Katyusha* rockets (pronounced 'kat-yoo-sha') had landed near the kibbutz, in the avocado fields, and had completely shredded some trees. Other *kibbutzim* in the area sustained similar damage and some had landed close to Kiryat Shmona, but thankfully no-one had been hurt. The *Katyusha* rockets were Russian-made anti-personnel munitions, launched from over the border in Lebanon by the PLO, the Palestine Liberation Organisation, at that time led by Yasser Arafat. They fragment when they explode into great shards of red hot and very nasty jagged metal pieces, specifically designed to rip apart human flesh. Some of the trees had literally been reduced to match sticks. These particular avocado trees were only about five hundred yards from the kibbutz dining-room, where hundreds of people had just been eating their lunch. They'd been instantaneously cut down and shredded while I was busy stacking dishes, quite obliviously singing along to *Hotel California*...

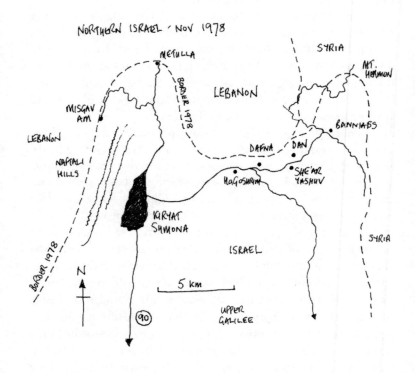

Northern Israel as I saw it in November 1978

AN EYE FOR AN EYE...

That night and for most of the next day the air raid was a major topic of conversation. I tuned the dishwasher radio to the BBC World Service and also managed to hear some Jordanian State Radio broadcast in English. The latter never referred to Israel by name but merely as 'The Enemy'. This all seemed quite bizarre and frankly a little childish to me. Israel's existence was an undeniable fact. It was real, so why not refer to it by name? Neither of these radio stations made reference to the rocket bombardment I'd just experienced. As I spent more time in Israel I realised these air raids were a common occurrence across the country and were not generally newsworthy to the international media. They were something the Israeli people just seemed to tolerate, or were forced to live with. I thought how unjust this was, a judgment perhaps based on my own ignorance and a naïve, but very British, sense of fair play.

The air raid *was* given some detailed and vociferous mention in the Israeli news broadcasts, as far as I could make out, both on the radio and the television. I heard 'Kiryat Shmona' and 'Katyusha' in the same sentence over and over. We asked Ezra about them and he was understandably very bitter and scathing in his condemnation of the attacks and hinted that Israel would probably strike back, in some form or another, if they continued.

It was only two days later, at three o'clock in the morning, when we were woken up by a noise that few Englishmen have ever heard, and would probably never experience in a whole lifetime. The first sound was a loud metallic clunking, squeaking, and very deep clangourous rumbling, some distance away from our room. It was very worrying, and as every second passed it drew ominously closer. Our room was at the bottom end of the kibbutz, not far from the main road.

This was where the disturbing noise seemed to be coming from, further down the road towards town. The ill-fitting wooden window frame and glass panes nearest my bed started rattling, with a noise like bees in a biscuit tin. The floor tiles groaned as though some great restless giant was burrowing underneath us. I heard dogs on the kibbutz start barking. I was sure then that we were experiencing the beginnings of an earthquake.

We were all awake together. Chris was first out of bed and immediately put the light on. The dusty shade hanging from the ceiling around the plain sixty-watt bulb was vibrating very slightly, trembling delicately at the edges like the fingers of condemned man.

"What the bloody hell's going on, Jonathan?" Chris exclaimed, seeing me awake, nudging Graham and looking at me, and then back at Graham, who was just beginning to sit up. I lay there in my bed not wanting to move, partly *unable* to move, perhaps subconsciously hoping that whatever was happening would happen less if I didn't stir.

I shouted: "It must be an earthquake!" as I looked around the room and noticed John's door was tight shut. I'd never experienced an earth tremor before, and this certainly felt as though it could be just that. I'd seen clips of earthquakes on the television and this seemed to be exactly the same. What else could it be? We peered out of the window into the darkness towards the road where the sound was coming from, but saw nothing. The noise was now becoming so loud it seemed as though it was almost on top of us.

John finally emerged from his room and strode calmly and stoically towards the toilet, without even looking at us. He disappeared into the toilet leaving the door open and stood taking a pee. The usual loud concentrated splashing in the toilet was drowned out by the increasing noise. Then he shouted one word in our direction:

"Tanks!"

"What?" Chris shouted back, an incredulous expression on his face.

"That's tanks, that is," John said again, in his West Yorkshire accent. "They're going off into the hills to get that lot for those bloody rockets the other day…"

"Bloody hell…!" Chris shouted. I rose from my bed and we opened our front door. Feeling a little braver, we stood on the step, jostling and pushing one another, but each of us not really wanting to be the first out of the door. I'd never seen or heard anything quite like it before. As they emerged from the darkness, I saw some enormous tanks lumbering slowly and heavily along the road, approaching the kibbutz. It seemed as though there were dozens of them, one after the other in quick succession, approaching Dafna only yards away from us just the other side of the fence. They trundled past the kibbutz and carried on along the road, clearly heading for the hills, their wide metal tracks rattling loudly on the smooth tarmac. The huge black shapes were quite indistinct at first. Their profile was low and rounded on top, and mostly in silhouette. Their main guns protruded an impossible length in front of them. At that moment I was struck by the incredible psychological power of a heavy tank, and by its sheer sonorous presence and seemingly unstoppable advance.

The convoy seemed to take hours to pass but was probably only about twenty minutes, and was followed by trucks and jeeps. It was obviously part of Israel's reply, as Ezra had mentioned. We found out later the tanks were American-built, 57 ton 'M60' 'Patton' tanks, renamed *Magach* tanks by Israel. We'd witnessed the early preparations for 'Operation Litani' by the IDF, the Israeli Defence Force, aimed at pushing the PLO at least 25 kilometres back into Lebanon, close to the Litani River. If successful, it would cause Kiryat Shmona and the surrounding *kibbutzim* to become out of range of the *Katyusha* rockets.

Chris put the kettle on and made tea. That's what the British do in circumstances such as these! He was due to start work at four o'clock on the conveyor with Graham anyway, so there was little point in returning to bed. Just before the two of them left for work, the occasional single vehicle sped past before, finally, all went quiet again. The air in and around our room was thick with the smell of diesel fumes. John and I went back to bed. I turned the light off and lay on my back, looking around the dark and, now very quiet, room. I expected to hear guns in the distance at any moment, but to my disappointment I heard nothing. Eventually I drifted back off to sleep.

My alarm clock woke me up just before six. I trudged up to the dining-room, still feeling very sleepy. I loaded the machine with soap and detergent, turned it on, and made a drink. I sat in the dining-room and lit my first Nelson of the day. I gazed into my coffee. The early morning sun was just beginning to stream in through the tall windows.

THE BANNIASS

The second week of December saw quite a few volunteers leave Dafna. In order to secure a place on the desired flight, in the pre-internet age, volunteers usually had to travel by bus to the airline offices in Haifa, on the Mediterranean coast, to book the flight in person. It therefore became common knowledge that when someone was planning a trip to Haifa, it was probably not simply for sight-seeing reasons. Even though it is a beautiful place and probably worthy of a visit, any such trip was therefore most likely the formal start of the irreversible departure routine.

Phil returned to England, claiming he would be back in Israel some time after Christmas. He wrote SHIT and BOLLOCKS alternately at the top of each page of my diary as a parting gesture. He also made an entry in my diary as follows: '*I talked to my very best friend Philip who I am going to give all my money to when I earn about £10,000 in the next few years. I will always remember my best friend Phil.*' I hid my diary in various locations other than under the mattress, but wherever it was kept it was clearly never left in a completely safe place. It was widely known that I kept a diary as I was often seen scribbling away. I decided then that I would take advantage of quieter moments to write, more perhaps when alone than in company. I never thought my writings were at serious risk or in danger of destruction. It was not as though I was forced to hide my diary every day inside a makeshift hole in the wall, to keep it from the prying eyes of some murderous occupying force.

Others whom I didn't know very well also left: Symon, Ged, Joe, Gerry, Sue, and Derek. Parties were held in their honour of course. Gerry and Sue were returning to England to resume their careers in nursing. We all crammed into kibbutz vehicles and drove into Kiryat Shmona to see them off, mainly at the insistence of the ebullient and ever happy Ethiopian Paul. We drank pints of beer and even chipped in together to buy a bottle of champagne.

One morning around that time we also discovered Chrome Dome had left without saying a word to anyone. I found this particularly strange and difficult to understand. He simply vanished.

Calling in at the kibbutz office and checking the post could be a highlight of the whole day. There was real excitement in the anticipation of receiving mail, rather like the purchase of a lottery ticket. Such excitement was rewarded if there was mail waiting, but there was obvious disappointment when, as was more usual, there was nothing. A decent piece of news from home could set the mood for the day, and often the same letter would be read over and over. I would sometimes sit somewhere comfortable with a coffee or a beer, and some Nelsons, and really enjoy reading letters from certain people, savouring every single word. I doubt they would ever know the true significance of those letters.

I was listening to more music I wasn't familiar with. Pink Floyd began to feature prominently and I finally understood what Gary meant about their song, *Welcome to the Machine*, and the relevance to the dishwasher. Ezra called in to our room one night with his Uzi submachine gun. He informed us that all the adults on the kibbutz over the age of eighteen had one. He kept his under the bed when he wasn't carrying it around with him. I was hugely envious. He let us have a play with it, but – luckily for everyone within a hundred yards of our room – he very wisely refused to give us any ammunition, despite our continued protestations. I can only imagine the dire consequences of handing a loaded Uzi to a group of drunken volunteers! I took photographs of each of us holding it and beaming broadly, gripping it tightly in our hands. I was surprised at how heavy and cumbersome it was, even without any bullets.

I continued working the dishwasher. I also continued trying to build a relationship with Chrissie. The night following the air raid I had a shower and put on my jeans and the only decent shirt I'd brought with me from England. I walked into the *moadon* at six o'clock when it was opened up, eager, excited, and thrilled at the prospect of spending the evening with Chrissie. Marianne soon arrived and I played backgammon with her for a while as she expounded all her knowledge of the band Supertramp and how brilliant they were. She must have seen my preoccupation with repeatedly glancing over her shoulder at the door, but she didn't say anything. She was probably too polite. Two hours passed with sadly no sign of Chrissie. After an evenly matched series of backgammon games Marianne insisted I accompany her back to her room to listen to Supertramp. By this time it was eight o'clock. Maybe Chrissie had forgotten about the arrangement? It could have slipped her mind, or she was probably busy with something else. I didn't feel inclined to knock on her door, as I knew she was sharing a room with Sarah, a friend from home with whom she was travelling. The arrangement had been made and it seemed that, for whatever reason, she had decided not to show.

Marianne and I left the *moadon* together and walked down to her room. I sat on her bed while she fiddled about with her tape machine. We had been there barely long enough to hear the first few minutes of the Supertramp album *Crime of the Century* when Wolfie walked in, clutching a full bottle of Israeli vodka. Soon after that, Christine and Karl arrived. To my amazement they all spoke English entirely for my benefit. I heard the occasional '*Ja, naturlich*' and '*vielleicht*' in amongst their English, and I felt honoured and strangely self conscious that they were making this extra effort for me. I was the only English person in the room and I was flattered. At ten o'clock, after all the vodka had been consumed, I thanked Marianne and staggered back to the *moadon* to find it was closed. This was not unusual for a Monday.

The next morning at work, Chrissie stated she had arrived at the *moadon* a few minutes after eight. I had apparently therefore just missed her. I believed her completely. She said she sat for a while talking to some other volunteers before leaving, at about the same time I had started being subjected to the Germans practicing their conversational English. I could tell she was not very pleased. I was incredibly angry with myself.

At the *Shabbat* Friday disco in the *moadon* on 15th December I was determined to make amends, so we both arranged to be there early. We then sat together for over an hour, talking, laughing and drinking Goldstar in a space of time which seemed to pass as though it had just been a few minutes. Eventually Chrissie left with Sarah and they both returned to their room. At last I was finally beginning to get the impression she perhaps enjoyed my company!

On Saturday morning we all woke up to a beautiful, clear blue sky. It was warm too, and unlike any weather we'd had for weeks. The rain had gone and the sparrows were back outside my window, flitting about and noisily chirping away. The weather was comparable to a pretty decent English summer's day. Ian was asleep in Graham's bed, apparently because Graham had spent the night in Ian's bed, for 'boning' purposes. Claudie, always welcome in our room, came round to speak to Ian about something, and as she walked in, he woke up. I listened to her sweet mellifluous French accent as she spoke to him. She sat with her back to me talking to Ian, her delicate frame perched gently on the edge of the bed, her curves perfectly filling her Levi jeans. I was still half asleep and tried to follow their conversation from across the room. It seemed Ian was very drunk the night before and had caused some sort of unspecified problem in their room. Claudie was attempting to reprimand him for it. Ian apologised, stating he couldn't remember the incident. This was not a surprise. Huge amounts of alcohol were consumed by volunteers, particularly on Friday nights. Not everyone reacted favourably to an excess of drink, or behaved themselves all the time. The kibbutz often represented a microcosm of human life, both good and bad. Otherwise polite and well-mannered people could become outrageously feckless and boorish when drunk.

Just as in the real world, these individuals were the ones to avoid.

John emerged from his room dressed, and left, stating he was going to visit Motty. No doubt he would also see Denis, who he was seeing quite lot of at the time. At breakfast in the dining-room, Graham, Chris and I decided we'd go for a run. We'd heard of a waterfall just up the main road called The Banniass and decided to investigate. We put on our shorts and the three of us set off at about eleven o'clock.

We ran out of the front gates of the kibbutz and turned left onto the road. I immediately noticed the smooth tarmac surface of the road had been very badly damaged in places, ripped up and scarred, from where the tanks had been driven along it a few nights before. We jogged seven kilometres up the road at a steady pace. As we ran we could see the tarmac was intermittently damaged for most of the way. The road swept up towards Mount Hermon at an ever steeper incline, making the run gradually slower and more painful. We stopped occasionally to take a breath and a few gulps of water from my green plastic, Israeli army canteen. We sat down by the road. It was then that I first noticed some curious thin metal signs every few yards hanging from the fence, lining the road. They were painted yellow with a red triangle and two Hebrew words in block capitals, the second of which ended with an exclamation mark.

Eventually we reached a small brown signpost on our right for Banniass. We walked down a track which tumbled abruptly towards a lush gathering of eucalyptus trees and some very tall, thick and healthy bamboo plants, which were obviously thriving by the water. The trees seemed to have hundreds of birds in them and the area appeared as a plateau of arboreal greenery full of life. A winding narrow path descended through the trees, and at the bottom of some huge stone steps hewn from solid rock was a waterfall: loud, cool and magnificent. Masses of water flowed solidly and spectacularly from gaps in huge rocks twenty feet above, and cascaded down into a deep pool about fifteen yards across. I saw a young figure sitting alone by the pool as we approached. As we drew nearer I realised it was a dark-skinned teenage boy. He promptly ran off into the trees when he saw us, and disappeared.

Hot and sweaty, we each jumped into the water, only to be instantly shocked at just how cold it was. But it was gin-clear and brilliant, foaming around us in masses of white bubbles as we splashed and swam around. It was well worth the exhausting trip, as it was a magical place. I swam about under and behind the waterfall, occasionally feeling the incredible weight and power of the water on my shoulders. It was truly an invigorating experience.

We climbed onto the surrounding wet rocks and looked around for somewhere to sit. There were ruins of a building nearby, so we sat for a while in the dappled sunlight which was breaking through the trees. Graham and I smoked a Nelson before contemplating the return journey. I had no idea at the time that the waterfall we were looking at was actually a source of the River Jordan. It was not officially in Israel at all, but part of the Golan Heights, which had been captured from Syria in 1967.

We started to walk back down the road, after unanimously deciding against running. The sun shone brightly in our faces. The Hula Valley stretched out before us, with the Naftali Hills and Kiryat Shmona on the right. The air was fresh and the countryside was busy and green after the recent rain. The snowy peaks of Mount Hermon looked wild and spectacular, quite close over our left shoulders. Looking down from the Golan Road into Northern Israel it seemed as though we were at the very edge of civilization.

We came to the fence again by the road with the signs hanging from it. I carefully clambered over the barbed wire.

"What are you doing, Biggles?" Graham asked. "I don't think you're meant to go over there," he said, moving himself closer to the fence.

"I'm just going to have a quick look," I replied. I glanced furtively around as though expecting to be shouted at, or worse, and began to explore some deep trenches and disused gun emplacements. Graham climbed over the fence and followed. There were rusty spent cartridge cases strewn across the ground and some old ammunition boxes with Arabic writing on the sides. Lengths of barbed wire were protruding from the sandy earth on spikes everywhere, reminiscent of photographs from the First World War. Clearly this had once been the scene of some bitter fighting in the not-too-distant past.

"Come on you two, get out of there!" Chris shouted. I could have wandered around for hours but Graham agreed with Chris and reluctantly we both climbed back over the fence. I pulled at one of the yellow metal signs, and when it finally came away I slipped it under my t-shirt.

We arrived back in our room at four o'clock, exhausted and hungry. John and Motty were in our room listening to music and drinking tea. There was a faint smell of toast and there were fresh crumbs on the floor around the fire. Motty seemed more than a little irate when he saw the sign I'd brought from the Golan road. He told me I should take it back, or at least throw it away. I asked him why, and what it meant. He said the direct translation was:

DANGER: MINES!

CLINIC!

Occasionally while operating the dishwasher, I would spike my hand on broken glass or cutlery stuck in the drains inside or under the machine. Usually this didn't cause a problem but on one occasion in December something had lodged itself inside the palm of my left hand and just wouldn't come out. My whole hand started to swell up like something from a science fiction movie and was becoming increasingly painful. I couldn't function properly with only one good hand at the dishwasher and began to lag behind a little. I could see some *kibbutzniks* had noticed quite a few clean plates and cutlery were making a second trip around the machine where I had missed them and eventually one of them came to see what the problem was. A middle-aged man marched up to me, and when he saw my swollen hand he just shouted one word at me: 'Clinic!' while pointing a finger in the general direction of the kibbutz clinic. I knew what he meant from all the descriptions Guy had given me about his visits there, so at eight-thirty that morning, just after breakfast when I had very few customers, I paid my first visit to the clinic.

The kibbutz clinic was a separate brick bungalow which consisted of a narrow and very plain waiting area inside the door, where half a dozen plastic chairs had been placed neatly in a line against one wall. Immediately off the waiting area was a small doctor's surgery, a treatment room and a dispensing area. All the rooms were spotlessly clean; in fact the clinic was probably *the* cleanest and brightest place on the whole kibbutz. There was a very pungent smell of antiseptic and iodine. The resident nurse was an imperious and matronly woman in her early fifties. In her younger days she had probably been quite good-looking. She possessed a huge inestimable chest which was impossibly held together inside her very smart, dark-blue, vaguely nurse-like uniform. She shook her head when she saw my hand and started muttering to herself in Hebrew. I was marched promptly over to a large and very shiny stainless steel sink adjacent to a hospital trolley. I was then instructed to sit on a chair close enough to the sink so I could easily reach inside it with my arm. She turned on the tap and steaming hot water began to fill the bowl, into which she then added what appeared to be a few drops of liquid soap. She whisked the water briskly for a few seconds with both hands then added some cold, before turning off the taps. My hand was then lifted up gently and lowered into the warm foamy water. I was ordered to leave it there while she reached into a nearby cupboard on the wall. There was no conversation of any sort between myself and the clinic nurse at that time, other than her occasionally polite but peremptory instructions. I didn't feel particularly inclined to talk to her at that stage either. She seemed very professional indeed and was completely engaged in her activity. I began to daydream a little, probably from the soothing, almost soporific effect of my throbbing hand submerged in the lovely warm water. I watched her take out a handful of white cloth from a large pile of linen in the cupboard, obviously freshly cleaned and pressed.

I was then left alone for several minutes with my arm soaking almost up to the elbow in the sink while she disappeared around the corner into another room. I could hear tins and packets being opened and some whisking going on as though she was baking a cake. I realised there was a radio switched on in the next room. The volume was very low but I could hear a man's voice chattering in Hebrew. There was a pleasant, soothing atmosphere in the clinic, and I felt very calm and relaxed.

Finally when the nurse came back into view she was carrying a large china bowl in both hands. With a surprisingly gentle touch she lifted my hand from the water and padded it dry very carefully with a towel. She then applied to my hand, from the bowl, some thick yellow poultice which had the consistency and feel of warm cloudy treacle. My hand was then bandaged with a sterile dressing and I was told to return the next day.

I went back to work, taking care with some difficulty to keep my bandage as dry as I possibly could. I finished at one o'clock when Ian arrived and took over. After work I decided to do some constructive wandering of the kibbutz grounds with my little camera. I took quite a few photos that afternoon, including one of Ishi standing with Chris and Graham outside the factory, the latter in his trademark and probably quite impractical black leather jacket. Chris took a photograph of me near the same location, with my freshly bandaged hand. I then strolled out the north entrance of the kibbutz and took another of the old bridge, having walked alone through the various fields and orchards. I sang Genesis songs to myself, sometimes out loud if I thought no-one else was within earshot. Those were the days before the iPod or even the Walkman. I then walked back to the kibbutz and drank tea and ate biscuits in the factory canteen with Ezra, Chris and Graham.

Chrissie was living with Sarah in one of the rooms adjacent to the road which led from the main gate to the dining-room, in a line of rooms known as 'volunteers' row'. I felt reasonably sure that if I knocked on her door I would at the very least be invited in for a cup of tea. This was a custom, almost a tradition amongst volunteers. Afternoons and evenings were frequently spent visiting one room then another, socialising in this way. So why shouldn't I just call in and see? I walked down volunteers' row towards Chrissie's room. I heard Sarah inside talking loudly and laughing. I paused briefly, but carried on past.

That night, Gary came round to our room with Ian when he'd finished his dishwasher shift, and brought a bottle of Israeli gin. Together with Chris and Graham, we drank the whole bottle. The next morning my hand was throbbing as though it had been crushed under the tracks of a passing tank. I was growing more than a little concerned. It was now almost the same size and possessed of the same amount of dexterity as one of my feet. I returned to the clinic and saw the nurse. This time there was also a young male present who I assumed, correctly, was a doctor. He immediately started to remove my bandage.

My fingers were swollen like thick Lincolnshire sausages, and my hand was all colours of the rainbow, with some deep blues, purples and yellow shades. And black. The nurse and the doctor chatted away to one another quickly in Hebrew. Then I saw the doctor pick up a huge needle and fix it to the end of a syringe. He then jabbed it firmly into my poor hand without warning, in the exact spot where it seemed to hurt the most. The pain was just excruciating. The two of them talked quite calmly for a few minutes, occasionally glancing in my direction. I was clearly the subject of a minor medical debate. It didn't occur to me that I was probably shrouded in a generally unclean odour of cigarettes and gin.

I sat for a few minutes until the doctor opened a drawer and took out some sterile packets. Using a shiny pair of elongated narrow scissors he cut open a thin sterile pack and removed a small blade from inside, similar to a craft knife. The nurse held my arm steady while the doctor made a small incision in the palm of my hand just at the base of my index finger. There was no pain as my hand was now quite numb from the injection, but what happened next just looked awful. Masses of disgusting, thick red and yellow material burst from my hand and plopped loudly into a steel kidney dish the nurse was holding underneath. The doctor squeezed the wound firmly with his fingers in an effort to extract everything he possibly could from the hole in my hand. When he was sure this had been done to his satisfaction, he then sprayed it all over using an aerosol with 'Ether' written on the side in English.

"*Tov!*" exclaimed the doctor, and "*Yofi!*" then turned, and left me with the nurse, clip-clopping away in his sandals on the brilliantly clean marble floor tiles. She carefully and slowly re-dressed my hand and told me:

"No work for five days, okay?" which I was delighted about, but then she said: "Here take these, they are antibiotic, yes? Take two, four times a day, and *no alcohol*, okay?"

My hand felt wonderful and I was free of pain for the first time in days. I was happy and relieved that it had been treated.

After lunch, Chris and I caught a lift from the kibbutz into Kiryat Shmona. He took a film to be developed at Martins photography shop, and I bought some more Camel cigarettes. My diary states we then went to our usual bar in the precinct, Yuval's, and both drank Coca-Cola. I find this astonishing. I know why *I* didn't drink any beer, but I don't recall the reason why Chris was drinking Coke!

When we returned to Dafna, Lynne, a rather large but friendly girl from Tasmania, appeared at our door asking for me. Lynne had been nick-named 'Goldstar' and was rumoured to be quite good at the shot-put back home. I had no idea why she had this nick-name, unless it was connected to her size, or if there was any truth about the shot-putting. I'd previously volunteered to assist her and French Paul in decorating the *moadon* for Christmas. She had no doubt seen my hand and was concerned I might no longer be able to help. She was unaware that I'd already spoken to Paul and assured him my bandaged left hand would not cause a problem. I was right-handed after all. My very modest artistic talent was becoming known among the volunteers. Not only had I drawn a Genesis logo on the wall near my bed and a decorative Bob Marley above Chris's, but also a Galit logo in Guy's room.

Lynne stood in our kitchen staring at me. She was actually quite pretty, with bright green eyes and freckles. But the other lads were scathing and cruel about her size. She certainly had an unmistakable presence. I informed her I was still quite capable and that nothing had changed. The rather vexed expression on her face faded to one of relief. She turned and stomped out the room, shouting a few words of Australian back at me: "She'll be right then, mate. Fair dinkum!" and disappeared.

John laughed and mumbled a derogatory comment about

her as she walked away. Then, with an entirely serious expression on his face, he told me that I was to be thrown off the kibbutz for damaging the walls with my graffiti art. He said he'd heard a rumour to this effect among some *kibbutzniks,* and the decision had already been made. To be 'thrown off the kibbutz' was the ultimate humiliation and ignominy. It could mean being black-listed across all *kibbutzim* in Israel. With nowhere to go it would therefore also mean an early and shameful trip home, never to return. I was worried, though I tried not to show it. He maintained this rumour was completely genuine for the rest of the afternoon, even quoting names of *kibbutzniks* he claimed had been involved in the decision.

Of course I believed him for a while, and even contemplated finding a bucket of warm water and a cloth, until he finally informed me it wasn't true.

THE CHRISTMAS TREE

French Paul was a lovely, softly spoken man in his late thirties. He had receding black curly hair and a black bushy beard. He was quite stocky, even thick set, but not at all short in stature. He appeared to be a physically strong man, and this was most likely due to his occupation back home, that of a farmer in northern France. He told me of many occasions when he and his farming contemporaries recovered munitions, and worse, from their fields almost on a weekly basis. They apparently disposed of most of the munitions themselves, but they notified the authorities whenever they recovered human remains. Some of the items often found their way into the local markets, as there was always a buyer for such wartime memorabilia. My French was poor as, sadly, was his English, so we couldn't communicate particularly well. But I enjoyed finding out about these things, and promised that one day I would pay him a visit to see for myself.

We now had some girls living next-door: Goldstar Lynne, Mary and Christine. Mary was English and from Southampton on the south coast of England, and was a little older than most of us. She had slightly curly, golden-blonde hair which just touched her shoulders and she always seemed very pleasant and happy. I'd seen her a lot as she worked in the kitchens, as did Lynne and Christine. Of course the best part of having these girls next-door was when their workmates paid a visit. Chrissie and Sarah often visited our neighbours and so I too became an occasional part of the furniture. In a room full of women I found the conversations refreshingly frank, straightforward and unguarded, compared to the more shallow topics and mutual piss-taking that occurs in a room comprised entirely of men. I was happy to use the pretext of planning for Christmas to sit in the room with Chrissie and the others, and they didn't seem to mind me being there. I was spending a lot of time talking to Chrissie, both at work and otherwise, and it was now obvious there may be something between us, though it was still almost impossible to spend any time alone together. But the ladies made tea and toast and waited on me, so I sat there on the bed with them like a Cheshire cat, happily lapping it all up.

While my hand was bandaged I filled my workless sick days without a problem. My parents sent me a *Flight Pilot's Diary 1979*, and the latest issue of *Aeroplane Monthly* magazine from England. I borrowed cassette tapes from anyone I could, and listened to a huge amount of music. Most of these tapes were home-made 'mix tapes'. They very often included some quite random and unrelated tracks from other bands on the end just to fill up the tape. As a consequence of this, when listening to someone else's tape and these tracks were missing, it seemed odd they were not there. Very often the tape machines the music was played on were not the best quality, so they chewed the cassettes frequently. I became quite an expert at splicing cassette tape with tiny pieces of sticky tape. It was useful to have a pencil around to help wind the tape in and out, as well as a roll of sticky tape. I was discovering some quality music of a timeless nature. Certain songs would from then on always trigger memories of Dafna, the people, and my time spent there. There was some of the amazing work of bands such as Pink Floyd, Led Zeppelin, Supertramp, Genesis and Santana, among others. Typical late seventies fare. Eric Clapton's *461 Ocean Boulevard* and in particular his version of *I shot the Sheriff*, always seemed to be played when most people had drunk far too much alcohol.

The antibiotic tablets I was taking for my hand made me feel a little drowsy, so I spent a lot of time sleeping. I also visited the *moadon* frequently with French Paul and Lynne, in order to help decorate the walls. Initially it seemed a daunting task, trying to transform the dark and austere interior into something resembling a welcoming and festive Christmas party venue. We drew the tables closer together in an effort to create a more intimate atmosphere, and hung home-made decorations from the walls. I wrote 'Merry Christmas' in as many languages as we could think of on large pieces of paper and stuck them around the huge room. It began to look quite appealing but it was still missing something.

While the others were at work I cut pictures of aircraft from my *Aeroplane Monthly* magazine and stuck them to the wall above my bed like a true teenager. Christmas cards started arriving from home so I obtained some string and hung them around our room. As the festive season drew closer there were more parties, and a tangible atmosphere of anticipation and excitement. Sadly I was unable to maintain my abstinence from alcohol as instructed by the nurse. I managed about forty-eight hours. My hand felt much better, and I continued taking the tablets, so surely it wouldn't matter?

Thursday December 21st 1978 started for us very suddenly and collectively at six-thirty in the morning, just as the first signs of early dawn began reaching across the dark Galilee sky. It was quite significant that we didn't panic or otherwise run for shelter into John's blast-proof room, or our nearby *miklat*. We just didn't bother. The first thing we heard and felt was a single deep thud which rattled our flimsy wooden windows and caused the floor to shake. Then there was another, followed a minute or so later by another. This was a series of short explosive thumps in the ground rather than a sustained and passing vibration as when the tanks had driven past. At each of these loud bangs the walls of our room shook a little too, which was extremely worrying. Rather late and ineffective I thought, an air raid siren started wailing away somewhere in the kibbutz. Dogs barked. I'm not sure how many of these bangs there were, but they continued for several minutes, very sporadic and intermittent, somewhere away in the near distance. Luckily they didn't seem to be getting any closer than at least a few kilometres away, but I know we were all listening intently for any signs they were coming nearer. The atmosphere in the room was suddenly brittle and intense, and I could just see in the early morning light the concern on my room-mates faces, despite no-one actually saying anything.

"*Katyushas* again..!" John finally said with his usual Yorkshire pragmatism, as he emerged from his room and walked over to the front door. He opened it and stood on the step looking incongruous in his sagging underpants and a t-shirt, toothbrush in hand, peering into the semi-dark distance towards Kiryat Shmona. He was in the process of getting up for work and seemed completely unconcerned by the noise.

"You'd better stay inside, Billy," Chris said to John, "Just to be on the safe side, you know?" but John remained at the open door scanning the horizon and occasionally looking skywards. *Katyusha* rockets were obviously raining down from above and landing probably in or near Kiryat Shmona, seven kilometres away. It certainly sounded as though the noise was from that direction. If the town was indeed being targeted it seemed the perpetrators may have finally corrected their aim. I remember wondering, rather selfishly, whether the rockets would manage to avoid our lovely bar in the precinct, the record shop, and the bus station. I also wondered why the Israelis couldn't put a stop to this bombardment, with all the military might at their disposal.

Before my visit to Israel, I had no real grasp of the wider political situation. I was suddenly being forced into waking up to the political realities of where I was living. At a very local level, some people were firing these awful munitions across the border quite randomly towards civilians. More importantly, they were actually exploding quite close to *me.* It was my opinion therefore, formed at that moment as our room shook and rattled, that whoever was responsible was utterly and completely in the wrong. Dependent upon your own point of view, and considering the full history of modern Israel, was there any justification in the targeting of civilians in this way? This conflict was now affecting me personally. Dafna was my new home, albeit temporary, and Kiryat Shmona was my local town, where my local pub was. They were both being attacked by these rotten terrorists.

The banging, and therefore the air raid, stopped as suddenly as it had begun. Thankfully, and with a huge sense of relief, as far as I knew none of the rockets came any closer to our kibbutz. I realised that in an attack such as this the chances of Dafna, and more specifically *our room*, being hit were very slim. It wasn't impossible but it was unlikely. I began to perhaps have some understanding, at a very humble level, that this type of mental assessment was probably how many people managed to function in such circumstances. A simple calculation based on space, numbers, and chance; a reliance on the sheer unlikelihood of becoming a victim. Like the hoped-for chances of winning the lottery, but in reverse. On this occasion I was able to hear the explosions, noises which were abrupt, threatening, and unconscionable. These sounds had been stark in their realism, as this time they were not masked by the noise of the dishwasher and my own idiot off-key rendition of *Hotel California*.

We walked into the dining-room for breakfast at eight o'clock. There wasn't the usual array of food on offer due to so many kitchen staff being away, sheltering underground. We spoke to a few *kibbutzniks* who were still around and managed to find out that Kiryat Shmona had indeed been hit, and several people injured, with even one person killed. All the kibbutz children had been taken into the nursery *miklat*, where they remained for the rest of the day. I saw a male *kibbutznik* lead his children underground like the Pied Piper, only to re-emerge much later. I wondered what the children were told about why they had to hide inside the various concrete *miklatim* on the kibbutz. Were they told it was dragons or evil men bringing down fire from the skies?

As we sat eating, in a dining-room which was unusually quiet and almost completely empty, we began to hear some other loud bangs. These were quite different. They were sustained and regular, and came from behind us up the road where the tanks had trundled off so noisily into the darkness a few days before. If an 'us and them' scenario was applied, then these latest bangs in the hills were 'our' guns, the IDF Magach tanks. They fired constantly for an hour, in obvious reprisal for the rocket attack, right up until nine o'clock, before stopping. I could only imagine the sheer terror and material damage modern tank shells could cause. I had little sympathy for any terrorist unfortunate enough to be at the other end of such a fearsome barrage from dozens of Magach tanks. It seemed that fire was being fought with fire. The motto of the Israeli Defence Force should perhaps be something along the lines of: *Killing Foe for Peace since 1948*.

I saw Ezra walk into the dining-room looking as though he was in a hurry, with his huge green kitbag on his shoulder and his Uzi, this time loaded with the magazine in it. There was another magazine fixed to the one in the gun, secured with thick black tape. He said he had to go. He'd been called up to his unit. I wished him luck and told him to keep his head down. He seemed serious and distracted. I'd never seen him like this. He looked very worried. He'd told us some horror stories before about comrades being captured by Syrian troops and sent back across the border bleeding half to death, having had their genitals cut off.

Just as we'd finished our makeshift breakfast, Mick's dog Blackie came scampering into the dining-room and up to our table, his little tail wagging furiously. He rolled onto his side on the floor next to my chair inviting me to tickle his belly, which I obviously felt obliged to do. Then Mick came plodding loudly into the dining-room, keys rattling on his belt, cursing and muttering under his breath.

"What's up, Mick?" I asked, as he noisily pulled up a chair and sat with us, continually shaking his head and chuntering to himself.

"That bloody scruffy grain grower's just dumped a load of stuff and cleared off without even seeing me about it! He's put it all in the wrong place and he knew that, the bastard!"

"What stuff?"

"Bags of feed and stuff for the cows and chickens that's just been delivered. I've got to move it all now. Bloody tons of it! The useless tosser!" I'd never seen Mick look quite so angry and I could see John was trying very hard not to laugh.

"Mick if you need some help, we can give you a hand,

can't we John?" I said to him, looking at John whose face then immediately changed at hearing my suggestion.

"Yeah, come on Billy, let's give the old sod a hand," Graham said, standing up. So then John, Graham and I jumped onto the back of Mick's tractor outside the dining-room and headed up towards the refit, the cow sheds, without really knowing what we were letting ourselves in for. We bounced our way across the kibbutz clinging onto the huge fenders, while Blackie was proudly ensconced in Mick's lap sitting bolt upright, looking for all the world as though he was helping him to drive.

We pulled up and jumped down outside a large brick barn with a corrugated iron roof. The four of us moved fifty large and very heavy sacks of feed under cover into the building. I wasn't much help, with my left hand bandaged, but managed to lift at least a few of them. We climbed back onto the tractor. We then set off again, but instead of heading back towards the dining-room we headed straight out of the north entrance of the kibbutz.

There was a *kibbutznik* at the gate holding an ancient bolt-action *'rega rifle'* as Ezra had described such old weapons; *rega* meaning 'wait a minute', and was a reference to how slow and laborious it was to use compared to an Uzi. I was surprised this chap was the only person guarding the top gate just after an air raid, until we passed an olive green army jeep parked surreptitiously among some trees and virtually out of sight. There were four Israeli soldiers in it, all armed to the teeth and looking very stern and serious, with bits of plants stuck in their helmets. They had streaks of black and dark green camouflage paint all across their faces and they looked as though they were part of a host of dark-skinned warriors from the Middle Ages, waiting for battle. Luckily they ignored us. Presumably the PLO wouldn't attack Israel on the back of a very old and crappy Massey Ferguson tractor driven by three rather silly looking Englishmen and a mongrel dog.

"Where are we going, Mick?" I shouted, barely making myself heard above the din of the old machine, and hanging on so tightly with my one and only good hand that my knuckles were glistening brilliant white.

"Christmas!" shouted Mick in reply. "We're going to look for a Christmas tree Biggles, for the *moadon*!" as we bounced around among the avocado trees and then into the apple orchard. It occurred to me at that moment that on one previous *Katyusha* raid not so long ago this was just where the rockets had landed. We lurched to a stop in front of a few very sad looking stone pine trees. The four of us, and Blackie, inspected the pitiful selection of potential Christmas trees on offer. Blackie promptly cocked his leg up against one of them in obvious disdain at the quality of the trees.

"This'll do..." Mick said, tugging at an eight foot pine sapling, and then reached into a tin box on the back of the Massey. He attacked the base of the tree with a one-handled band saw like a man possessed, and in a few seconds it was down. Sticky sap was all over his hands and there was suddenly a very strong pine smell all around us. We loaded it onto the back of the tractor, Mick lashing it on with a length of oily old rope, and set off back to Dafna.

We passed the army jeep again, chugging along on the old tractor, and we must have looked like a bunch of lunatics on day release. We drove straight in through the open gates, Mick shouting '*Shalom!*' to the bemused guard, and up to the *moadon*. We found a massive pot to stand it in. Our tree then stood proudly in the back corner of the huge room, ready to be decorated.

THE ROMANCE

Christmas Eve

The next night, Friday, we threw a party in our room. We didn't often host these social events as we'd seen the mess they would usually cause, but we were probably overcome with Christmas spirit, so what the heck! We started off with only one bottle of vodka and no glasses, so we played 'pass the bottle' around the room, and it was a great success. As more people arrived and crammed their way in, more booze came with them. It seemed at one stage there were a hundred people in our room. Pink Floyd screeched away on an old monotone tape machine in the background, almost completely drowned out by all the merriment and talking.

At around midnight most of the party, including myself and Chrissie, walked a short distance down the road in the direction of Kiryat Shmona, about a mile, to Kibbutz HaGoshrim. We'd once been invited there by some other English lads we met in the Kiryat Shmona bar. We all rolled into HaGoshrim past the guard at the gate, who only asked us a few brief questions before allowing us in. It was probably quite obvious that a bunch or Europeans and Americans were not actually members of the PLO. The HaGoshrim disco was inside a huge *miklat,* which struck me as an excellent idea, particularly after recent events. It had obviously been in there a while too, as there was a proper wooden bar and even a hand pump for the beer, straight out of a barrel.

We returned to Dafna at about three o'clock, though I can't be sure of the time. I do remember, just as it was getting light, I sprang out of bed, desperate to get back to my own room, before suddenly realising I was in my own bed all along. Later that morning I woke up at about nine o'clock.

Chris wasn't in his bed. I'd seen him arm-in-arm with a girl earlier, at HaGoshrim, but then lost him. I drifted back to sleep and was woken up with a start at eleven o'clock by Goldstar Lynne screaming in my ear:

"Biggles! Biggles! We've gotta decorate the *moadon*, mate, get yer arse up there!" in her broad Aussie drawl. She then disappeared out the door, slamming it hard and muttering curses to herself. I sat on the edge of my bed. My head was pounding and I felt terrible. I brushed my teeth, the simple act of which almost always made me feel a little better, and slipped my coat on. I had no need to dress as I'd slept in my clothes all night. I walked into the *moadon*. French Paul and others were blowing balloons up and decorating the tree. They wanted me to write some more 'Merry Christmas' greetings around the hall. I needed food first, so made my way to the dining-room and ate some bread and eggs, and drank copious amounts of sweet tea.

Back at the *moadon* and feeling slightly better, at French Paul's dictation I drew 'Merry Christmas' in seven more languages on some large screens at the back of the hall. San Francisco Mary helped us with Chinese, thanks to her oriental heritage. Ezra had already shown me how to write the words in Hebrew and Arabic. No-one could think of any more. The inside of the *moadon* looked like a Christmas party venue for some very optimistic but impoverished United Nations troops. After lunch the hall was closed. It was finally ready. I followed Lynne and Christine back to the dining-room.

In the kitchens almost all the female volunteers were busy making trifle and cakes, and around the hot ovens there was a wonderful aroma of cake mix and home baking. Chrissie and English Mary invited me to sample their freshly baked buns, so I took two and began eating one of them. They both laughed and shouted at me for being greedy. I stood for a while talking to Chrissie in the warm and happy atmosphere, then Chris and Graham walked into the kitchens, wearing shorts. They were both red-faced and panting like a pair of hunting dogs. They told me they'd just spent the last thirty minutes running around the kibbutz perimeter. I showed them the iced bun in my hand and pointed to a large tray where others were laid out fresh from the oven. I took another, just as Chris and Graham were caught taking a handful each. All three of us were then chased out of the kitchen and banned from returning for the rest of the day.

We walked back to our room together, carrying an uncut loaf of bread and our stolen buns. The sky was blue and clear, and the sun was quite warm on our faces but low and autumnal. Leaves were falling from the silver birch and sycamore trees and there was a cool, fresh chill in the air. We lit our paraffin heater in the room and made toast. Chris turned on the radio and we listened to the English language radio station 'The Voice of Peace', or *Kol HaShalom* as it was also known. This was a pirate station, apparently broadcast from 'a ship somewhere in the Mediterranean'. It was actually anchored in international waters just off Tel Aviv and was part-funded by ex-Beatle George Harrison.

It became very dark quite suddenly; the transition from day to night seemed to take barely a few moments. Our room was again a very warm and cosy sanctuary. At six o'clock 'The Voice of Peace' as usual broadcast *Twilight Time*, sung by The Platters, which eventually became as familiar and reassuring as the BBC's *Lilliburlero*. These sounds formed part of the rhythm of life on the kibbutz, along with the smell of toast and paraffin: pleasurable, ritualistic and comforting. *Twilight Time* on the radio became like an evening dinner gong, signifying the time we should all make our way to the dining-room. If not working, we'd usually shower and wear clean clothes for the occasion if possible, particularly on a Friday *Shabbat* night. Those taking their meal break from the factory would eat in their blue work clothes, as would those on duty in the kitchens. When working on the dishwasher the evening meal break consisted of a few stolen minutes here and there spent sitting with other volunteers, while all the time keeping a close eye on the plates and cutlery generated by diners.

The night before Christmas Eve, the girls from next-door along with Chrissie and Sarah, came to our room, bringing with them several bottles of wine. They were laughing and talking loudly to one another and it seemed as though they may have had a few glasses already. We were all very civilised and polite and everything was going well until one of the girls decided to use our toilet. We heard a scream and she ran out of the toilet back into the room. Pooh had started to bubble over the top of the toilet bowl onto the floor, accompanied by a disgusting smell. It had obviously become blocked and we were suffering some sort of backlash from the drains. John and I quickly took a look, and I'm sure I recognised one of my own as it seemed to climb out of the toilet bowl before flopping with a splat onto the floor tiles. John found a stick from outside but it was no good, we'd already lost. The girls returned to their room in disgust.

On Sunday 24th December, the Christmas Eve weather in the Upper Galilee was just like an English summer's day. The clear skies and cool breeze had now gone, to be replaced by some very calm, warm air. There were some voluminous dark clouds gathering together and building up around the Golan Heights and Mount Hermon.

I visited the clinic in the morning and finally had the bandage removed from my left hand. It was back to full working order and completely healed. I'd also finished taking my antibiotic tablets. The daily work list would no longer show my name with the word 'sick' adjacent to it.

The *kibbutzniks* began celebrating their own festive season on Christmas Eve, when I noticed a very large, nine-branched candelabrum appeared in the dining room. The first candle was lit that night. I assumed the Jewish 'Festival of Lights', or *Hanukkah* always coincided with Christmas, but this was actually the first time it had done so for quite a while. I also thought *Hanukkah* was connected to Christmas in some way but it has nothing at all to do with it. The festival itself should start at sundown on the twenty-fifth day of *Kislev,* a month which roughly overlaps November and December. Ezra had told me all about it in great detail a few days before, and Mick knew some vague details too. According to the *Talmud*, a lamp was lit in the Holy Temple in Jerusalem following its recapture by the Maccabee Jews in 165 BC. It was thought there was only enough oil for the lamp to burn for one day, but instead it burned continuously for a further eight days, thereby symbolising a miracle. We needed a small miracle of our own, too. Our room smelt like a very busy sewage works. I called by the kibbutz office and informed Yonatan that our toilet was blocked. He assured me it would be fixed as soon as possible.

Chris, Graham and I hitched into Kiryat Shmona to see if we could buy some decent booze, rather than the usual offerings on display at the kibbutz shop. We came back with eight bottles altogether; brandy, whisky, vodka, wine and vermouth.

We started preparing our selection of drink at five o'clock in the afternoon. We squeezed a dozen large fresh oranges and added some water to the resultant juice. We tried in vain to create a pleasant and appealing beverage which was strong and intelligently mixed, yet subtle enough on the palate to interest the ladies. We soon gave up on this pretence and simply mixed it all together. It seemed whichever way it was mixed it tasted awful. We rather optimistically named our concoction 'Christmas punch'.

Just as it was ready to drink, we started to welcome a succession of eager and curious visitors. Firstly Christine called in from next-door and promptly helped herself to a glass, and then Gary arrived. The nearest thing to Christmas music we had on tape was *Moonflower* by Santana, so at Chris's insistence we put this on, even though it is not in itself the least bit Christmassy. Our room gradually filled up and I drank three glasses of punch and two bottles of Goldstar before we all walked up to the *moadon* at six-thirty. We sat down to eat a turkey dinner, on the evening of Christmas Eve. It was surprisingly good, and was followed by trifle which the girls had made. I was aware the trifle was on the menu, but had no idea how the turkey dinner had been produced, and who had cooked it.

Later, the tables were moved to the side of the floor and loud music was turned on. I sat chatting to Chrissie for most of the night, but we were both quite drunk. Sadly, for my part, it became just another drunken night in the *moadon*, and I was yet again no closer to achieving any semblance of a civilized relationship with her. The floor of the dimly lit room filled with people dancing and smooching. As the night progressed, there were plenty of people falling over and rolling around being sick. Nice. I really struggled to stand or even sit upright, and only just managed to reach the outside of the *moadon* before throwing up against the wall. I knew I was in a bad way and had to leave. Without returning inside, I decided I should get to bed. I staggered in a zigzag manner down through the kibbutz, across the grass, as though I was trying to avoid being shot at by a sniper. I lay down on my bed and passed out.

CHRISTMAS DAY

I didn't wake up until eleven-thirty on Christmas Day. Chris wasn't in his bed. Graham looked as though he was dead. I also felt as though I'd died in the night. The door to John's room was slightly open but no-one was in there. I washed my face, brushed my teeth and put on my boots. Outside the air was warm and humid, despite some very dark, dense-looking clouds jostling around threateningly above, so low over my head I felt as though I could reach up and touch them. Mount Hermon and the rest of the Golan hills were completely obscured. A very fine drizzle was falling, like a mountain mist, and this conspired with my still semi-drunken state to give the day an eerie sense of calm. My head was pounding, so I walked very delicately in tiny gentle steps along the path and across the grass to the dining-room. As I walked, droplets of moisture gathered on my face and clothes. It actually felt quite refreshing, so I took deep breaths of the damp air as I walked. As well as a hangover, my chest felt tight, probably the result of smoking a whole pack of Nelsons during the evening.

Chrissie was sitting alone in the volunteers' area of the dining-room, at one end of a table, reading a letter from home, left hand clasped around a glass of Turkish coffee.

"Happy Christmas, Jonathan," she said, seeing me, smiling. As I moved to sit down next to her she handed me two letters addressed to me, from England. "I picked up your mail…" she said, looking at me, putting her own letter down, open on the table.

"Yes, yes, Happy Christmas…thanks for that," I replied, picking them up and pulling out a chair. I was very pleased to see her, and was surprised and a little flattered that she'd thought to collect my mail. The two letters from home had been delayed a week due to a postal strike in Israel. Chrissie and I talked of the previous night and we compared hangovers:

"What happened to you last night?" she said, smiling.

"I was a mess. I threw up outside. Sorry about that, but I just had to get home. Sorry." I shook my head a little and my brain screamed at me in protest, as it was still sloshing around in Christmas punch.

"I went to bed too," Chrissie said. "Jeez, I feel rough today. I drank a whole bunch of beer that's for sure. I'm not going to drink that much ever again!"

I thought for a moment how improbable it was, to drink a *bunch* of beer. I'd only ever heard this word used to describe flowers before.

"I'll just be a minute…" I said, standing up slowly. I wandered into the kitchens. I needed some stodgy food, so I crept into the back and filled a large bowl with rice and hot milk. I added two heaped tablespoons of sugar and returned quickly to eat it. Chrissie looked puzzled and smiled.

"You shouldn't eat so much starch," she said, giving me health advice as she lit a cigarette, reaching across the table for a tin ashtray. She leaned her head back a little and then blew smoke straight above her head. Her blonde hair was caught briefly for a moment in her collar before it then fell down her back.

"What are you doing today, Jonathan?" she asked, taking a sip of coffee from her glass. I then noticed Sarah and Christine walking into the dining-room together, chattering busily to one another. Sarah could see where we were sitting, and began making her selection at the first food trolley.

"I don't know. Probably spend time in the room with the lads, as usual. Are you doing anything? Someone told me yesterday there's a disco up the road tonight. Are you going?" Between mouthfuls of warm milky rice I scanned her facial expression closely for any clue as to how she would reply.

"Sure. What time?"

"I think we're all going at about nine o'clock," I replied, elated that she'd agreed, just as Sarah came over and sat down next to us. Sarah was a lively extrovert, who always seemed confident and friendly. She talked very quickly. I didn't often get on with people who spoke in this way, probably because I tended to speak slowly, and was sometimes accused of speaking in a mumbled and languid manner. This was something I've made conscious efforts to overcome. I could tell she was not at all enamoured by me or my presence, as she was one of those people who would frequently say to someone else when I spoke: 'What did he say..?' This was always an indication we were not quite connecting. Maybe she felt I was a threat to her, and her relationship with Chrissie. They *were* travelling together, and I knew they were planning to see the rest of Europe before returning to Seattle.

"Hello Sarah," I said, as I slurped the last of my breakfast. Some of it accidentally dropped from my spoon and fell messily onto my clothing. I tried to scoop particles of rice back up, drawing my spoon over my shirt as I did so. I was suddenly acutely aware of how very awkward and English I probably seemed, at least to her.

"Oh, really!" Sarah exclaimed, seeing the mess I'd made on my shirt. She then turned away from me and said: "Chrissie there's some folk dancing in here this afternoon, shall we check it out later?"

"Yeah, I guess…" Chrissie replied. She threw a sideways glance in my direction. It was a tiny, almost indistinct, secretive glance on the back of a lovely smile.

"Merry Christmas, Sarah," I said, before standing up and walking over to the dishwasher.

I returned to the room and had a shower. Chris then walked in, as did John, a short while later. Both were tight-lipped as to where they'd been all night. We were all hung over so we turned the radio on low and tuned in to the 'Voice of Peace'. They seemed to be playing Beatles music all day long, and very little else, which was fine. It made a change from the usual pop songs.

We were all lying on our beds, dozing, when Christine from next-door walked in. She made us all a cup of tea. I'm not sure why she did this, apart from the fact that she sat and drank some of it herself and then washed all the cups. We were always very happy to let her carry on doing things like that if she wanted to do it! Then Perry came round with some huge Jaffa oranges, which we knew would come in very handy for squeezing in order to make more punch. Perry quite often made such spontaneous gestures of generosity and goodwill, similar to Christine's tea making. Sadly I suspect we did not express our gratitude as much as we should have, to either of them.

At some point in the mid-afternoon, and probably at about the time when we all started to feel well again, someone asked if there was any vodka left. I don't remember who it was. It certainly wasn't me. At least I don't think so. The suggestion was not met with surprise or derision of any sort, but merely some curious glances around the room. Then:

"Whoa! Billy! What happened to all the booze from last night, mate?" Graham shouted in perfect Brummie towards John's room.

"It's in the kitchen!" John shouted back from inside his room, his door wide open. John never seemed to drink or lose control as much as everyone else, and was always tidy and methodical. He had collected the remaining booze and stood the bottles neatly by the sink in the kitchen. Graham sprang off his bed and took a large plastic jug from the cupboard and began squeezing Perry's oranges. A few short minutes later we were all drinking an orange punch containing vodka, brandy and wine, both red and white. It lacked a few ingredients but it was as equally disgusting as the awful cocktail we'd made the previous day. It *was* Christmas Day, after all. So it started all over again.

I sipped my drink a little more cautiously than the night before. An evening with Chrissie was coming up, so I didn't want to end up in the same disastrous condition. When The Platters gave their nightly rendition of *Twilight Time*, at six o'clock I walked across to Tim and Ian's room with John. I listened to Genesis's *Supper's Ready* all the way through and almost fell asleep. John nudged me awake before we all walked up to the dining-room. That evening, as no-one was at work, all the volunteers ate together at their end of the huge room. There was a lively, convivial atmosphere, probably helped by the drink, but no doubt mainly brought about by the festive season. We ate little, drank a few cups of tea, and smoked endless numbers of cigarettes. Almost everyone smoked, and as usual in the dining-room after dinner, we stubbed out our cigarettes rather disgustingly in the food remnants on our plates. Then at around eight o'clock, our room became the rendezvous point for the evening and the forthcoming trek up the road. There were twenty-five of us who trudged noisily out of the main gates at nine o'clock for the three kilometre walk up the road to Kibbutz Dan.

John, Tim and Ian (not Ian Anarchist, but yet another rather tall, thick-set, fresh-faced Yorkshire man who'd moved in with Tim after Guy had left) led a rendition of *Ilkley Moor baht 'at* as we walked. This is a song about a man who climbs Ilkley Moor in Yorkshire while not wearing a hat (the 'baht 'at' part means 'without a hat'). He catches a cold and dies. He is then buried. Worms eat his body, and soon some ducks eat the worms. Then his surviving friends and relatives eat the ducks, thereby indirectly eating him. It is the unofficial anthem of Yorkshire. They were surprised and impressed when they realised I knew all the words, and sang along with great enthusiasm. I walked with Chrissie in the very shabby but exuberant crowd, a bottle of vermouth in one hand, which the two of us shared all evening. I occasionally sang Genesis songs completely out of key as usual in between further renditions of *Ilkley Moor*, while chatting to Chrissie. She in turn told me about some of her favourite music, including Joni Mitchell's song about a Christmas tree. I listened politely but I'd never heard of Joni Mitchell let alone any of her songs. Anticipation mounted as we trudged along the dark unlit road. The fine mist from earlier in the day had now turned to rain, but it was still surprisingly warm.

When we arrived at the kibbutz gates, our clothes had become quite wet but we were not in the least dispirited. We were directed to the *moadon,* which was similar to ours, by a uniformed guard carrying a loaded Uzi. The people of Kibbutz Dan were incredibly generous, and they must have known we were coming. We were all provided with turkey sandwiches and a vodka orange punch. I sat with Chrissie, leaning against a wall on the floor of the *moadon*, where we shared the last of my Camels and the vermouth. Chrissie had confirmation, if any was needed, that I had a poor sense of rhythm for dancing, so this was not pursued beyond a few comical and very clumsy attempts on my part! But it was great to talk, and we both remained at a happy and quite coherent level of inebriation without becoming ill.

Chrissie spoke enthusiastically about growing up in the Pacific North-West. She described in great detail her life in close proximity to vast open stretches of true wilderness. She spoke of seeing giant red-wood trees, killer whales, Mount St. Helens, of long exciting ferry trips to Vancouver Island, the ocean, and California. In return, I mumbled something about my local pub, *The Hare & Hounds*, and warm Sheffield beer known as *Stones Bitter.* I also told her of my passion for aeroplanes and my recent flying experiences. She seemed impressed. She spoke with gentle equanimity in her soft, distinctive, and to me, mesmeric and sexy West Coast accent. I realised she was actually a tiny bit self-conscious, and in possession of a degree of quiet diffidence, but this was at the same time balanced by a surprising amount of focus and determination. She told me how she missed her dad, who'd not long since passed away, and there were aspects of my behaviour and personality that reminded her of him, in a nice way.

"How old are you, Chrissie?" I asked, "twenty, twenty-one?"

"No. Keep guessing!" she replied, laughing, and looked at me intently with her blue eyes focused directly on mine, like a pair of lasers cutting through the smoky gloom.

"You're twenty-two then?" I stated, not wanting or daring to go any higher.

"Jonathan, I'm twenty-three, almost, in a few months. But twenty-two now, you're right. Not that it matters anyways…"

"No not at all, so what?" I replied, lifting the vermouth bottle and taking another gulp.

"Why, how old are you, Jonathan?"

"Eighteen, just," I replied. I felt an overwhelming urge to lie, to say I was twenty, or older, but settled for the undeniable truth.

"Wow," she said, smiling, "you're way too young! You're just a baby!" she said, immediately contradicting herself and laughing. Then I laughed too, and Chrissie took the bottle from my hand. She paused briefly, and then looked at me.

"Ever been to the States?" she said, before raising the bottle to her lips and slowly taking small sips of vermouth.

"Er, no, not yet. Maybe you'll have to invite me?" and I reached forward and eased the vermouth from her hand and swallowed a mouthful myself. We were very delicately fencing with one another and teasing information from each other. It was all part of the wonderful experience of getting to know someone new. All the time I wondered where and how far it would lead. I stood the bottle on the floor between my legs and opened a new packet of Nelsons, removing the cellophane and dropping it by my side. It seemed that a significant part of the fun attached to being a smoker was the occasional grand unveiling of a crisp new pack. The clean, bright contents of twenty cigarettes lined up in two neat rows were the promise of so much smoking pleasure ahead. It was almost like starting smoking all over again. There was safety in a full pack too. There was nothing more disappointing or useless than an empty pack. I put two cigarettes in my mouth and lit both together, then handed one to Chrissie. She laughed. I'd seen it done in the movies, somewhere, and I know it sounds like a really cheesy thing to do, but at that moment it just felt right.

"You'd like it. There are lots of open spaces. You could sing your Genesis songs as loud as you liked!" and we both laughed. I think I was probably too stupid at that point to feel any embarrassment regarding my poor singing, but it was clearly a great source of amusement to Chrissie, so it didn't seem to worry me.

"Maybe you should get some singing lessons first though…" she said, and we both laughed again, blowing smoke up into the noisy, crowded room, adding to the foggy and sweaty atmosphere. We smoked and talked, and sipped the vermouth together until the bottle was empty.

There were a lot of people shuffling about, supposedly dancing to the latest pop songs. I remember a very tall man in the *moadon* of Kibbutz Dan that night, with a long greying beard and very long, thick, straggly black hair. He was probably in his late thirties and was dressed in white robes which touched the floor, with open-toed sandals occasionally visible. For most of the evening he stood in the middle of the dimly lit room holding a burning candle in each hand at arms' length, repeating:

"It's my birthday! I'm Jesus Christ!"

Chrissie and I left together, at about two o'clock, after most of the others had already left. We had obviously been too engrossed in one another's conversation to realise people had been drifting away for the last hour or so. We walked down the dark road as the rain seemed to be falling heavier than ever. We quickened our pace and in no time at all we were back at Dafna, standing together in the rain on volunteers' row just outside her door. Chrissie opened the door slightly and peered into the darkened room. Sarah had already returned from Dan and was fast asleep in her bed. She shut the door again, smiling, and we stepped a few feet back and stood in the relative shelter of the new rooms that were being built onto volunteers' row. Standing at the very end of this concrete row gave an illusion of an elongated corridor, like the inside of a huge submarine. The buildings were in the final stages of construction, and the walls had not yet been painted so were plain and grey. Rain water ran down some of them, turning the surface a deeper blue-black shade, at the same time filling the air with the smell of damp cement and plaster. We managed to find a small covered area sheltered from most of the rain.

"Goodnight…" I said, taking hold of her right her hand with mine. I was fishing for a response and was rewarded

149

when she reciprocated by gripping it tightly. I could feel droplets of water running uncomfortably down the back of my neck inside my clothing. The rain was falling loudly around us, and a preponderance of tiny rivers flowed quickly around our feet. The light from a plain white street lamp near the road created a subtle reflection from the concrete walls and cast a pale ethereal glow across both our faces. For a moment we just looked at one another without saying a word. Chrissie moved closer to me, pulling my hand gently, and the distance between us fell away and was gone. Her hair was now darker in the wet, soaked and smooth on her head. Damp blonde ringlets were covering her collar which she was holding tightly against the rain with her left hand at her neck, the very ends of her hair being the only betrayal of its true colour. Her face was wet and on her nose a raindrop formed which fell just as she raised her left hand to brush it away in a gentle, almost childlike manner. She seemed more delicate and feminine than before; small, submissive and vulnerable. Her deep blue eyes were as wide and beautiful as the warm azure sky which greeted me the first morning I arrived in Israel. I released my right hand from her grip and took hold of her slender waist with both hands and kissed her. She kissed me back. We kissed gently at first but then with long, slow, exploratory kisses for what seemed hours. I hugged her and she spread her arms around my shoulders, holding me tightly as though she would never let me go. Her eyes were closed and I could just hear her breathing, close, deep, and gaining intensity, above the pouring rain.

"I've wanted you to do this for weeks..." she said softly.

"So have I," I replied. We kissed again.

I'd like to say Chrissie's kisses tasted of sweetened strawberries and so on. But they actually tasted of vermouth, cigarettes, and garlic, lots of garlic. But they were nonetheless quite wonderful.

Top: John on his way to work at the factory in his kibbutz work clothes, Nov 1978.

Bottom: 'The Old Bridge', Nov 1978.

A photograph of the sign I took from the side of the Golan road. It hangs in my study today.

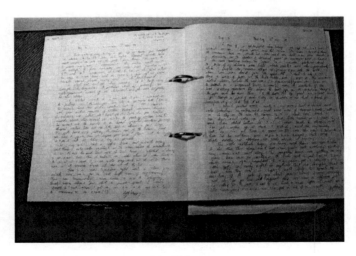

My Diary

Coupons for the kibbutz shop, Dafna, circa 1978

Top: L to R: Ishi, Chris, and Graham, (wearing his trademark leather jacket), outside the factory, Nov 1978.

Bottom: Letters from home. John and Chris sitting on our front step, having just collected the mail, Nov 1978.

שאר ישוב

כרטיס כניסה

לקולנוע

№ 23973   5.00

A ticket for Moshav She'ar Yashuv cinema.

*The business end of the dishwashing machine: A volunteer
working hard to keep pace as the clean items roll out from
inside the machine (left of picture)
to be quickly sorted and stacked.*

Top: Self sitting in Dafna's 'P-51', Nov 1978.

Bottom: Kiryat Shmona, Nov 1978.

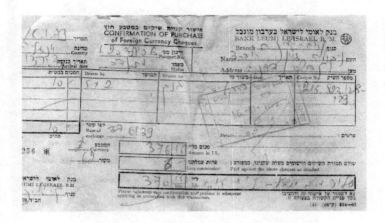

One of my receipts from the Kiryat Shmona 'Bank Leumi'
dated 15th January 1979, showing £10 in two five pound notes
produced no less than 370.15 Israeli Lira.

Four 'Egged' bus tickets from 1978/79. I suspect the ones for
31 Lira represent a trip to Haifa.

Top: Self with bandaged hand outside the factory, the snow-capped hills of the Golan behind, early Dec 1978.

Bottom: L to R, Chris, Graham, Guy, John, and Ezra on Chris's bed in our room, Nov 1978.

Top: Barclay, Chris, John, and Graham sunbathing outside our room on part of the miklat, all dressed in blue kibbutz clothes, Feb 1979.

Bottom: L to R, Barclay (in the hat) John, Graham, (minus beard) and self, Feb 1979.

Top: Chris and Gary looking out from the 'Monastery of Temptation' across the Jordan Valley, Jericho in the near distance.

Bottom: Returning to the kibbutz bus at the foot of the 'Mount of Temptation', March 9ᵗʰ 1979.

Top: 'Solomon's Pillars', Southern Negev.

Bottom: L to R, Graham, Gary, Wolfie, Chris & John desperately trying to get the stove going, Dahab, March 11ᵗʰ 1979.

Top: Dahab, Sinai, March 1979.

Bottom: May 5th 1979, first in the pool!

מועדון וריאטי בישראל

ELTON JOHN   אלטון ג'והן
RAY COOPER   ריי קופר

כרטיס כניסה

יום ראשון 6.5.79   בשעה 8.30   בערב
היכל התרבות ת"א

שורה	כסא	גוש
№ 38	16	א

המחיר -.**250** ל"י

החכנסות מהופעות אלטון ג'והן בישראל למרכז וריאטי לאבחון ושיקום חילד והמשפחה

*My Elton John concert ticket dated Sunday 6th May 1979,
in Tel Aviv.*

*Home, from left: Claudie, Gary, Mary, Ian and Chrissie, at
my parent's house, England, July 1979.*

MISGAV AM

I returned to our room at three o'clock in the morning, very wet and tired, but deliriously happy. I hung my clothes up to dry as best I could and climbed into my creaky little iron bed under the window. I lay awake for some time thinking of Chrissie and listening to the other lads snoring loudly. A kiss very definitely changes the relationship between two people. In particular if the kisses are repeated, and they are long and passionate. Suddenly we were more than just friends, and there was an expectation of more. The first kisses were over, so I therefore had implied permission to kiss her again. The rain was now falling heavily, and was pattering down very hard on the roof. As I drifted off to sleep I was already looking forward with great anticipation to the next day.

I slept right through until nine o'clock in a very deep, restful sleep. The other lads were *still* snoring when I woke up, so I walked quickly up to the dining-room to catch the end of breakfast.

Gary was the only volunteer still eating, so I sat with him. My tray was heavily laden with the last of the morning's eggs, bread and semolina. I drank tea and smoked cigarettes after breakfast while talking to Gary. He was delighted when I informed him I'd finally made some progress with Chrissie.

I then called by Chrissie's room on the way to the kibbutz shop to ask if she needed anything. Of course it was *not* on the way to the shop at all and involved quite a detour. I just wanted to see her again. They'd been to breakfast earlier, so both Sarah and Chrissie were sitting on their beds quietly reading and listening to the radio. Chrissie said I could buy her some cigarettes. She seemed reassuringly pleased to see me, so I skipped and bounced my way across the kibbutz like a love-struck village idiot. I walked straight into the shop and immediately accosted the poor unsuspecting female *kibbutznik* behind the counter with some very dubious Hebrew:

"*Shalom! Bokertov! Nelson filter, bevakasha.*"

"*Echad?*" replied the woman, sternly, after a slight pause, appearing a little surprised. She looked at me rather inquisitively. She was standing at the till, poised to turn around and reach for the cigarette display behind her.

"*Ken, toda roba,*" I replied confidently, handing over some very ancient and tattered kibbutz coupons, my last remaining for that week. I was handed a single pack of Nelsons. I was about to leave when I noticed some crates of beer on the floor near the counter. Quickly and absent-mindedly I abandoned any attempt at Hebrew, and said: "Oh, and some of these too…" I picked up seven bottles and placed them on the counter.

"*Sheva, beseder. Esrim va shmoneh lirot,*" she said quickly, clearly testing my Hebrew. She then picked them up one at a time from the counter and slotted them into a brown paper bag. My wallet was still in my hand, and she could see I was hesitating, obviously making an attempt at translating the number in my head, before she said: "Twenty-eight lira, if you pay with money. You have coupons?"

"No. No more coupons. I have thirty lira." I handed over the notes, which she rung into the huge till, and then passed me my change.

"*Toda,*" she said, as I picked up the bag and moved to the door.

"*Toda,*" I replied, and then: "*L'hitraot,*" as I walked out of the shop, 'See you later'.

I returned to Chrissie's room and sat on the end of her bed. My beer bottles in the bag clunked loudly onto the hard tiled floor. We drank tea, smoked, and the three of us recounted events of the night before. Soon after my arrival Mary, Sandra, and Christine came in, crowding into the room and sitting across the two beds. More tea was made and I could see where the afternoon was heading. I just wanted to take hold of Chrissie and throw her onto the bed right there and then. Instead, I found myself frustratingly engaged in some of the usual women's chatter that had very suddenly become shallow and irritating. It seemed destined to carry on for hours.

"Call in after dinner…" Chrissie whispered in my ear, as I stood up to leave, clearly noticing how frustrated I was. She kissed me quickly, almost furtively, on the cheek as I stood near the door.

Back in my own room I put the beers in the fridge and drank yet more tea. We all lay around on our beds, not really doing a great deal apart from some occasional flurries of less than energetic cleaning, tidying, and farting. Graham had clearly trained his bottom sphincter so incredibly well that he could virtually fart on command. Not only that, he seemed to have pitch control too, as though he could make his back-side talk. There was little wonder therefore, that Chris was often heard accusing Graham of talking out his arse. There may well have been an element of truth in this. But there's a down side to everything of course; the smell was atrocious.

It became clear that in the last few days there had been quite a lot of 'boning' going on, among my fellow room-mates. This was the main topic of conversation. It seemed that apart from drinking and smoking to excess, the other main hobby on the kibbutz was bed-hopping. I was the only resident of our room at that time who was not yet regularly absent from my own bed. I was asked about Chrissie, despite the fact they clearly knew everything there was to know anyway. It seemed there were no secrets that could be kept for very long on the kibbutz, particularly when it came to relationships.

At about four o'clock in the afternoon, we started to entertain visitors. Dominique and Sue called in, and then Motty arrived and made us all tea and toast. As soon as he'd eaten some toast Motty left. Then Geordie came in, with Ethiopian Paul. At six-thirty we all ate dinner in the dining-room.

That night we spent half an hour helping a *kibbutznik* move an ancient upright piano across the kibbutz. We had to lift it into the back of his van first, and it took a dozen of us to do it. I tried to play 'chopsticks' in the vehicle as we moved, but failed completely. We were thanked profusely before we were all returned to the dining-room. I walked down towards volunteers' row, to Chrissie's room.

I knocked on the door and recognised Sarah's voice shouting: "Come in!"

I sat on a flimsy wooden stool, rather hesitantly, between both beds, not wanting to appear too eager. Sarah was busy folding clothes and tidying, talking in her usual lively and ebullient manner, while Chrissie was sitting on her bed, quietly writing. I smiled and she smiled back. I wanted to kiss her again. I wanted some more of those long kisses we had the night before. But it was clearly impossible in the circumstances. The three of us talked about Christmas, and any new gossip we had, mainly about who was doing what to whom. The way she was talking I guessed that Sarah had met someone on the kibbutz very recently, but I was obviously not privy to who this person was. She seemed excited and occasionally giggled, looking around at Chrissie every now and again with a knowing look and secretive, churlish grin. I took out my cigarettes and offered one to Chrissie and she took it. Sarah didn't smoke and so refused one.

After an hour I stood up to leave and Chrissie came over to the door with me. We kissed for a few moments just outside the door.

"I'll see you at work in the morning, Jonathan, okay?"

"Yes, of course," I replied, resigned to the fact that I'd seen as much of her as I was going to for that night. I kissed her again, a lovely long, proper kiss, tasting her cigarettes and garlic, then left.

I walked up to the cinema and saw the first few minutes of a Spanish film, with the usual scratchy Hebrew subtitles, called: *The Call of the Crow*. It was awful, mainly because I didn't understand a word. I returned to the room and John was about to leave for a night shift on the conveyor. It seemed Christmas 1978 was suddenly well and truly over.

I was back at work on the dishwasher at six o'clock the following morning. In a way it was great to be back in the work routine. It was good to be sitting with Chrissie at the morning coffee break again. As we all dispersed to return to work after coffee, Chrissie took my hand and said to me:

"Come round this afternoon when you've finished…"

At the end of my shift when Ian took over, I went back to the room. I took a shower, and changed. The weather had turned cool again, fresh and windy, the warm humidity from Christmas having completely gone. Everywhere volunteers' rooms were warm and cosy, their paraffin heaters hissing and bubbling away quietly. Chrissie's room was less than a minute's walk from ours, just along volunteers' row from Sick Mick's room. Arab builders were working on the new blast-proof rooms adjacent to the older buildings in the row, fixing the roofs and tiling the floors inside. I spoke to them quite often, even though the majority of them didn't seem to speak any English. I managed to learn a few words of Arabic such as: *Marhaba* meaning 'Welcome' or 'hello', and the usual reply: *Hamdullah* which I took to mean 'Fine thanks', and was used in this context, but literally translated means: 'Praise to God'. Another greeting of course was: *Salaam alaykum* meaning 'Peace be upon you', to which you would normally reply: *Alaykum salaam*, 'and peace upon you.' I'd heard Israelis often use the Arabic word: *Yella* or *Yalla,* meaning 'go' or 'come on'. The Arab workers were a friendly and happy bunch. They didn't seem to live on the kibbutz, though they frequently ate in the dining-room. It seemed they arrived for work each day, and then left at night. I had no idea where they lived, presumably somewhere in Kiryat Shmona.

I knocked on Chrissie's door and walked straight in. She was alone in the room and in the middle of dressing after her shower. She was naked from the waist up, with her back to me. She slipped a t-shirt over her head and pulled it down around her waist, lifting her long blonde hair from the neck of her shirt with both hands so it cascaded down her back. She turned and faced me; her t-shirt was stretched and amply filled in all the best places. She walked straight over to me and gave me a hug and a great big kiss on the lips.

"Are you going this afternoon?" she said, in a cheeky and exuberant voice. She was clearly in a very good mood.

"Where?" I said, slightly bemused, and very distracted by the sight of Chrissie's t-shirt and its sudden close proximity.

"Swimming of course. You'd forgotten hadn't you?"

Yes, I had. There was a bus at two-thirty to another kibbutz near Kiryat Shmona called Misgav Am, to their indoor pool. This had been the reason we'd obtained passport photos weeks before. It was for 'security reasons'. Chrissie was pushing a towel and swimming costume into a bag, just as Sarah walked in. I ran back to our room to find my swimming trunks and towel, before returning to Chrissie's room. The three of us then walked up to the dining-room together and climbed aboard the kibbutz bus, an orange and white monster with huge wheels, which looked like an old 'Mack' truck converted to carry passengers. Chris and Graham were working, and I know, like me, they had forgotten about it. But John arrived with Denis, his Israeli girlfriend.

At just after two-thirty the bus set off. It was probably only half full. A *kibbutznik* was driving and there were two others in the bus with us, sitting at the front talking to the driver. I didn't know any of them at the time, though their faces were familiar. I began to recognise Dafna's *kibbutzniks* with a vague familiarity as you would your own co-workers in a large corporation. There were some *kibbutzniks* we knew well and who clearly enjoyed the company of volunteers. There were others, the majority perhaps, who merely tolerated us and were disinclined to become particularly friendly. I don't blame them really. The through-flow of volunteers was huge. Very few ever stayed or kept in contact once they had left the kibbutz.

All three *kibbutzniks* on the bus had with them loaded Uzi submachine guns. The driver put his on the floor of the bus near his feet; the other two cradled theirs, on their laps.

The journey from Dafna to Kiryat Shmona was as

unremarkable as usual. By now I'd travelled along that particular seven kilometre stretch of road many times before. I had become quite a confident hitch-hiker, at least between these two places. I'd gratefully accept a ride in anything heading my way, from trucks and vans, to tractors and cars. The short journey was easier by Egged bus, and was only two lira each way, but hitch-hiking was often much quicker, and sometimes a lot more fun. It was now so familiar to me I knew every slight bend and incline in that small stretch of road. But then, as we approached the town the bus took a sharp and unexpected turn to the right and started to climb. We passed around the outer edges of the town on its northern side and drove towards the hills. The road narrowed as we drove further from the town, seemingly in direct correlation to the gradient ahead of us. We passed through some small settlements and what appeared to be guard posts, with groups of soldiers standing with M16 assault rifles slung to their front, smoking and looking very bored. Several army jeeps passed us in the opposite direction, and then the road became quiet. The land around us was sparse and empty. I saw some of the same yellow signs hanging on the fence by the road as in the Golan, warning of mines. The road then became steeper and even more winding.

We turned off to the left and into an even narrower road. I saw a sign at the junction pointing to a place called Metulla. I learned later this was a border crossing with Lebanon, and was also known colloquially as: *The Good Fence*. But we'd left this road and were now trundling along a single track road similar to a narrow English country lane. It was clearly becoming increasingly difficult to negotiate in such a cumbersome vehicle. The huge engine at the front of the bus strained and groaned, and the driver crunched the gears downwards from third, to second, then right down to first to meet the impossible gradient. I then heard shouts from the front of the bus:

"Ken! Ken!" and *"Beseder!"* meaning 'yes, yes, alright!' mainly from the driver to the other two men standing next to him cradling their guns. Clearly there was some debate at the

front of the bus as to who would make a better driver, or possibly whether we'd make it to our destination at all. As we climbed higher I realised just where we were being driven. Misgav Am was one of the settlements high in the Naftali Hills above Kiryat Shmona, the lights from which formed part of the magical display I'd seen at night for the first time a few days after my arrival. I was thrilled at being on board the bus and eagerly awaited the view from the top.

We finally levelled out and Kibbutz Misgav Am came into view. It really was straddling the very top of the hill. Kiryat Shmona and the Hula Valley were on our left, and Lebanon was on our right. As we approached I noticed the rolls of barbed wire fence around this kibbutz were far more substantial than those around Dafna. An armed guard stopped us at the gate and climbed on board. He scanned our faces with a serious expression and spoke to our three *kibbutzniks*. Our driver handed him some papers which he then sifted through, retaining some of them. There was then some relaxed conversation before the guard jumped down the steps and off the bus. He waved us on through the gate.

We were driven into Misgav Am towards the indoor pool, a large smart-looking modern building near the centre of the kibbutz. It appeared to be quite a recent construction, and was surrounded by a landscaped lawn area with trees and shrubs dotted around. In the changing rooms I spoke to John as we undressed. I was then pleasantly surprised to see a fantastic full-size heated pool. There were a few Israeli families swimming and talking quietly, so I sat on the side and slid myself into the water. It was warm, relaxing and invigorating. Chrissie appeared at the door from the female changing rooms and looked gorgeous in a one-piece bathing costume. We swam lengths together, occasionally chatting to John and Denis. We spent a very relaxing fifty minutes or so in the pool before we climbed out to get dressed.

Just as twilight began to fall, we walked a short distance from the pool, led by a local *kibbutznik*, to their dining-room. Similar in size and initial appearance to Dafna's dining-room at the main entrance, we walked in and were told to help ourselves to hot tea or coffee and biscuits. As yet unremarkable, I was drawn to the far end of the dining-room where the corner consisted of huge picture windows from floor to ceiling. I stood with my glass of coffee, open-mouthed and in complete awe of the view. Clouds were drifting by, *below* the windows, giving the impression we were high up a Swiss mountain at the very top of the world, or drifting along in some huge airship. I'd never seen anything like it. Chrissie and I sat together at a table close to the windows sipping coffee, staring out at the colossal view. Thin grey clouds drifted slowly past, a hundred feet below us, gently tracing the contours of the hill. The very tops of the passing clouds occasionally caught a reddening glow from the setting sun, and their movement around us caused an illusion that it was we who were moving, and not the clouds. Far across the Hula Valley I could see large blue-grey clouds hugging Mount Hermon like elongated balls of darkened cotton wool, seemingly at the same level we were. I stood up close to the glass and tried to look down. It seemed this whole side of the dining-room was suspended by tall steel joists, and protruded from the hillside in a spectacular manner.

Misgav Am was an amazing place in a beautiful but vulnerable location. It formed part of the border with Lebanon and as such was always going to be at risk from terrorist attack. This kibbutz was far more remote than most. Just over two years after my first visit, on the night of April 7th 1980, terrorists broke through the perimeter fence from over the border and managed to gain access to one of the children's dormitories. They sprayed the inside with machine-gun fire while the children slept. A young child and a *kibbutznik* were killed before there were further deaths in the fire-fight between Israeli soldiers and the terrorists. The incident was a tragedy and came as a terrible shock. For years the people of Misgav Am had been trading happily and freely with the nearby Arab villages in southern Lebanon. The terrorists were not local people. They were not even Lebanese.

As the sun slipped away and dusk fell, we boarded the bus for the return trip to Dafna. To my astonishment I then saw another old aircraft wreck, right in the middle of a sloping grassed area, parked facing the fantastic view. It was a small 'L-19' single engine Cessna *Bird Dog* spotter plane, in drab green colours and Israeli Air Force markings. There were large wooden chocks wedged under the front of the main wheels, and it actually appeared perfectly airworthy.

The return drive down the mountain road towards Kiryat Shmona was very interesting. Hundreds of lights began twinkling across the valley as it grew dark. They stretched far away south into the distance, in lines and grouped together in clusters. The long approach road into Misgav Am was lit by street lights, and was obviously one of the lines of lights visible from the town below. The main part of the steep winding road, however, was not lit at all. It was definitely challenging for our driver. Luckily we managed to negotiate the worst before it became completely dark.

ROOM 17A

New Year's Eve, as you might imagine, passed in a very similar manner to the Christmas festivities. We all danced around in the *moadon* drinking to excess as usual. I spent all evening talking to Chrissie.

January 1st 1979 fell on a Monday. Luckily we were given the day off. We were all nursing some pretty severe hangovers. No-one was expected to work, unless you specifically volunteered to work extra hours to collect a 'free day'. The *moadon* floor was again completely awash with booze and other detritus, so quite a few of us, including Chrissie and I, assisted in clearing it all up.

In the first few days of January I noticed a calendar hanging in the kibbutz office with the new year of '1979' written among some Hebrew. There was also another number, '5739' adjacent to it. On closer inspection and after asking about this from the short, crotchety woman behind the counter, I found out this was actually the date according to the Jewish calendar. The Jewish New Year or *Rosh Hashanah* had passed months ago, in early October 1978. I realised for the first time in my life, thanks to my own ethnocentricity that of course our Western Christian calendar relates back to the time of Christ. Many countries had never even heard of Jesus Christ, so had therefore developed their own date systems. It is purely by accident of fate and fortuitous worldwide agreement, therefore, that our system is used across the whole world.

On January 7th I found an entry in my diary that had *not* been written by me:

'*Very good day today. Been boning all night long. I'm falling in love slowly. I'll let you know for future reference.*' It was Graham's handwriting. Yet again I needed a safer place in which to hide my scribbling. But I guess there was a little truth in at least *some* of his observation. Chrissie and I were spending a huge amount of time together. Despite this we maintained an outwardly cool and pragmatic approach to the relationship, as did other volunteers who found romance on the kibbutz. There was very little in the way of public demonstrations of affection or hand-holding and so on. I'm not sure why this situation existed, but it did.

Chrissie's room-mate, Sarah, had found romance too. I was told she was seeing a young Israeli chap on the kibbutz. Luckily for us, she was away from the room overnight on a regular basis. Inevitably there were occasions when we knew in advance Sarah would possibly be away over night, and when she had *agreed* to be away *all* night. We could then push the two iron-framed single beds together into the centre of Chrissie's room. This was the usual volunteer's make-shift double bed. It was incredibly uncomfortable, particularly with the very prominent steel spine running down the centre and the very real risk of the whole thing parting in the middle without warning. At the time of course, this bed was the greatest and most fantastic place on earth.

During January, there was seasonal work to be undertaken on the kibbutz. I was relieved of my regular dishwashing duties in order to help out in the orchards. I didn't know it at the time but I was never again to work another shift on Dafna's dishwasher.

The apples needed picking, and there were two shifts, 6.15 a.m. to 12 noon or 9 a.m. to 3 p.m. It seemed to rain for most of January, particularly when I was picking apples, so I was very glad when the last of them had been gathered in. But no matter how wet and cold I became while trudging around among the trees and baskets of apples, always prominent in my mind was the exciting prospect of returning to Chrissie's room after work, when we could shut out the rest of the world for a while.

We visited Kiryat Shmona together once or twice a week, and sat in Yuval's bar in the precinct, drinking pints of beer, smoking and talking. The fifty pounds I once had in the kibbutz office rapidly diminished as I would occasionally take five or ten pounds of it into the town and change it for Israeli *Lira*. The exchange rate was brilliant. I began to rely on the 'wages' we were given by the kibbutz. I realised Chrissie had access to quite a lot of money. She had saved thousands of dollars to fund her trip around Europe. She needed to be prudent with it though, as it had to last. She still had a lot of travelling to do.

Quite often during those first few weeks of the New Year, when it rained it did so in an almost biblical manner. Storm clouds in the form of tall, dark, undulating cumulus seemed to gather quickly around Mount Hermon and then descend from the Golan Heights, sweeping across the whole of Northern Galilee. The nearby hills vanished completely in the heavy and fast moving low cloud that came with it. The rain fell harder, faster, and more ferocious than any I'd ever seen before. It was often accompanied by some stunning and fantastic displays of lightning and extremely loud thunder. The dry earth was instantaneously transformed by flash floods in a few short minutes, causing small rivers everywhere to sweep up dirt and debris, which then poured down the roads and paths, gathering in hollows or low ground before soaking away. Quite often the rain would last for hours, or even days at a time. Frequently it would stop as suddenly as it had started. The sun would then return and very soon the earth would revert to its previous dry condition, as though it had never rained at all.

I was hardly spending any time with the lads in my own room; not that they were even there themselves for much of the time. My bed was now empty and unused most nights of the week when I stayed at Chrissie's, thanks to Sarah staying with her kibbutz boyfriend. So it went on, as though everyone was now involved in sharing someone else's bed.

A cool and wet January passed quite quickly. The weather began to change and warm up in February, as though the two months of December and January were the only few weeks that could possibly be described as 'winter'. Sometime in early February a new volunteer arrived and took up residence in our room, adding to the cramped conditions. Barclay was Scottish and had a reasonably strong accent, but was also well-spoken and patrician, as Phil had been. He was tall and had long black hair that reached down beyond his shoulders. He looked and sounded a lot like the comedian Billy Connolly. On the increasingly rare occasions when I stayed overnight in the lads' room, the conditions were made more bearable due to the fact we were not usually all present at the same time. Even so, Barclay had moved yet another bed into the room, and so it was now very crowded.

Also in early February, Yonatan stood down as the Volunteer Leader and an Englishman called Robin took over. He was a nice chap in his early thirties with short curly blonde hair and beard. He was immediately more approachable than Yonatan, and sadly I suspect I pestered him frequently for a variety of reasons from then on.

On the 1st February 1979, Israel seemed to be thrown into something of a national panic. The media and newspapers were in frenzy when the Ayatollah Khomeini returned home to Iran after fourteen years in exile. There were jubilant scenes in Tehran as he walked down the steps of a plane from Paris. Thousands of grown men marched through the streets of the Iranian capital bashing themselves on the forehead with lumps of wood, causing injury and drawing blood in the process. Frankly it all looked rather silly, like a clip from a *Monty Python* movie. I couldn't quite imagine the Archbishop of Canterbury leading a similar procession around the grey and austere streets of London. For days this was the predominant topic on the television news and in the English language *Jerusalem Post* newspaper. No-one could envisage the consequences for Israel, but Mr Khomeini was certainly not making any peaceful overtures towards the country at all.

Once all the apples had been harvested I spent some time back in the factory working the zipper. By now I was very experienced, being in my fourth month on the kibbutz. I found myself performing the role of the *kibbutznik*, acting as 'boss' of the machine to two other volunteers. I didn't request this 'promotion', it just seemed to be a natural progression. Arnon simply approached me in the factory one day:

"Jonathan. You work the zipper. You operate the machine, *beseder?*" and walked away. I worked with several new volunteers including Barclay, Glyn, and Val, and enjoyed the work. If you are able to have fun and an occasional laugh while working, it can really make the whole experience so much more rewarding. This sounds obvious now, but I was still very new to the world of work!

Towards the end of February the weather really started to heat up again. The rain was reduced to a few short showers on the occasional day, and it was mainly sunny, becoming much warmer all the time. In February, Chrissie and I dared to make representations to formalise our relationship by asking Robin about the possibility, however remote, of obtaining our own room, just the two of us. There were other couples living together so we decided to give it a try. Sarah continued her relationship with Benny, her young *kibbutznik* boyfriend, but it often seemed unpredictable and capricious. She would sometimes return to her room – as she was quite entitled to do – thereby immediately frustrating any prospects of our own romantic intentions. The concrete flat-roofed constructions in volunteers' row were now finished, and so we tentatively asked about the pair of us sharing one. Robin initially met the idea with some scepticism and seemed reluctant to pursue our request. I suspect this was probably due to him not yet realising whether the rooms would be ready and available. The next day he surprised us both when he came up to us at lunchtime in the dining-room, with two shiny new keys in his hands:

"There you go. It was only finished last week and still doesn't have a proper number on the door. It's room 17a. Look after it!" and he smiled as he handed the keys to Chrissie before walking away. Both keys were attached to a thin brown cardboard tag, on which was written a few scribbled words of Hebrew and the number 17. There was a single Hebrew letter after the number which looked similar to an English capital 'N'. This was the Hebrew letter *aleph*, or 'A'.

Chrissie and I looked at one another and laughed. I couldn't believe it. Our own room! For me it was like Christmas and my birthday all in one. Still incredibly selfish and naïve, the first thought that flashed through my head like a lightning bolt was: 'Wow, I'll be able to have a shag absolutely any time I want!' I clearly had a great deal to learn about relationships.

Chrissie and I hastily finished our meals and slipped away from the dining-room. We headed towards volunteers' row, and talked excitedly as we made our way along the line of new blast-proof rooms. We checked each of the doors in turn, until we found one with '17a' scribbled on it in Hebrew, very untidily in pencil. Just for an instant I thought to myself how I would no doubt be able to write those numbers in a better and neater fashion.

The room had a sliding door, and Chrissie inserted one of the two identical silver keys into the lock and turned it gently. The door to our brand new home was heavier than I expected. When it opened we saw before us a square, dark, cave-like little room which smelt strongly of plaster and fresh paint. It was literally one single room, not much larger than a prison cell. There were no toilet or shower facilities, as these were shared, a few yards across the way in volunteers' row. We walked inside. In only a few short steps I'd crossed the tiled floor and reached the far wall. I took hold of the winding handle at the metal window shutters and opened them up as wide as they would go, letting in more light. There were two single beds in the room, the standard steel-framed articles, and two new mattresses, still in their clear plastic wrapping.

We moved in that same afternoon, Wednesday 28th February 1979. I didn't think to carry Chrissie over the threshold at the door, but it nevertheless felt significant and exciting. It was a lovely warm afternoon and ideal weather in which to move house. I was thrilled about the whole thing, as was Chrissie. I took my key from the key-ring and held it reverently in my hands as though it was the Queen's key to the Crown Jewels. I wrote '17a' along with our two names underneath on the back of a blue ten *lira* kibbutz coupon, and fixed it to the door with two drawing pins. We were effectively setting up home together, and I could only half believe it was really happening. We made up the two beds as one double after we'd pushed them together in the centre of the room under the shuttered window. I lashed the legs together tightly with some rope from the factory, in the hope the beds wouldn't part in the middle. Chrissie hung two cotton sheets on the walls, fixing them with drawing pins. I acquired a small table from somewhere, I forget exactly where, and this became our bedside table. We managed to furnish our little room quite well. A small, green, angle-poise lamp sat on the table, next to an alarm clock, an ash tray, a glass bowl containing sunflower seeds, and a hairbrush.

I returned to my old room to collect my diary. I informed John and Graham I was moving out. They both laughed, and then cheered. I ran back to 17a. In that short space of time, Chrissie had obtained a green plastic tube to use as a vase and had filled it with wild flowers. She also had a small wooden *Villiger* cigar box that looked like a very distressed musical box, which she also placed on the table. This contained some letters, personal effects, and kibbutz coupons. I had no idea where this box came from, because as far as I knew, she didn't actually smoke cigars. When I placed my copy of *A Postillion Struck by Lightning* on the table, it was completely covered and wonderfully cluttered, as though we'd lived there for months.

The first night we were resident in room 17a, at around nine o'clock, we heard the Israeli Defence Force rattling sabres in the Golan Heights. I stood outside our room and tried to look up into the hills, but couldn't see much at all through the darkness. A military convoy passed by the kibbutz, parts of which made the very unambiguous and now familiar clangorous rumbling sound unique to tracked vehicles. The main noise, however, came from above. Helicopter rotors were thudding overhead, punctuated by the occasional scream of fast jets flying low and then up over the hills. This was a very tangible show of force over the Golan Heights. But for whose benefit?

On the first morning of our official cohabiting, I sadly had to force myself very reluctantly from our bed at 3.45 a.m. in order to start work on the zipper at four o'clock. I hated getting out of bed so early, mainly because Chrissie didn't start in the kitchens until six. I thought how very unfair it seemed that I had to drag myself away from such lovely feminine warmth, in our lovely warm, cosy bed, just to go to work!

That morning I worked with Glyn, a curly-haired English lad with a marvellous sense of humour, and Val, who had long black hair and was from Geelong, near Melbourne, Australia. It was enjoyable work, and because I was in charge, I made sure we had plenty of breaks. After work I returned to our room to find a note on the very neat and well made bed. Chrissie had written a few lines on the back of a blue ten *lira* kibbutz coupon (perhaps an indication as to their relative value) before she went to work: 'J: PLS HAVE THIS FILM DEVELOPED AND PICK UP THE OTHER ONE FROM MARTINS, THANX. DON'T FORGET THE LAUNDRY. LOVE, C.' I smiled when I read the note, in particular the last part. It was only one little word but its significance was beyond its size, and I was flattered. It seemed there was now a formal acknowledgement there was some love in our relationship.

I had intended to hitch into town straight after work, but decided to wait, so we could both travel together. I kept forgetting to collect the laundry, hence the reminder in the note. I walked across to the kibbutz laundry and picked up Chrissie's coat. Then I called in at my old room on the way back to collect the last of my belongings. Barclay had been working in the fishponds with John that morning, and had brought some huge fish back with him in a bucket, alive. They were splashing and flopping about in the bucket of water, and he was in the process of lifting them out one at a time, killing them, and gutting each one. This was all being done rather messily just outside the room when I walked up. Presumably the fish were to be prepared for cooking. It was a little more upmarket from the usual toast and jam. I picked up my green nylon sleeping bag from my bed and walked towards the door to leave, as John said:

"How's married life then Biggles, settling in alright are you?" and laughed.

"Do you want some fish there, Biggles?" Barclay shouted, in his distinct but refined Scottish accent. There was a profusion of blood and guts slopping around over the rim of the bucket and onto the front step of the room. His hands and arms were covered in blood right up beyond his elbows, and he held a huge carving knife in one hand. Some bright red flecks of fish blood were spattered in lines across his face and over his clothing. I remember thinking how surprised I was at seeing so much red blood coming from fish. For some reason I didn't think they bled the same way we did.

"No thanks, Barclay. Thanks anyway…" I said, walking away, feeling as though I'd somehow made a lucky escape.

John laughed again, and shouted after me as I made off: "Biggles…" followed by: "Regards to the wife!"

At three o'clock, Chrissie and I locked our room and hitched into Kiryat Shmona. It was a nice feeling, locking our room together, as it was doing anything and everything with Chrissie. We visited Martins, the photography shop, and each collected a film we'd had developed. I bought some more Camel cigarettes at the tobacconists, and we decided to have a drink in Yuval's bar, so we could properly examine our latest photographs.

We then met Perry and his Argentinean girlfriend Raquel, who were already in the bar.

"Hi there, Jonathan! Hi Chrissie!" Perry said, jumping up from his seat instantaneously, as if someone had just passed a current through it. He started pumping my hand vigorously, as though he'd not seen me for weeks.

"Are you missing my machine, Jonathan?" he said, beaming broadly and moving to sit back down.

"I don't miss working in the evenings, Perry, to be honest," I replied, "and I don't miss being wet through all the time." Raquel giggled coyly as Perry nudged up closer to her on the brown leather bench seat. She took a sip of her drink, which was dark and bubbly, like Coca-Cola. The tall glass had a small paper umbrella sticking out from the top, among a lot of ice and several generous slices from what must once have been a huge lemon. I stood at the bar and ordered two pints, leaving Perry and Raquel with Chrissie for a few moments. When I sat down, pint glasses in hand, Perry beamed at me, grinning like a schoolboy with a naughty secret.

"We want to congratulate you both, don't we Raquel…"

"What about?" I said in reply, curiously, seeing an equally bemused expression forming on Chrissie's face.

"About your good news!" and he laughed again, looking around the table at Raquel, then back to Chrissie and me. For a second or two I had no idea what he was talking about until he said: "*We've* been living together for six months, and we're very happy. Congratulations!"

Raquel then said: "Isn't it wonderful?"

Chrissie laughed out loud when she realised, and so did I. It was almost as though we were newly-weds. I half expected them to shout '*Mazal Tov!*' at us at any moment. I suppose it was pretty close to it, and just short of the real thing. In kibbutz terms it seemed very much like the real thing. But how on earth had they found out so soon?

"How did you know?" I asked Perry, genuinely curious.

"Raquel and I want one of those cute little rooms too, don't we Raquel?" and Raquel giggled again, "So we asked Robin about it. He told us you guys were having one. We could be neighbours!"

Chrissie looked at me and I looked at her, and we both laughed again, trying our very best to disguise the real reason for our laughter.

The four of us laughed and joked, and the conversations were light and frothy. We sat in the bar with Perry and Raquel until six thirty. We watched the sun descend at a seemingly slower pace than usual behind the hills above Misgav Am, as though it too had been sipping beer all afternoon. The warm sunset glow eventually gave way to the inky darkness above the town, and a very slight evening chill followed. We were slowly becoming quite happily inebriated, until the four of us left the bar and wandered over to the bus station to look for our number twenty-seven bus. I climbed the steps up to the record shop and found a vinyl LP of Pink Floyd's *Wish You Were Here*. I asked the proprietor to play it for me. He seemed to approve as he raised his thick black eyebrows:

"*Ken, beseder,*" he replied, nodding, before quickly slotting it onto the turntable in his usual apparently carefree but casually expert manner. Weeks ago I'd acquired a taped copy of this album from Tim, and had played it constantly in Chrissie's room, probably far too often. It became something of an anthem for our relationship. There was quiet in the bus station as Pink Floyd was loaded onto the record player, and the speaker hanging on the wall started to crackle into life. The air around us was heavy with the familiar and ubiquitous smells of spicy *falafel*, diesel fumes and Time cigarettes. Buses were coming and going, and groups of young Israeli soldiers loitered around, chatting to one another and smoking. I began to notice some soldiers had their unit insignia on shoulder tags which hung like a loose epaulette from their left shoulder. There was quite a wide variation of badges. I made a mental note to ask Ezra about this when I next saw him.

Chrissie and I stood leaning on the rail overlooking the bus stop as Perry talked at us for a while, in an even more animated manner than usual.

"You'll get fed up of hearing this…" Chrissie whispered in my ear, stealing a kiss at the same time, as Dave Gilmour's solo guitar playing filled the bus station, echoing loudly and magnificently from the corrugated iron roof above.

"Pink Floyd or Perry?" I replied, to which we both laughed.

"I won't anyway," I said. "It will *always* remind me of you…"

At seven o'clock our bus arrived and we had to leave, just as the track *Welcome to the Machine* started. I was about to explain its significance to Perry but didn't get the chance. Maybe another time.

THE KIBBUTZ TRIP

Masada

Exciting rumours were flying around between the volunteers of a kibbutz trip to the south of the country. Gossip in all its forms and on any subject seemed to spread around very quickly, like wild fire. No-one seemed to know any firm details, or even if there was any truth in the rumours. Tim and Ian held a party in their room that night to celebrate six months since Tim's arrival on Dafna. I still remembered Tim's five-month party, and his four-month party. Several new volunteers had recently arrived from New Zealand, and some were proudly wearing t-shirts with slogans across the chest: *All Blacks Grand Slam 1978.* This clearly referred to their national rugby team's recent international success. Proud Yorkshire man that he is, Ian made his own version of this on a plain yellow t-shirt, and wore it at the party. He'd written: *ALL WANKS GRAND SLAM 1978* untidily in thick black pen across the front of an otherwise decent t-shirt. I spoke to Robin at the party and he finally and officially confirmed there was to be another five-day trip at the end of that week. Without being specific, he said it was to be a journey that would take us almost as far south as the kibbutz dare take us, with some interesting stops along the way. This time Chrissie and I would both qualify for seats on the bus.

I worked the zipper all week, mainly on day shifts until Friday 9th March, the day of the trip. I enjoyed the day shifts more than any other, as I would then be able to spend all night, every night with Chrissie in our room. I had little comprehension as to the extent of the kibbutz trip and exactly what lay ahead. There didn't seem to be a written itinerary of any sort, though no doubt one did exist somewhere, as it all seemed well rehearsed by the *kibbutzniks*. I was extremely pleased to be going this time. Chrissie and I had by then spent a full week together in room 17a.

I became acutely aware of the imponderable and innumerable differences between living with a woman, rather than sharing a small room with several other men. Besides the obvious, the room always looked clean and tidy. There wasn't much farting and belching going on either. No hairy-arsed buttocks to greet me in the mornings. Chrissie's bottom was not quite as hairy as Graham's! Chrissie had obtained a sweeping brush, probably from the dining-room, and there was always a container of fresh flowers on the bedside table. I doubt, on reflection, that I ever made the bed, and I remember she regularly swept underneath it too, which seemed a waste of time and effort as no-one ever looked under there. There was always a warm and slightly delicate, feminine atmosphere in the room, despite its initial austerity and utilitarian design. We had to keep our clothes on the bed, side by side, as we didn't yet have a wardrobe of any sort. Seeing Chrissie's clothes sometimes lying on top of mine somehow symbolised a greater and less formal closeness between us. When we were together in the room I enjoyed the sheer proximity of her loveliness. I wanted to be close to her, and I could reach out and touch her at any time. The constant and repeated sight and sound of a woman dressing, and more importantly, undressing, even in the dark, was a wonderful and sensuous new experience.

The huge orange and white kibbutz bus was parked outside the dining-room. Luggage panels were wide open at the sides, and steel cooking pots and a gas stove were being loaded, along with large stringy sacks of vegetables and fruit. Dozens of loaves of bread and large packs of margarine in cardboard boxes were all pushed into the capacious storage compartments. Gas cylinders were loaded aboard along with square water containers encased in polystyrene, the same as the ones used when working in the fields. We were allowed a few minutes to eat an early breakfast in the dining-room before being instructed to climb aboard at six o'clock. There were nineteen volunteers and three *kibbutzniks* on the trip. I sat in the middle of the bus at a window seat, with Chrissie on my left. On her other side across the aisle was Sarah, sitting next to San Francisco Mary. English Mary sat next to Sandra. Reminiscent of any decent school trip, all the 'bad boys' ensconced themselves across the wide bench seat at the back of the bus: Tim, Ian, John, Graham, and Chris. Gary and Claudie sat just behind us and in front of us were French Paul and Marianne. Ian Anarchist sat with Geordie John and Wolfie with Christine, no doubt so they could converse in German. All three *kibbutzniks,* Ethiopian Paul, Sofa, and Ishi, had their Uzi submachine guns with them, loaded and always at hand. Sofa, who looked not unlike Eli Wallach in the film *The Magnificent Seven*, drove the bus, his Uzi hanging casually next to him on the door. He took it down from there after only a few miles and laid it on the floor, as it kept repeatedly banging on the side of the door every time we went around a bend. The early morning sun was just streaming into view as we pulled out the gates of the kibbutz. A loud cheer rose up from most of the volunteers as we left Dafna.

After we'd passed through Kiryat Shmona, we headed due south on Highway Ninety. Descending from the Upper Galilee down towards the Kineret, I had the sudden realisation that this was the first time in three months I'd been beyond the immediate vicinity of Dafna. I was thoroughly enjoying being away from the kibbutz and was tremendously excited. The bus drove straight through Rosh Pina past the junction with Highway Eighty-Nine, the main road west which ultimately led to the coast. We carried on heading south. My second sight of Tiberias and the Sea of Galilee was no less fantastic than the first. It was a lovely day, and the water looked as deep blue as the sky above, and very inviting. We stopped only briefly in Tiberias for a comfort break before pushing on.

The early spring countryside was green and lush, and the road fell down low into the valley, following the River Jordan. The hills of Samaria were on our right and the mountains of

Jordan immediately to our left, just a few miles away. Occasionally we could see clusters of large, dark brown tents in the distance towards Jordan, pitched in the desert, apparently miles from anywhere. These were Bedouin people, who were living the same nomadic lifestyle as they had for centuries. Then, in complete contrast, we saw a reminder of the modern world. We passed an Israeli army base on our left which must have contained several hundred Magach tanks parked in the open. There were soldiers visible, climbing about on some of the machines, their engines turning over, creating a heavy fog of diesel smoke that slowly drifted around them. They looked as though they were ready to be called into action at a moment's notice.

At around mid-morning, the lads at the back of the bus started passing around a couple of bottles of vodka and orange. They then started singing. There were rugby songs, football songs, and the inevitable *Ilkley Moor*, led by John and Ian.

The landscape then became noticeably more arid as we journeyed south. There was a radio in the bus but sadly it was barely audible above the singing, chattering, road noise, and the huge ancient twelve cylinder diesel engine rumbling away at the front. At one o'clock we reached Jericho. We didn't stop in the town but cruised slowly through it. Jericho had not a single tall building and appeared as an oasis, with tall date palms and cypress trees seemingly between every flat-roofed house and lining every street. It was quite a biblical vista and looked exactly as I had imagined it would. The bus then left the main road and onto a dusty and very rough track, pulling up outside Jericho at the foot of some steep cliffs. The air brakes on the old bus hissed like a sigh when we came to a halt, as though it was pleased to be given a rest. The door opened and we all climbed out and stood looking down across at the town, happy to be off the bus and on our feet. Bread, tomatoes and hard boiled eggs were unloaded for lunch. High up the cliff face behind the bus I saw areas of smooth walls with sharp angular edges protruding from the surrounding rocks. I could just see rectangular windows in neat rows, and walkways with steel railings jutting out impossibly from the rock, hundreds of feet up. In my ignorance I hadn't a clue what I was looking at. I asked Gary and he told me we had arrived at 'The Monastery of Temptation.' I stood chewing my egg and tomato sandwich as the dry atmosphere and early afternoon sun began to cause small beads of sweat to form on my forehead.

There was a steep rocky path behind us rising at forty-five degrees to the dirt track, which seemed to disappear around the side of the mountain. When lunch was finished and all was packed away we were led up this path, towards the Mount of Temptation. Apparently this was the site where Jesus spent forty days and forty nights being tempted by the devil. Greek Orthodox monks arrived in the sixth century and built a monastery around the cave where Jesus was thought to have stayed. It was an extremely improbable and dangerous place to build anything, let alone a monastery.

Some monks were still in residence, so we were instructed to respect their privacy. It was still a fully functioning monastery. Once inside, it was the strangest place I've ever seen, hanging so precariously as it was from the side of a cliff. I did notice one of the toilets, which was quite astonishing. Inside the small wooden shed-like room, there was a pretty ordinary looking dark wood toilet seat built onto a wooden box about knee-height. There was no cistern or flush of any sort. I looked into the toilet itself and it merely consisted of a hole in the floor which fell away to the rocks several hundred feet below. These rocks far beneath appeared to be of a slightly darker brown hue than all the others. The ancient planks in the wooden floor creaked and groaned as I walked on them, as though the whole thing would collapse at any moment.

There were narrow iron walkways connecting the buildings, fixed into the precipitous rock face with steel bolts. These mountings moved very slightly at the weight of human traffic, and the rusted iron handrails were clearly in place to prevent you from falling to your death. An amazing view was gained from the monastery across Jericho and the Jordan Valley, and it was quite breathtaking.

Back on the bus, we seemed to drive in a generally downhill gradient for quite some time until we reached the shores of the Dead Sea. With no air conditioning in the old bus, all the windows were flung open as the atmosphere around the Dead Sea seemed particularly hot and dry. At first sight, the water appeared as fresh and inviting as any other lake anywhere in the world. We followed the shore line for several miles until we reached a beautiful oasis called Ein Gedi. There were some shops and bars and it all appeared to be extremely cosmopolitan and civilised. Much of it was shaded by a huge number of very tall and heavily-laden date palms. The bus pulled up in a car park area close to the water, where there were freshwater showers and a changing area on the beach. For most of us, including me, it was our first visit to the Dead Sea.

The water was very warm, and I waded in up to my waist. Without much thought to the salt content of the water and its possible effects, I leaned forward and tried to dive in. After the initial surprise of being physically unable to push myself under the surface, the next thing I felt was some extremely painful stinging in my eyes. I quickly ran out of the water and up the beach to the showers. I rinsed my face and washed my eyes thoroughly. I was then joined by quite a few others who had the same problem. We returned to the water and tried again. I walked into the sea very slowly on the soft muddy sand, and then gently leaned back. The buoyancy of the salt-rich water held my weight on the surface, and it was an amazing, unique sensation. I floated around for a while in the Dead Sea like a plank of wood, unable to sink, with no requirement to move around in order to stay afloat.

It wasn't long before we climbed onto the bus and carried on south. We soon arrived at our next destination. This place was unknown to me, but if you have any Jewish connections at all, then you would probably realise the significance of it to Judaism. We had arrived at a place called Masada.

In essence, Masada is a huge flat-topped mountain standing alone on the edge of the Judean Desert, overlooking the southern end of the Dead Sea, like a metaphor for Israel itself. We pulled up in the car park outside a very plain, flat-roofed building which was apparently a youth hostel, and where we were to spend our first night. Looking up at the mountain from the east it seemed very formidable. In the early afternoon we started the long walk up the steep eastern zigzag path. It was a climb of thirteen hundred feet. There was a perfectly decent cable-car at Masada, from the car park near where we had parked, right up to the summit, but it was decided we would walk. Our group reached the top surprisingly quickly. Some members of the party obviously saw it as a challenge and raced their way up.

We spent some time relaxing, drinking water, and taking in the amazing panoramic view before exploring the site. A tourist guide had been provided for us, and I was fascinated to hear of the mountain's history. Masada had originally been constructed as a palace by King Herod in 30 B.C. After his death a number of Jewish zealots fled to the mountain to evade the Romans during the rebellion in 66 A.D. It was then fortified, and even had its own rainwater catchment system, with arable areas where crops were grown and animals were reared. As the rebellion continued, Masada was surrounded by an entire legion of Roman soldiers who laid siege to the place for several years. The Romans were continually turned back by the defenders who stubbornly refused to surrender. The only way the mountain fortress could be conquered was to form a huge ramp of earth and stones, eventually amounting to thousands of tons, which were slowly piled up against the mountain on the western side. The Jews of Masada could observe the gradual construction of the ramp, and harried the Romans as best they could, while still refusing to give themselves up. When it became clear the Romans would eventually succeed in climbing the mountain, a collective decision was made to ensure the Romans a hollow victory. They knew they would all be forced into slavery or worse if they were captured alive. The men of Masada drew lots. Ten of them were chosen to despatch everyone on the mountain before the Romans could reach them. On one very sombre night in 72 A.D. whole families laid themselves down together on the sandy earth to be slaughtered. Finally the last ten turned their weapons on one another.

Amazingly there's a huge amount of Herod's Palace on Masada still available to see. The ramp is still there today, as are the remains of the Roman camps around the mountain on all sides. There are some intricate mosaics on floors, walls, and in bath houses, and quite a lot of the original architecture. Some parts of the palace on the northern side are located spectacularly on the very edge of a sheer drop, falling away a thousand feet. There were some gruesome archaeological discoveries in the nineteen-sixties, when the skeletal remains of many of the residents were discovered. The whole site has been a very rich source of ancient artefacts.

I found it an incredible and thought-provoking place to visit. Today, new recruits to the Israeli Defence Force swear an oath of allegiance to their country in a ceremony held on the top of Masada. The rock stands as a symbol of Jewish defiance, and there's a proud saying in Israel: 'Masada shall not fall again.'

MASADA
FROM THE EAST

EILAT

An alcohol-free early night in the youth hostel ensured we were all awake and up promptly the next morning for another six o'clock start. The next stage of the journey consisted of driving virtually the full length of the Negev Desert, south along Highway Ninety. For most of the way the road was dead straight. It was at one such straight section when Gary shouted at me to look out the back window of the bus. He was standing up talking to Tim at the time, and I have to say, I didn't see it at first, and probably wouldn't have done until it was right on top of us. In the far distance, only a few feet above the ground, as though travelling on the road itself, something was approaching us at an astonishing speed. There was a dirty dark smoke trail spiralling behind the object in huge billowing circles. It was made even more mysterious as it was approaching in complete silence. As it drew nearer I realised what we were looking at. When it closed to a few hundred yards I finally identified a pointed nose, cockpit, and twin tail fins. A few seconds later it rose up and flew straight over the bus. I could see it was an Israeli Air Force F-15 Eagle. The aircraft thundered overhead in a split second and carried on along the road in front of us before climbing and banking away to the right over the Negev Desert. The pilot applied re-heat to the engines and the exhausts glowed bright yellow and orange like two miniature suns, before disappearing from view. It occurred to me that an aircraft capable of such high speed could easily fly over 'enemy' territory within seconds, either by accident or design. This fact must have been foremost in the minds of the pilots, on both sides.

It was close to lunchtime before the bus turned off the main road to the right at a small green sign stating 'Timna' in Hebrew, Arabic and English. The huge wheels of our bus threw up great clouds of thick yellow-brown desert dust behind us, and the track seemed to deteriorate the further we drove from the main road. After ten minutes we stopped at a flattened square of desert, presumably made to resemble a car park. There was a cliff face 300 yards away, with several separate, prominent and rounded segmented ends jutting out. It was in fact a natural phenomenon known as Solomon's Pillars. They were tall, sandstone columns of rock weathered and worn into shape, and had a fabled connection to King Solomon and some ancient mining. It was another spectacular sight we were able to explore, and was the backdrop to where we sat in the increasing heat and penetrating dust to eat our lunch.

The rock formations were impressive, but at the other side of the car park were some huge sand dunes, as high as a house, which were part of the southern edge of the Negev Desert. This was *real* desert, and I needed to get closer to it. Claudie had the same idea, so we trudged up the shifting sand together, struggling to make progress as it immediately gave way and spread under our feet. Finally, at the top of the first dune, we paused and looked across the empty miles of wilderness. The view was simply awesome. Sand dunes stretched away into the distance as far as the eye could see.

"*C'est magnifique, non?*" Claudie said softly. She shaded her eyes with the flat palm of her right hand like a navy salute, as she stared across the seemingly infinite desert.

"Yes. Yes, it is, it's really amazing," I said in reply, a little lost for words. The sun was very strong and we were both panting and sweating as we gazed around us. I heard Gary shout from the car park below. After a minute or so, we both turned and ran as best we could back down the hill of sand. I fell and rolled awkwardly, sand flying everywhere, before finding my feet again. Claudie laughed. I felt sand in my hair and inside my clothing. As we walked up to the bus, Claudie offered me a Time cigarette. I took it, and we paused briefly together as she lit them both with a match, before we climbed aboard the bus.

Gary said to me: "She's always wandering off is Clauds, have you noticed? You can be out somewhere and suddenly she's gone, just bloody wandered off."

We reached Israel's most southerly town, Eilat, in mid afternoon. Eilat sits geographically at the very top of the Red Sea, and it was much hotter than where we'd started our trip in the Upper Galilee, 560 kilometres further north. Our bus parked outside the Eilat youth hostel and we spent some time helping to unload the items we needed. We were then told we had three hours before we were to be back at the hostel for dinner. We grabbed our towels and made for the beach.

The closest I'd been to swimming in waters such as the Red Sea was probably 'The Blue Grotto' off the south coast of Malta in the Mediterranean Sea. There the water was clear and quite warm with a lot of marine life to see. But this did not even come close to the experience of swimming in the Red Sea. The water was very warm and gin clear. The sea appeared to be absolutely filled with life; tropical fish of every size, shape, and colour, the likes of which I'd only ever seen before in aquaria, or some very large pet shops. Those who wanted them had use of a mask and snorkel, and the view using these was utterly extraordinary. Chrissie and I swam together for a while and were joined by Gary and Claudie. The two girls looked tremendous standing in the water, like extras from a Bond movie. Gary pointed across the sea to a town in the distance at the other side of the Gulf of Eilat:

"Akaba, over there, look, Jonathan," he said. "Remember, in the film, *Lawrence of Arabia*?" as we stood waist deep in the blood-warm water. Gary rubbed spit into his mask, his long black hair was lying thin, straggly, and wet on his shoulders. Of course, I thought to myself, this was also known as the Gulf of Akaba. Across the water just a few miles away was the town that was so heroically seized from the Turks by Lawrence and the Arabs in the great Arab Revolt of 1917.

"Amazing isn't it, that it's so close," Gary remarked, "but you can't go there, sadly, because they won't allow you to cross. Claudie and I tried it once before, but there's no border crossing, you see. Shame really." And he crouched down into the water and paddled away, his snorkel hissing and spitting as he breathed. I would have loved to have been able to visit Akaba. It was extremely frustrating to be so close and yet so very far away.

We all helped to some extent in preparing the evening meal in the enormous youth hostel kitchen. I peeled a few potatoes, and eventually we ate chips, salad, eggs, and lots of bread and margarine. That night, as the sun sank low over the Judean Hills, casting a deep red glow across the Gulf towards Jordan, we all left the hostel together in search of some night life. The skin on my face felt tight from the sun and sea water. We all had red, glowing complexions. Those who'd been to Eilat before led us to one of the few bars there seemed to be in the town at that time, a place known as 'Henry's Bar'. On the outside it appeared as a rather dreary and unprepossessing shack of a place, but on the inside it was far more promising, like a popular student bar at an English university. I don't know if the proprietor was actually called Henry, but it was a surprisingly capacious little place close to the sea, with a very powerful sound system, and beer sold on draught, poured into large pint glasses. From the outside fire-escape, which was a rusty, iron construction, and looked as though it had been stolen from the monks high up in the cliffs above Jericho, you could stand drinking and smoking while looking across the water. The many lights of Akaba flickered in the distance, some of which were reflected in the still calmness of the Red Sea. Just for a moment I wondered if there was an equivalent bar in Akaba, where drunken revellers were gazing across in our direction.

Very soon most of us were fairly well inebriated and the music seemed to become much louder as the night progressed. I remember being jostled around in a crowd of people, some of them Dafna volunteers, and some strangers, all apparently dancing in their own individual and drunken manner, singing along in unison to Eric Clapton's *I shot the Sheriff*, and Bob Marley's *No woman, no cry*. The stiflingly hot air in the place was dense and cloudy with smoke that I only later realised was the sweet and distinctive new-mown hay smell of cannabis.

Just as I thought the trip couldn't possibly get any better, we climbed aboard the bus the next morning, though not quite as early as usual, to be told we were to venture further south into the Sinai Peninsula. There was no border control of any sort, just a small group of Israeli soldiers who casually waved us on by. At that time the whole of the Sinai was occupied by Israel, and had been since the Six Day War in 1967. From Eilat we drove south along the coast road for several hours. We stopped a couple of times to stretch our legs and frequently passed the rusted hulks of destroyed military vehicles, all of which we were told were Egyptian. They were riddled with bullet holes.

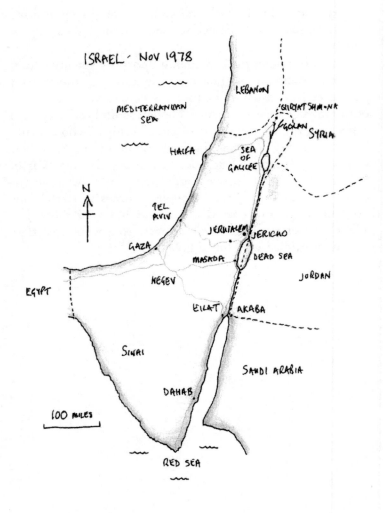

A map of Israel in 1978 drawn by me with no acknowledgement whatsoever of any official 1948 borders.

THE SINAI

The Sinai seemed vast, probably due to the fact that it contained very little of anything. I sat with Gary for a while as Claudie was sitting at the front of the bus, and Chrissie sat with Sarah. Gary and I were both huge fans of the David Lean film, *Lawrence of Arabia*, and it seemed some of our trip actually retraced small parts of Lawrence's journeys. I found this tremendously exciting and Gary spoke with predictable omniscience on the subject, and as usual I was hugely impressed. By late morning we reached the end of our travelling for the day and indeed the furthest south we were to reach on the trip. We were about two-thirds of the way down the coast. There was very little that was distinguishable as anything resembling a building of any sort, and the bus pulled up off the road virtually straight onto the beach. Date palms fringed a beautiful wide, gently curved bay adjacent to the blue sea under a cloudless azure sky. Across the water were a range of deep red sandstone hills. These barren mountains appeared to cast their colours down onto the water, which suggested a reason why the sea had acquired its name. We were led to some rough timber constructions which looked as though they had been thrown together from large pieces of driftwood and very old palm leaves. These were our 'rooms' for the night. We were charged two U.S. dollars for each 'room' by local Bedouin. This was the only accommodation available on Dahab beach. There was no electricity and no flushing toilets, but there was some tap water. The toilets consisted of wooden shacks, each covering a hole in the ground. In the dry desert atmosphere, these were not as bad as you would imagine.

The snorkelling was even better at Dahab than Eilat. A coral reef stretched some fifty yards or more from the beach in places, and had to be crossed before it was possible to swim properly. The only way to do this was to swim completely horizontal, like a flat plank of wood, using the mask and snorkel. I lowered myself into the water and began paddling with my flippers. The razor-sharp coral passed only a few inches beneath me as I slowly propelled my way through the water. I passed over some small gaps, one of which I saw was occupied by a brown and white striped fish the size of a football. It was sitting quietly a couple of feet below and probably didn't see me. I noticed it had some very long and fearsome spines like those of a porcupine protruding from its dorsal fin and tail. I drifted slowly over it, taking care not to startle it in any way, as the spines seemed particularly unfriendly.

On reaching the edge of the reef I was unprepared for what I saw next. The coral fell away vertically like an underwater cliff for hundreds of feet, dropping down and becoming dark blue and then inky black far below. It was an incredible sight. I was swimming over the very edge of a precipice. I was a very inexperienced diver at that time and we had been warned of a possible likelihood, however small, of hammerhead sharks being in the vicinity. I could have swum further out into the Red Sea away from the coral and over the deep blackness, but contented myself with drifting along the end of the great drop close to the coral edge. I was joined by small fish of all colours, swimming around me and past me, seemingly unconcerned by my presence. I then saw some much larger fish which initially gave me quite a fright, but I was very reassured when they seemed to pay me no attention whatsoever. Occasionally I would stick my head out above the water to check my position, and I found I had moved quite a considerable distance along the beach.

Every now and again I would say to myself, 'just a few more minutes,' before carrying on for five or ten minutes more each time. It was some of the best snorkelling anywhere in the world and utterly unforgettable. I paddled gently back across the coral, thankfully not repeating my close encounter with the brown and white spiny fish I met on the way out. I later discovered this was probably an Angel fish. Contact with the spines can cause paralysis and death.

In the late afternoon one of the huts became an improvised kitchen. Graham, Gary, Wolfie, Chris, and John took it upon themselves to connect the gas cylinder to the stove and compete for position as alpha male and head chef. I kept out the way, but I did manage to take a photograph.

I heard Wolfie's gruff, peremptory German voice above the others shouting: "I can get zis verking you know, ja, I know how to do zis…" sounding like a long-haired, bespectacled and bearded Arnold Schwarzenegger. He was eventually drowned out by the more numerous Brummie accents and then John's Yorkshire, all making their suggestions as to how the thing would light, which they seemed to have great difficulty with. Finally they managed to get it going without blowing themselves up and the first pots of peeled vegetables were placed on the burners. While it had taken five men half an hour to light the stove, the girls of the group had peeled all the vegetables, cut the bread and prepared plates and cutlery in a perfect display of domesticity and multi-tasking. At dusk we all sat on the fine warm sand with our plastic plates laden with food, looking across the dead calm Red Sea at Saudi Arabia.

Chrissie and I went for a gentle, after-dinner stroll along the beach as the sun set, and I took some photographs with my small *Kodak Instamatic* camera. It was not an instrument that would serve to do justice to the true beauty of the place. There were few references to the real, outside world in Dahab, and so time really did seem to stand still. We rented our own open hut on the beach facing the sea. Everywhere around us seemed to be cast in a deep red glow as the sun fell quickly behind us in the Sinai. The hills of Arabia were at first scarlet and then very deep ochre. This was reflected in the water, and turned the surface of the sea almost the same colour. Small waves only a few inches high lapped up onto the sand as though the warm water was as tired and happy as we were. The night sky was filled with stars, some of which seemed to reach right down to the ground. It was as if we were sitting in our very own private planetarium. There were no street lights, no road or traffic to speak of, and no sound but for a few volunteers chattering and laughing, and the occasional grunting of a nearby camel.

In the morning we were all awake with the sun, and helped to load the bus. There was just time for a quick dip in the sea before breakfast, and then we were off again heading back north. It seemed a shame to be leaving such a paradise so soon. All along the beach in among the date palms, Europeans were living under the trees in sandy caves and make-shift huts, somehow surviving there for days, weeks, or even months, judging by the appearance of some of them. I could see the attraction, and understood how easy it would be to give in to the temptation to live there for as long as possible. There was always someone to trade with for food and cigarettes, and at least there was a source of fresh water, but very little else. No shops or buildings of any sort. It was an unspoilt paradise. I am told there are hotels there now.

JERUSALEM

We drove all the way back up through the Sinai and stopped for lunch at Eilat. There were a few shops where some of us bought cigarettes and beer before returning to the bus. We were all noticeably quieter than on the outward journey and many of us dozed and slept as best we could. Most conversations were hushed and subdued. We trundled along Highway Ninety adjacent to the western shore of the Dead Sea, and again passed the palm trees of Ein Gedi. At the northern end of the Dead Sea we turned west.

The bus began climbing and at times slowed to a near walking pace. Cars and other buses, and even larger trucks passed us as we seemed to struggle up the winding road into the hills. Grey clouds obscured the blue sky above and it became noticeably cooler the higher we went. The dry warmth of the desert was gone. But this all added to the atmosphere of our destination. We approached Jerusalem on Highway One, the Jericho Road, from the Judean Hills and I saw a sign pointing to Bethlehem which was only a few kilometres away. I would challenge anyone to admit their first glimpse of Jerusalem was not one of the most breathtaking sights they have ever seen. The city appears quite suddenly as a jewel nestled among the barren hills, regal and resplendent.

It was close to dusk when we pulled in and unloaded at the youth hostel. The air was much cooler than the desert but still quite warm by British standards, for March. After briefly settling in, we walked together as an untidy group into the Old City. We ate *falafel* from one of the many food stalls. The final minutes of daylight were reflected in spectacular fashion in the golden 'Dome of the Rock' on Temple Mount. Long shafts of fading light struck the dome at sunset, as though directed by divine intervention from behind exiguous breaks in the gently rolling clouds. A myriad of ever-changing colours ranging from deep red to bright orange gambolled and sparkled from the magnificent golden roof. There were calls to prayer echoing across the walled city in Arabic, and the narrow and congested ancient streets were alive with chattering locals and rather timorous and bewildered tourists. We didn't venture far, due to the fact it was now dark and we had no clue as to where we were going. The youth hostel was close to the Jaffa Gate on the western side of the Old City, so after a couple of hours we returned, very tired after the day's travelling and eager for an early night.

After breakfast we were gathered together at nine o'clock in the common room of the hostel, as a guide had arrived to take us around the Old City. He was a native Arab whose face was dark brown and lined like old boot leather, and was probably in his early sixties. He seemed quietly enthusiastic and very pleased to be tasked in showing us around. He was a very small figure and wore an Arab head scarf, a *kafiya*, in the manner of Yasser Arafat, but his was red and white. He also carried a stick with him which he used to great effect in pointing at his subject matter. It is probably essential to be accompanied by someone who knows the geography and history of such a place, as there is so much to see.

Within its magnificent walls, the Old City is very small and divided into four sections: The Jewish, Armenian, Christian, and Muslim Quarters. Firstly we were led through the Jewish Quarter to the Western Wall of Temple Mount, more commonly known as The Wailing Wall. This is the most sacred place on earth for Jews. The huge blocks of stone form part of the remains of the Second Temple from the time of King Herod. We stood in awe at the sight of it, its significance and its sheer proximity. Being non-Jews we assumed we would merely have to content ourselves with standing some distance away but we were wrong. The Wall was partially fenced off with an area fifty yards deep in front. We were each given a paper *kippa* to wear on our heads, and were allowed to approach the Wall and touch it. There were a few tables with small pieces of paper and some pencils available for general use. Some of us, me included, wrote a short prayer in the form of a wish, and neatly folded it up. I don't quite remember what I wished for, but I jammed the piece of paper as tightly as I could in a wide gap between two of the enormous bricks in the Wall. Thousands of others must have done the same as almost all the gaps within easy reach were filled to bursting with rolled and crunched up bits of paper. All around me Orthodox Jewish men dressed from head to foot in black robes and hats were chanting and nodding their heads, tightly gripping their copies of the *Talmud*. Their long black ringlets of hair over each ear swung back and forth in time with their movement. It seemed they only just avoided banging their heads on the rough yellow-brown surface. Some even appeared to be actually kissing the cool stone. I wasn't particularly moved by any specific religion at that time. I found all this overt and emotive reverence shown to a large stone wall very curious. Faith is clearly a matter that cannot be fully explained and is a deeply personal issue. This wall obviously held equal importance to these men standing next to me as the devotees of the Ayatollah in Tehran banging their heads in the street with pieces of wood.

Chrissie and the other girls were at another section of the Wall as they were not permitted to stand with the men. Our group was gathered together again and we were led onto the nearby Temple Mount. We walked past the rather grey and austere al-Aqsa Mosque and towards the great golden Dome of the Rock. To my surprise we were allowed inside, once we had removed our footwear at the door. The outside of the building was incredibly beautiful, consisting of millions of coloured pieces of mosaic and segments of marble, predominantly in various bright shades of blue. There were large sweeping inscriptions from the *Koran* completely encircling the outside walls. Inside was equally beautiful and quite breathtaking. There was a large, flat, mustard-coloured slab of rock twenty yards across sitting in the very centre of the floor. It was discoloured and worn smooth around the edges, no doubt by the touching of hundreds of generations of eager hands on its surface. It was four or five feet high in places and it was protected by a modest velvet rope suspended from small brass posts all the way around it. This was the rock on which the prophet Mohammed stood when he ascended to heaven on his night-time journey. Somewhere on the surface of the rock was his sacred footprint. At one end the rope fence was quite close to the rock, so as we shuffled past I deftly stepped over it and reverently but quickly laid a hand on it. It was cool and smooth to the touch. I was fully aware of its significance to millions of people.

I noticed what appeared to be bullet holes in the ceiling on the inside. I asked about these and was told by our guide that a Jewish extremist had entered the building with an Uzi and sprayed it with 9mm bullets. I guess there are bloody idiots everywhere, but an idiot with a gun is the worst kind.

From Temple Mount we were led into the Muslim Quarter and onto the Via Dolorosa. This was the start of 'The Way of the Cross', otherwise known as 'The Fourteen Stations of the Cross'. This extraordinary little street began where Jesus was firstly condemned and then led carrying his cross through the streets to his crucifixion. Each of these 'stations' is marked on the nearest wall in Roman numerals and a Latin inscription. Not all of them refer to points on the route where Jesus fell while carrying the cross, though some do. Others make reference to him meeting his mother, and the final four refer to his crucifixion. If you are in any way a religious Christian you will know the significance of this walk through the streets of old Jerusalem up to the Church of the Holy Sepulchre, where the last four 'stations' are located. Our guide spoke clearly and succinctly, describing the events and history in vivid detail. It was not at all difficult to imagine Christ himself struggling along the same street as a condemned man. I may indeed have been seeing some of the same sights he saw on his fateful journey. Few dispute his existence but it is your own faith which dictates to you whether or not he was the Lord of Lords, King of Kings.

Our guide informed us the Arabic name for the city is *al-Quds*, 'Holy Sanctuary' or 'Eternal Sanctuary', and he was clearly very proud to be associated with it. He continued to lead us up the Via Dolorosa, and at the top of the hill we were ushered inside the very ornate church built over the place where Christ's journey with the cross came to an end. I saw at the back of the church, roped off in a similar fashion to the Holy Rock in the great Dome, a small hole in the ground perhaps six inches in diameter. It was decorated with silver in a blazing star pattern. This was the hole in which the cross had actually stood when Jesus was crucified.

At an opportune moment I stepped over the rope barrier and dropped one of my hands into the hole. I was discreetly shouted at by a man who appeared to be a priest, dressed in a black skirt and blouse, and wearing a very tall hat like a wizard. But I'd done no harm, and apologised. I had touched all three now, each of the sacred places from all three religions. I don't really know why I had collected these sacred touches as I did, other than the fact that I was drawn to them, and was unaware of another opportunity to do so again. I do know that non-Muslims are no longer permitted to even see the Rock under the great Golden Dome, let alone touch it.

I continued to be moved by what I was seeing in Jerusalem. If there will ever be a Biblical Apocalypse, and the Seven Trumpets start blowing, with the Guards of Magog swarming around, then I have no doubt it will be right there within the walls of that very special Old City. Indeed, it seemed highly likely that while we were there, we would witness Roman soldiers marching the streets and alleys, asserting their authority, or see an angel standing in the sun. Our brilliant little guide then went on to tell us some of Jerusalem's violent and bloody history. It has to be a city that has been fought over more than any other, as it has changed hands dozens of times. On each occasion there was huge loss of life with rivers of blood running through the streets. There cannot possibly be anywhere else on earth as controversial as this place and at the same time held in such reverence by so many.

In all these tiny streets there were locals, mainly Arabs, selling souvenirs. There was a wide range of items available, anything from gold and silver jewellery, to t-shirts, hats and leather goods. I bought a black and white *kafiya* head scarf and a square ceramic wall tile decorated with three words in Hebrew, English and Arabic: *Shalom, Peace,* and *Salaam.* As I walked with Chrissie I was asked by some of the shop-keepers we passed how much I wanted if I was to sell her, or swap her for something. I declined all offers. I really had no use for camels or donkeys. I had no idea what I would feed them on.

Our tour finished at two o'clock and we thanked our guide. We were told we had a few hours at our leisure before we should return to the youth hostel. It was around that time that it started to rain, and it became quite a lot cooler than we had been used to. In fact Jerusalem is quite high up and it is not uncommon for there to be snow in winter. We followed our noses and found another *falafel* bar, and then strolled around the Old City. I've no doubt we didn't appear particularly reverential as we walked and ate, and we were becoming quite wet as the weather deteriorated further. Some of the streets were no wider than corridors and were covered over, so we lingered a little longer in these. All the time we tried to avoid direct eye contact with the eager *souk* traders.

Israeli soldiers were of course everywhere, standing and talking in small groups or walking around in pairs, wide eyed and serious. Their M16s and Uzis were fully loaded and slung to their front rather than the more relaxed manner of over their shoulders. They were the modern day Roman Army, irresistible and all-powerful. Their twentieth-century green uniforms and guns made them look particularly incongruous in the ancient streets.

Eventually, back at the hostel, we prepared our final meal. It was our very own memorable 'Last Supper' of the trip. After the meal most of us stayed in all evening. There was a superb view of the Old City from the flat roof of the hostel, and we drank some Grenache red wine which had apparently been brought from Dafna in the bus. It was a very calm and civilised end to the five day trip, as darkness fell and the evening call to prayer rose up again all across the magnificent ancient place. The rain and dark clouds somehow added to the atmosphere, like that of an old Cecil B. DeMille or William Wyler epic. At any moment it seemed a youthful and athletic Charlton Heston might ride furiously past us in his splendid four-horse chariot.

THE SINGLE LIFE

Purim

To say we were all a little subdued when we were driven into the gates of Dafna the next day is probably a great understatement. I then realised how Chris and Graham had felt when they returned from their trip down south. We'd been on quite an amazing tour of The Holy Land and had visited some of the greatest places in the world. Now we were back. I was pleased to return to room 17a with Chrissie though, but unhappy at the sight of the work list that night. I was to work conveyor on the ten o'clock night shift until four the next morning.

After work I climbed into bed a few minutes after four o'clock. I was utterly exhausted. I probably fell asleep in minutes; my arm snaked around Chrissie's waist, drawing my body up close to her lovely warm femininity. Sadly our alarm clock shattered my deep sleep just before six o'clock, when Chrissie had to get up for work in the kitchens. I slept on until almost lunchtime, when I strolled sleepily and very hungry into the dining-room.

Chrissie and Sarah were seated together slightly separate from the other volunteers at the end of the table, and were obviously in very deep conversation. Sarah appeared stern and seemed mildly angry at something. Chrissie appeared distant and distracted, looking almost confused at something Sarah was telling her. I took a tray and selected some food, then walked over towards their table. Sarah rose to her feet as I approached and left with two words to Chrissie, which I also heard:

"Tomorrow then, okay?" This was spoken in quite a stern and peremptory tone. I sat down.

"Okay?" I said, leaning my head around over the table for a better look at Chrissie's face. I slid my tray down and pulled up a chair next to her. Her hair was obscuring much of her face, like half-closed curtains, hanging straight down and hiding it from view. Perhaps this was intentional.

"What's that all about?" I asked, though not particularly interested, until I then saw Chrissie's face, serious and wistful, with some obvious sadness forming in her expression.

"You know she's split up from Benny?"

"No, I didn't know, but go on…"

"Well, she split up from Benny a few days ago. It turns out he was a lot younger than he originally claimed to be."

"So, what's the problem there?" I asked, not feeling any need to remind her of our own age difference.

"That wasn't everything. But anyways, she says she's had enough."

I picked up my cutlery and started to eat. I felt relaxed and refreshed after a decent morning's sleep. The food was quite good too. I'd obtained some fried eggs left over from breakfast. I also managed to salvage a bowl of cold semolina, which was very thick and lumpy, like cheap, badly mixed wallpaper paste, just as I preferred it. I was about to ask Chrissie exactly what Sarah had had enough of, when she said:

"We're going to Haifa tomorrow, Jonathan…"

She looked towards the kitchens, avoiding eye contact with me. I suspected I knew the reason for such a trip to the coast but needed to ask her anyway. Maybe there was a chance it wasn't for anything other than some sight-seeing? Could it be they just wanted to spend more time together, after all, they *were* supposed to be together, until I came along and split the two of them up.

Before I could ask, Chrissie said: "We're going in the morning, early, to book our air tickets."

Just for a moment I had a little difficulty swallowing my cold semolina. Suddenly it really *did* acquire the appearance and texture of wallpaper paste. The only thing I could say, in a slightly croaky and incredulous voice was:

"Why?"

Chrissie turned to face me: "Jonathan, we've already been here longer than we'd planned. I didn't expect to get a room with you or *anyone* other than Sarah, and so what we've had has been a bonus. It's been lovely, it really has, but we have to move on. We have the whole of Europe to see yet, and I have to be home before September. You do understand, don't you?"

No, I thought. No I don't understand. Let her go on her own if she wants to go now. Or tell her to wait a while. But don't leave yet. Not yet.

"Yes, I suppose so," I replied, confused and shocked, hiding my true feelings as best I could. What about our room?

"I'll write. But you won't be able to write back, because I'll be travelling all the time. Maybe we can meet up somewhere, in Europe, or even England? When are you going home?"

"I always said, well, that is I'd *planned* to go home after six months, early May..." I replied, stumbling for words a little, a thousand conflicting thoughts flying around in my head, most of them miserable and bleak. I wasn't at all prepared for this. I knew it would have to end sometime but surely not until May? I was even considering staying on a little longer, if we were still together and living in our lovely little blast-proof room. But now this possibility, this ephemeral dream had been instantaneously and irrevocably turned to dust.

"So, there, we'll meet up later in the year somewhere..."

"Right. So that's it. There's nothing I can do about it I suppose. I don't want you to leave, you know that. We've only just got our own room. Can't you go later?" My voice probably sounded rather pleading and a little desperate, and I still hoped I could persuade Chrissie to stay, but she had clearly decided, with some obvious persuasion from Sarah, that the time had come to leave Dafna.

"Jonathan, we're going to Haifa tomorrow. I'll try to stay for my birthday, but then we'll have to go."

Chrissie's birthday was 28th March, which was only two weeks away. Two tiny, short, precious little weeks. Then what would I do? I didn't even want to give it another thought.

The next morning we were both up and dressed at five-thirty. We kissed before Chrissie left the room to call for Sarah. They had both booked a free day for their trip to Haifa, and left at six o'clock in the back of a kibbutz van, bound for Kiryat Shmona bus station.

I worked the zipper all morning. I was distracted by thoughts of Chrissie leaving, and Glyn's jokes and impressions were not as funny as they usually were. The boots were coming through in small numbers from the conveyor, so I called a break and wandered into the factory canteen. John and Graham were sitting at the table laughing, pushing great handfuls of biscuits into glasses of hot Turkish coffee. Folds of soggy biscuit fell away into their sludgy coffee and onto the table. Graham had shaved off his beard in February and now maintained a few days' stubble, intermittently becoming clean shaven, clearly not allowing the beard to return in full. Looking at the two of them I realised just how much I'd neglected my friendship with them in the last few months while being so close to Chrissie.

"Biggles!" John shouted as I walked in, "having a coffee with us?" and he pushed the biscuits in my direction across the table.

"Why not," I said, and spooned a small mountain of the earthy dark brown powder into a glass then filled it with hot water from the steaming urn. I stirred my coffee and dropped my packet of Nelsons on the table. I sat down. I wanted to tell them all my inner most private thoughts and worries, but held back. Men just didn't do that sort of thing. I wanted them to give me reassurance and to tell me everything would be okay and not to worry about a life on Dafna after Chrissie. But I just talked about the factory, the zipper, and pulling boots. I sipped my coffee and dunked half a dozen of the thin biscuits into the glass. The next day would be Friday, 16th

215

March 1979. Not an ordinary Friday, apparently. John said it was *Purim*. It was an important festival, and the whole kibbutz was throwing a party. It was a celebration of Jewish deliverance from the Persian Empire, as told in the Biblical Book of Esther, or so I found out later. Dressing up and being very silly was apparently encouraged.

"It's fancy dress, Biggles, everyone will be dressing up. I mean *everyone*! And getting pissed!" John said. There was nothing remarkable about getting drunk on a Friday night, I thought.

"Yes Biggles, we've all got to dress up. What are you going as?" Graham paused, and then said: "Give us a fag will you?" and reached across the table for my cigarettes. He took one, and lit it with his own matches.

"I don't know. I've no idea," I replied absent-mindedly, "I'd not given it any thought at all. I'll have to see. I'm not sure." I drew on a cigarette and my thoughts wandered away through the open factory window. The clean blue of the sky contrasted sharply with the black dirt and soot on the inside of the glass and the surrounding wall. Unless I consciously kept a firm hold of my thoughts, they would quite often drift away, like chimney smoke on a summer breeze. While John and Graham continued talking about *Purim*, I was thinking about Chrissie and what would happen to us. We'd been together since that first kiss in the rain in the early hours of Christmas morning. It seemed I was not making my own decisions unilaterally any more, as everything included Chrissie. This would soon come to an end.

Chrissie and Sarah returned in the late afternoon. I was very pleased to see her. I was given the bad news. She was flying out of Israel on the morning of Friday 30th April, but leaving Dafna the day before. We opened a bottle of red wine and shut out the rest of the world. We hid in our little blast-proof room holding onto each other as though it was the very day of our separation.

At seven-thirty we ate a late meal in the dining-room. Most of the volunteers were still there, sitting around chatting to one another. Having finished eating, they were now drinking tea, smoking and playing with the remains of their meals on their plates. The scraps of food were dotted with the usual cigarette ends sticking out like miniature grave stones. All were discussing *Purim* and their fancy-dress outfits. I still had no idea.

On the day of the festival I worked at pulling boots on the conveyor from four o'clock in the morning until ten. I was actually beginning to get the hang of it at last, and no longer had any cause to clamber over the machinery like an idiot, or ask for the whole thing to be stopped so I could catch up. I developed more blisters on my hands, but the skin finally hardened and became as thick as leather. I felt fitter and stronger, both physically and mentally, than when I first arrived on Dafna, and was subconsciously developing a quiet determination of my own.

I needed some inspiration for a fancy-dress outfit. Some volunteers were going to extraordinary lengths in producing quite elaborate costumes, keeping them secret from the rest of us, and taking the whole thing very seriously. It was rumoured there would be a prize for the best one. Gary suggested I dress myself up as an RAF pilot, but I couldn't find an appropriate uniform. My eventual outfit was rather pathetic compared to some, and kept falling to pieces. I made a pair of wings from cardboard, and glued handfuls of filthy feathers from the chicken shed onto them. I made a large beak and secured it to my face with a length of elastic. I wore some blue and orange flippers on my feet. I was going as a bird, and I looked like an over-sized Dodo. I looked and felt like a complete idiot.

Chrissie dressed herself up as a 'loose woman' in an extremely short skirt and tight fitting blue top, with a serious amount of make-up on her face. None of the girls on the kibbutz ever wore make-up of any sort, and I had no idea where she had obtained it. Seeing Chrissie like this was a real shock. She actually looked ravishing, and I didn't think it was safe for her to leave our room! The amount of lipstick and powder on her face was in fact probably little more than would be usual for a night out in a big city. It just seemed unusual in the context of our surroundings. This was perhaps a glimpse of how she would appear under more normal circumstances out there in the real world.

Purim started as the sun went down, but the festivities which were held in the dining room didn't get fully underway until after nine o'clock, once the evening meal had been cleared away. There was a huge amount of booze available including cans of beer, which were a rarity, and plenty of wine in bottles on the tables. There was music and dancing, including a live band. It all led to a fantastic atmosphere. From a volunteers' perspective, getting drunk and fooling around on a Friday night was the norm, but I'd never seen so many *kibbutzniks* in this state before. Tim, Ian, and Donald appeared dressed as 'The Gumbies', characters from *Monty Python*; quite an easy outfit which merely consisted of a knotted hanky on the head and Wellington boots on the feet. The three of them wandered about all evening shouting: 'My brain hurts!' in thick Yorkshire accents. Mick appeared looking suitably absurd in a long frock and huge wig. He looked like a bespectacled Winston Churchill dressed in drag.

Towards the end of the evening and after much alcohol had been consumed by all present, three finalists were chosen among the volunteers. French Paul was brilliant dressed as 'Asterix the Gaul', Julie looked marvellous as the 'Statue of Liberty', but the winner, for sheer comic effect, was Gary. He was dressed as a pregnant woman, complete with beard, and his hair in two long plaits. He was wearing a pink night-dress down to his knees and had a large bump stuffed underneath. The main problem with it though, and the part which caused the most hilarity, was that his 'bump' kept descending almost down to his knees, as though his poor unfortunate woman had completely prolapsed.

The party continued well past midnight. Chrissie and I returned to our room at around two o'clock.

ALONE AGAIN

On the Saturday *Shabbat* after *Purim*, Kibbutz Dafna was extremely quiet. I doubt anyone made it to breakfast. Chrissie and I stayed in our room and only ventured out in order to use the toilet across the corridor in volunteers' row. We didn't get out of bed or get dressed all day.

For the next week I worked day shifts on the conveyor, the calluses on my hands intermittently hardening and bursting in a repeat process, which eventually caused my palms and fingers to look fat and rough, like those of a biblical galley slave. The Tuesday night film at the kibbutz cinema was *Cross of Iron*, the incredibly powerful and brilliant Sam Peckinpah anti-war movie starring James Coburn, set on the Eastern Front in World War Two. It is a film about overcoming hardship and betrayal amidst the madness and futility of war. I was wounded in action myself again when I managed to crack my head very painfully on the conveyor welly-boot extractor. I took a day off sick due to some quite severe headaches. No doubt I was probably a little concussed, but with all the latent alcohol in my system I suspect I wouldn't have known. I also worked with Graham, pulling boots, and enjoyed his company. I was glad to be home in bed with Chrissie every night too. Graham asked about her, and he informed me he had been experiencing some romantic encounters of his own. He was seeing an English girl who had recently arrived in a small group. Kim was also from Birmingham, and I gathered that the two of them were quite serious because he never stopped talking about her.

The Friday night disco in the *moadon* seemed strangely irksome and irrelevant. Chrissie and I didn't stay very long. In the morning the two of us behaved like a pair of indolent bed-ridden sloths, until we finally surfaced and walked together to She'ar Yashuv cinema in the afternoon. We saw a

Burt Lancaster film called *Twilight's Last Gleaming*. This seemed to act as the catalyst which signalled the beginning of all that week's 'lasts' that we were to experience together; the *last* Friday night disco, the *last* walk to She'ar Yashuv, the *last* trip into town, and so on.

Walking back along the entrance road from She'ar Yashuv after the movie, the late afternoon was calm and warm. Somewhere in the *moshav* a fire was burning, as wood smoke drifted slowly across the road. We actually held hands, an act so simple and yet so often overlooked, but which can be incredibly intimate. My carefree singing days were over, and an unwelcome seriousness had descended over our relationship.

I booked three free days leading up to Chrissie's departure. We took a trip into Kiryat Shmona and drank pints of beer in Yuval's bar. Monday 26th March 1979 was also another milestone date for the State of Israel. There was huge excitement everywhere about a momentous event which everyone hoped would be just the first of many such celebrations for Israel: a Peace Treaty was signed in Washington between Menachim Begin, the Israeli Prime Minister, and Anwar Sadat of Egypt, under the watchful supervision of U.S. President Jimmy Carter. At that time Israel was surrounded on all sides by despotic and tyrannical police states and stood as a beacon across the Middle East as the only democracy, so this was a very welcome and promising development. The *Jerusalem Post* front page that day was dominated by this story, as were most of the inside pages. It wasn't until then that I realised just how precarious the peace was with Israel's Arab neighbours. This would in fact be the first and *only* peace treaty with an Arab nation. All that existed so far with its other neighbours was merely a 'cease fire'. No wonder Jordanian radio referred to Israel as 'the enemy', and why Israel kept hundreds of tanks and troops in a permanent state of readiness along its borders.

It was brilliant news though, and I was pleased for both countries. A victory for peace and common sense, I thought.

For Israel the price was high; it meant the phased withdrawal from the whole of the Sinai Peninsula. Such a huge piece of real estate, spectacularly captured in battle by Israel in 1967, was to be handed back to Egypt as 'Land for Peace' as it became known. Israeli troops and police were soon to be seen forcibly evicting their own citizens from settlements in the Sinai in order to fulfil their treaty obligations. The buildings they had left then had to be immediately demolished, not from feelings of spite and resentment at handing them over to the Egyptians, but in order to prevent Jewish radicals returning and occupying them. This was a process which was repeated years later in Gaza.

That night Chrissie and I watched *The Sweeney* in the television room, along with most of the other volunteers. As soon as it finished everyone else stood up to go, leaving the two of us sitting alone together. At midnight the Israeli National Anthem, the *Hetikvah* (meaning 'The Hope') was broadcast, and transmission came to an end for the day. I walked across the room, turned the television off, and sat back down in my seat next to Chrissie. Sitting beside her, I looked into her eyes. The expression on her face had changed and in the soft light of the room she looked very pretty. Her eyes seemed particularly blue.

"Babe, it'll be okay you know," she said, fixing her eyes on mine.

"I know. I hope you're right. Just look after yourself…" I said as I stood up. We walked back to our room across the dark pathways of the kibbutz, arm in arm.

The next day we walked together to the old bridge for the final time. We sat on the sun-bleached boards listening to the water. The sun was as bright as ever and it was just as peaceful. But it was somehow not the same place any more. I lost much of my love for the old bridge in those few minutes we sat there that day. Suddenly I didn't want to be there any longer. I helped Chrissie up, and we walked back to the kibbutz. I felt restless, angry and sad all at the same time, and I held onto Chrissie's hand tightly as we walked.

The night before Chrissie left the kibbutz, Chris and Graham very kindly threw a party for her and Sarah in their room. It was also Chrissie's 23rd birthday. I hadn't known much about the British band Led Zeppelin before I arrived at Dafna, but that night their classic song *Stairway to Heaven* seemed to be played over and over. Maybe I was just noticing it more. I drank far too much, as did Chrissie, but we managed to find our way back to room 17a for our last night together.

At breakfast the next morning I began to sense an odious countdown towards the middle of the day, when Chrissie and Sarah were intending to leave the kibbutz. I wasn't consciously counting down the last few hours, but as each one passed I tried in vain to make the next one pass a little slower and savour each individual minute. I watched Chrissie pack her belongings into her backpack, and realised just how much of the contents of our little room she was taking with her. I asked her to make an autograph entry in the back of my diary. She did so with this:

'Jonathan: There's so much I could say, but I don't know how to say it. I just wish we could have had a month of moonlit nights on the beach at Dahab. Maybe I'll see you in England? Love, Chrissie xxxxx'

At twelve o'clock Sarah knocked on the door. She was happy and talkative as usual, but as we stood at the door to our room I noticed Chrissie had tears in her eyes. We locked the room together for the last time, and then I walked with them both through the kibbutz, out the gates, and onto the road. I had planned to wave them off from there, but a van emerged from the kibbutz heading in the direction of Kiryat Shmona, so I too jumped aboard. Sarah chatted away and I held Chrissie's hand discreetly but tightly as the countryside flashed by and the town loomed ever closer.

We were dropped off in the bus station just before one o'clock. Sadly we didn't have to wait long before bus number 841 from Tel Aviv pulled in, and the passengers alighted. To my surprise I then saw both Chrissie and Sarah had started crying. I put an arm around Chrissie first, and then Sarah. The two of them cried quite unashamedly for several minutes before Sarah pulled out a tissue from a pocket of her white jeans and patted her eyes. Chrissie took out a handkerchief from her coat and blew her nose. People started to congregate around the bus. The driver stood up and routinely turned a handle a few times above his head, changing the number of the bus to 840. He then climbed out of the cab with a cigarette in his mouth. This was the one-fifteen *Egged* bus to Tel Aviv.

At five past one, the driver finished his cigarette and helped some passengers load heavy cases into the luggage compartments under the bus. He then climbed into his cab and people started boarding. I shook hands with Sarah and kissed her on the cheek before she stepped up to the driver. He sold her a ticket before she then turned to find a seat. I kissed Chrissie several times, and held her so tight her feet lifted from the oily, diesel covered tarmac floor of the bus station. I lifted Chrissie's backpack onto the bus and she stood on the bottom step. She leaned over and I kissed her again. Some passengers pushed their way past us while climbing aboard. They muttered loudly in Hebrew, as there wasn't much room on the steps of the bus. Two soldiers ran up with full kit-bags, laughing, their M16s over their shoulders.

"Jonathan, I'll see you soon okay?" she said, as I let go of her hand for the last time. She had to move from the steps further into the bus to allow the soldiers room to climb on board.

"Take care," I replied, feeling more than a little shaky, in a sudden panic at the realisation of what was about to happen. I wanted to jump onto the bus with them. Maybe I could see them off in Tel Aviv, or at the airport?

"Babe, it's gonna work out fine. I'll see you in England okay?" she shouted, just as the driver started the engine. The folding door of the bus hissed and slammed shut, loud and harsh in its finality. I saw Chrissie buy a ticket, and then the *Egged* bus was reversed a few yards before turning and manoeuvring straight, in preparation for heading out of the bus station. I couldn't see up into the windows very well from where I stood, so I ran up the steps to the record shop in the hope of gaining a better view of the bus. I saw Chrissie, standing in the aisle about halfway down the bus. I could see she was looking in my direction. I waved, but was unsure if she could see me. In a few moments, and in a cloud of diesel smoke, the bus was gone.

So it was that we were parted. Not by relationship breakdown amid perhaps some tired, fading love, or the more usual mutual mistrust and animosity, but by pure accident of circumstance. We were ended unfinished, unresolved, but nonetheless ruthlessly broken apart quickly and irrevocably in a moment, like porcelain slipping from the hand and shattering on a cold stone floor. Suddenly I felt like a little boy lost, standing there, staring into the empty space the bus had occupied only a few minutes before. Chrissie had been my friend, lover, and beautiful guardian; eyes so blue and hair as golden as the Dome of the Rock.

I sat down and leaned against the outside wall of the record shop. My first impulse was to light a cigarette. I took out my Nelsons and lit one. I drew in the first smoke and blew it out in a long, withering sigh. A huge emptiness and deep feeling of loss descended over me. An Abba song was playing from the speaker above my head, *Hasta Manana ... till we meet again, don't know where, don't know when...* and so on. Then, as though the proprietor of the record shop had seen me and understood my predicament, or was perhaps just taking the piss, Boston's *More than a feeling* came on, particularly loud.

I don't remember how long I sat there listening to music, but after a while I noticed one of Dafna's *kibbutzniks,* Yisrael from the fishponds, driving near the bus station in a white Ford Transit van. He pulled up and began loading some boxes into the back. I walked over and he recognised me, so I helped him load the van. He was collecting newspapers for the kibbutz. I then had a free ride back to Dafna.

One of the worst aspects of seeing Chrissie leave was then

returning to our room alone. I walked along volunteers' row in a near trance-like state. I unlocked the door and stepped inside. The flowers were still in the vase on the table. I noticed she'd forgotten her small wooden cigar box with her kibbutz coupons inside. I'd written: 'Chrissie's box' on the lid, among some Pink Floyd and Genesis lyrics.

There were no welcoming kisses or soft American accent to greet me, with: 'Hey babe, nice day on the zipper?' There were only my clothes left on the bed, and the room seemed cave-like and empty. I saw Chrissie's room key lying solitary on the bedside table. I don't remember her putting it there. I came to the conclusion it is always easier to be the one leaving, rather than to be the person who is left behind.

I found a few inches of Israeli '777' brandy left in a bottle on the bedside table. For the next few hours that afternoon, I wallowed in some miserable self-pity, sitting alone in room 17a on our double bed, sipping brandy, smoking Nelsons, and listening to Pink Floyd. The title track of the album, *Wish You Were Here*, along with the brandy and my present state of mind, set me blubbering away like a petulant two-year-old child.

BACK WITH THE LADS

That night there was a party. Hank was leaving. He was much more civilised than the rest of us in that he threw a barbeque rather than an ordinary party. I didn't really know him as he seemed to socialise with Tim and Ian and various *kibbutzniks* most of the time. He was American, a lot older than I was, and came from California. He was tall and quite good looking in a Lee Marvin kind of way. He was well-built, had collar-length, curly fair hair and beard, and always seemed to wear light brown cowboy boots. He also used some very colourful swear words, some of which I'd rarely heard before. Most of them were associated with the female genitalia. I was quite drunk when I arrived at the party, and sat for most of the evening slumped against his cassette player with my head against the speaker like a gate-crashing vagrant. I was still very much in the depths of self-pity. No-one paid me any attention as they knew I'd just seen Chrissie off earlier in the day. Later I sloped off to bed, not feeling particularly sociable.

I thought about returning to England. I hated living alone in room 17a. I expected Chrissie to walk in at any moment so felt an urgent need to abandon the room. It was rapidly beginning to resemble a plain, monastic cell, rather than the happy, fervent place it had once been. Perhaps I could return to my old room, and live with the lads again? My bed was apparently still in the room, but it had been joined onto Graham's bed to make a double. Chris was regularly missing a few nights a week apparently, as was Graham. It seemed Barclay had the room to himself for most of the time. My old bed was now part of a communal 'boning bed' and I would need to reclaim it.

I'd not kept up to date with quite a lot of news among the volunteers. I had a chat with Graham in the dining room, and he filled me in on a few important issues. Chris now had an Israeli girlfriend, Raquel, who was tall, slim, and very pretty. She was in the army and was stationed not far away in the Golan Heights, at a mysterious place called El Rom, which sounded like a town from a *Spaghetti Western*. Graham was still seeing Kim, and John was still with Denis. There were rumours Barclay was seeing a gorgeous new Swiss volunteer with the unlikely name of Doris. Quite a few new volunteers had arrived and I now felt very much like a Dafna veteran.

On Friday 30th March I spent all day working at the north end of the kibbutz wearing thick protective gloves, reinforcing the barbed-wire fence. It was exhausting work and quite dangerous handling the barbed-wire, and I cut myself several times. It was great to be out in the open air. I worked with several *kibbutzniks* and a new volunteer called Richard, a Canadian from Vancouver Island. Two new American lads had moved into the room across from 17a so I spent a few hours that night after work chatting to them, along with Eddie and Glyn. But each night I returned alone to my empty little blast-proof cell.

On Saturday 31st March everyone crammed into the television room at nine o'clock to watch the Eurovision Song Contest. Israel was hosting the event live from Jerusalem and there were high hopes for their entry *Hallelujah!* sung by three men and a woman known as 'Milk and Honey'. With the recent signing of the peace treaty with Egypt still fresh in everyone's mind, it was fantastic to see Israel win the competition. The Israelis were justifiably ecstatic.

I sat with Ian Anarchist at breakfast the next day. He told me he was going to Haifa with English Mary in a day or so in order to book their ferry tickets to Greece. I didn't know anyone else who was close to leaving Dafna so I decided to tag along. I took my air ticket from the office and collected my 'wages' for the month, 240 *lira* from Robin. On Monday 2nd April I booked a free day and rose at five o'clock to go with Ian and Mary. The bus ride from Kiryat Shmona to Haifa was excellent. We followed Highway Ninety south to

Rosh Pina before turning right, onto Highway Eighty-Nine, and over the hills of Northern Galilee towards the sea. I vividly remember the Elvis Costello song *Oliver's Army*, on the radio as our modern coach weaved its way along the high winding road, while looking out at the superb panoramic views across the hills. At Nahariya we turned left along the coast through Acre and finally on to Haifa. The bus terminated in the city centre. We soon found the offices Ian and Mary were looking for. They booked their tickets on a ferry leaving for Greece on 12th May. I saw the El Al Israel Airlines office and stepped inside. I booked my flight out of Israel.

I reserved my seat on a flight leaving at one o'clock in the afternoon on Monday 7th May. It was over four weeks away, but I decided I may as well book it while I was there. A number of us had bought tickets to see Elton John in Tel Aviv on Sunday 6th May, so this would be an ideal time to leave, just after the concert.

Haifa is an industrial city with a huge sea port and docks area. But unlike Tel Aviv it has some high hills behind it with Mount Carmel standing proud above the city, dominating Haifa Bay. Mount Carmel looked fabulous. It seemed as though it was completely covered in bright red flowers from rhododendrons in full bloom. We spent a few hours wandering around before we found our bus which took us back across the Galilee Hills to Kiryat Shmona.

We reached Dafna in time for the evening meal. I found Chris and Graham in the dining-room just as Robin came over to speak to me. He asked me about the room and whether I still needed it. There was a waiting list for the new blast-proof rooms and they were meant for double occupancy. I told him I was very willing to give it up and move back with the lads, if they'd have me.

"Yoh coming back to us then Biggles?" Graham asked, in his broadest Birmingham accent, while chewing on a full mouthful of his meal.

"Yes, if that's okay. You heard what Robin said. He wants me to move out my room."

"I'm sure we can squeeze you back in. Alfie here's hardly ever there anyway are you mate? Neither am I actually, as it goes!" Chris said, smiling, looking at Graham while sipping black tea from his Duralex glass.

"Alfie?" I said, looking confused. Who the hell was Alfie?

"Alfie's Graham's new nick-name," Chris said, noticing the expression on my face, "there's a few things you've missed while you've been with that woman of yours you know!"

"Yes, I know. I'm aware of that," I said, wistfully, as I was suddenly reminded of where most of my attentions had been for the previous three months. I wondered where she was now, somewhere in Europe with Sarah.

"Tomorrow then, Biggles, okay?" Graham said, nodding at Chris.

"Yes, that's great, thanks. I'll check the work list and sort it out tomorrow then."

I worked the early shift on the conveyor, four o'clock until ten in the morning. I returned to 17a with a cardboard box from the factory. I stripped the bed and untied the legs, returning our double back to two singles. The bedside table seemed like a shrine to Chrissie, as I realised when I came to collect it all. It was just as she'd left it. The flowers were now dead, so I put the remains in a bag along with the vase, and threw them away without ceremony. I noticed dust had started to gather under the bed. Everything else, including Chrissie's little wooden box, I gathered together and took with me. The sheets still smelt of the two of us and more particularly Chrissie, so I kept them and made my bed with them back in my old room. Then I locked 17a for the last time and took the keys to Robin. I don't know if he was aware of the significance in my returning those keys, he probably was. By this time I was glad to be away from that room and back in some company. Back to the spiders' legs peeking out from the Y-fronts, hairy bottoms, the belching and the farting. I'd been in a pretty intense relationship and now it was gone. There was some adapting to change that was urgently needed. So I moved back in with the lads at three o'clock on the afternoon of

Wednesday 4th April. It took me about ten minutes to complete the move.

I was welcomed back in the room with some grudging acceptance and: "Right, you're back then…" from John, and some unintelligible grunts from Chris and Graham, and that was it. I felt like an errant son returning from university.

All that afternoon we lazed around on our beds listening to the radio and various home-made tapes. I sat on our front step for a while with a glass of sweet, milk-free tea, and my Nelsons. I found my smoking habit was a great comfort. It's actually true what the old advert used to say: 'You're never alone with a cigarette.'

I heard songs from a little-known and very under-rated Pink Floyd album called *Obscured by Clouds* drifting from the open door of our new neighbours' room. When the track *Stay* came on, I glanced across the road to see a bright red tractor, dragging a plough across a field of very dry earth. Huge clouds of yellow dust were being thrown up around the cab. Large birds whooped and dived around the back of it, like gulls following a trawler. The machine was becoming difficult to see clearly as a result, coupled with the effect of the heat haze shimmering like a mirage across the ground around it. This image has remained with me ever since, and is always present when I hear that particular song, even after so many years. It is uncanny how this can happen, when certain things like music or odours act as the trigger for powerful memories. Apparently a very old veteran from the First World War was once asked if he could remember the serial number of his personal issue 'Lee Enfield' rifle. He stated he had absolutely no idea. When he was handed a smelly piece of cloth soaked in gun oil from the same war, the five-figure number came back to him immediately.

My bed was now under the window again. I could hear the sparrows chirping on the roof and in the stone pines nearby. I took out my diary and started writing. John was in his room with the door closed, and Chris was asleep on his bed in the opposite corner. Graham was at Kim's, and quite likely to stay the night. Barclay was sitting in his armchair, an article of furniture he'd purloined from somewhere, quietly reading.

I worked the conveyor on nights for the next couple of days, then a day shift on Friday. Tim and Ian held a party, as they were both leaving Israel the following Sunday. The party was in the *moadon* that night, and I had rather a lot to drink. I had developed an infection of some sort in my right ear and as a consequence the world became a very lonely place. All I could hear was my own breathing accompanied by loud sloshing noises when I ate or drank anything. It was very painful, so I made another trip to the clinic. By this time I knew the nurse so well she was becoming my matronly surrogate mother. She patted me endearingly on the head, before handing me some more antibiotics. I was told to finish the course and not to drink alcohol while taking the tablets. She may as well have told me not to smile or have a good time. As if I wasn't miserable enough.

THE GOLAN TRIP

On Saturday afternoon I walked with John, Kim and Val to She'ar Yashuv cinema to see a Mel Brooks film: *The Twelve Chairs*. It was very funny and I enjoyed it. That night there was yet another leaving party for Tim and Ian. It was well attended, and as usual everyone present drank to excess. I tried to restrict my intake due to the tablets I was taking, and managed quite well. Ian treated us all to a final, slurred, and very drunken rendition of *Ilkley Moor*. They finally left the next day.

On Monday I worked a day shift on the conveyor. At twelve o'clock Ishi turned off the machine as it was constantly faulty. There were problems with the boot moulds. I was amazed at this, and they must have lost a huge amount of production as a result. I sat in the sun on the loading ramp at the side of the building and smoked a Nelson. There was a pedal bike leaning against the wall so I sat on it and decided to go for a ride.

I rode across to the *refit* (the dairy), where I knew John was working that day. When I arrived on the bike John was driving a tractor up to the *refit*. I helped him feed the cows for a while, and also met Alan, a new British volunteer from County Durham in the North of England. Once the cattle were fed I jumped back on the bike and headed out towards the top gate of the kibbutz. I stopped briefly at the north gate, from where I had a clear view of the Golan and Mount Hermon. It was as spectacular as ever. I pedalled out of the gate and into the kibbutz fields. There was a clear blue sky and it was a very warm spring day in the Upper Galilee. Yellow sand lilies and crown daisies were in full bloom, competing for space in the dry but recently moistened earth with the ubiquitous red poppies. The air was thick with the heady perfumed scent of hundreds of fruit trees in full blossom.

In the top field I found Claudie working among some young avocado trees. She looked lovely and was quietly singing to herself as she occasionally did, in French of course, utterly absorbed in her work. I didn't see anyone else around but I knew there were others nearby. We chatted briefly, and I stood straddling the cross-bar of the bike while we both took a break and smoked a Nelson. Then I saw Mick and Blackie through the trees. His old tractor was parked at the end of the row. I could hear him shouting at his dog and talking to him as though he was human and understood every word. It was a very peaceful and idyllic scene and I envied them their work.

I'd been gone for over an hour, so I rode frantically back to the factory. I needn't have been so concerned, as on my return it was all quiet. The conveyor was still dead. I made myself a Turkish coffee in the canteen and sat outside on some boxes near the loading ramp for a quiet smoke. After a few minutes I was joined by Chris and the old man, Zelig, who he'd just been talking to. I'd seen Zelig quite frequently wandering about, trying to keep himself active. He apparently used to work the dishwasher years ago. Very often he would smile at me and say hello when I worked the dishes, slaving away amidst all the heat and steam.

Zelig was probably the oldest *kibbutznik* resident on Dafna. He spoke mainly Yiddish, which sounded like a mixture of Hebrew and German, and he seemed to be smiling constantly. He was a happy soul but he always seemed to have a strangely distant and melancholic look in his eyes which I'd seen only once before, in the face of the old jeweller who mended my watch strap in Kiryat Shmona. Zelig seemed to pay the female volunteers quite a lot of attention, and in his own way flirted with them outrageously. Chris carefully helped him to perch on top of one of the boxes next to me, and the three of us sat drinking our coffee in the sun. Zelig nodded, and then muttered something which sounded like: "*Gut, yah?*" or similar, and he raised his left arm, pointing up at the sun, high above us in the vast clear blue sky. It was then

I saw something and at first I didn't realise what I'd seen, so I quickly but discreetly took another look. This second glance confirmed what it was, yet at the same time I couldn't quite believe what I saw. On the inside of Zelig's left forearm was a very untidy tattoo. It was a series of six numbers, as though they had been very roughly and painfully drawn into his once young but now withering and aged skin, like human bacon. This lovely little old man obviously had a secret from his past which was more terrible than anything anyone could ever imagine. He spoke very little English, so I couldn't ask him about it. Not that he would have wanted to tell me anyway, or that I would have had the courage to ask. Zelig was a 'camp survivor', as they were known. One of the few remaining. As a young man he'd been a prisoner in the extermination camp at Auschwitz.

At three o'clock the conveyor was *still* not fixed, so Ishi told us that we could finish work and go home. Chris and I returned to our room. After a shower we made omelettes with cheese, tomatoes and onions, and spent the afternoon in typical manner, lazing around on our beds, alternately listening to the 'Voice of Peace' and the BBC World Service. While I was at work the previous day, and barely as Tim and Ian had stepped out the kibbutz gates, the other lads in our room raided their old room and stripped it of chairs, rugs, posters, bedspreads, pots and pans, in fact everything and anything that wasn't nailed down. This behaviour was something of a tradition among a lot of volunteers. Our room now looked fantastic, and was very well equipped! Just before the shop closed we pooled twenty-five *lira* each in coupons and bought a thirty-bottle crate of Goldstar beer. If an excuse was needed, then it was probably to celebrate the re-furnishing of our now luxurious accommodation.

I worked the conveyor with Vancouver Island Richard for several days in a row on a variety of shifts. I wasn't bothered what shift I worked any more. Richard and I seemed to get on well and one night close to midnight we 'borrowed' a couple of unattended push bikes from outside the dining-room, and decided to have a race around Dafna. For half an hour we rode around a very dark and quiet kibbutz. We chased one another up and down the paths onto the roads, around the buildings, and eventually paused for a rest outside the dining-room. Just as we'd stopped and were standing with our bikes, the night patrol jeep came tearing around the corner with headlights blazing. We didn't want them to see us, so in a panic we both dived off our bikes and into some bushes. The jeep roared past and pulled up nearby outside the *moadon*. We watched as two people climbed out of the back before the jeep sped off again, heading back to the top end of the kibbutz. The two dark figures from the jeep started walking towards us. I was sure we were in trouble. Richard suggested we should ditch the bikes and run, but as they grew closer I recognised them. It was Kim and Graham. The driver of the jeep, one of the *kibbutzniks*, Iran, had given them a lift from Ethiopian Paul's place. Kim and Graham turned and walked down a path towards Kim's room.

Thursday 12th April was *Pessach*, or 'Passover', and we were all given a day off work and a small gift from the kibbutz. This was very nice, but for a whole week there was no proper bread available, just some very flat, tasteless, dry cardboard. This was in fact unleavened bread, and was an integral part of *Pessach*. I sat on top of our *miklat* in the sun reading *Exodus* by Leon Uris. I had been on Dafna for five months. I was still in agony with my ear infection.

On Saturday 14th April we were taken on a one-day trip in the kibbutz bus. We climbed aboard at nine o'clock in the morning, and turned left out the gates of Dafna. We were heading for the hills, with three armed *kibbutzniks* in charge as usual. There were very few of the 'old' volunteers on the bus, as the day trips were not particularly popular. I hadn't been any further into the Golan Heights than the Banniass waterfall, so was keen to go. We were to spend the whole day touring the Golan, and our first stop was the ruins of a Crusader castle called Nimrod. This was a few kilometres up the road from the Banniass, on a small hill of its own overlooking the valley. There was a brilliant view from the Nimrod castle, typifying the sort of prime location at which such structures were originally built.

The bus strained and groaned up the steep road and we eventually stopped at the top, close to the peak of Mount Hermon, 9000 feet above sea-level. There was thick snow on the mountain some way off, sadly too far to reach, but we found some nearer the bus, in shaded areas behind some large rocks. This discovery inevitably led to a snowball fight among most of the volunteers. It seemed particularly strange, suffering the pain of chilblained fingers in freezing snow, considering how warm it was further down the valley.

We were just yards from the cease-fire line with Syria, and on a clear day the Syrian capital, Damascus, was apparently visible from where we stood. Sadly it was quite hazy when we arrived and visibility was limited to a few miles. There was a ski-lift which headed up towards the summit but it didn't appear to be in use at the time of our visit. There wasn't nearly enough snow, though in December and January there may well have been. I couldn't imagine Mount Hermon would ever become an internationally renowned ski resort to rival the French Alps. It was located on the top of a disputed border region between two belligerent nations.

There was a cool breeze on the summit, and though it was a sunny day we were very glad we had our coats. The rusted hulk of an abandoned tank was sitting by the road, complete with huge gun and even a machine-gun still sticking out the front. A few of us clambered onto it and peered inside. There were spent machine-gun cartridges littering the floor and even a few live rounds. I had no idea what sort of tank it was but it didn't appear to be an Israeli Magach like those which so frequently passed Dafna. There were quite a few Israeli soldiers in the Golan Heights, as you would expect. I saw a large flat-roofed, two-storey building painted in drab green, which was bristling with some extremely tall aerials and transmitter masts. A bright blue 'Star of David' Israeli flag flew proudly high up above the building, bold and prominent as it fluttered gently in the crisp mountain air.

We passed a sign for 'El Rom' on our right, where Chris's current girlfriend was posted. The road then turned in spectacular fashion down towards the Sea of Galilee. We were now on the eastern side of the water, and it seemed strange to be looking across the Galilee from this direction for the first time.

We arrived at Hammat Gader near the south eastern tip of the Sea of Galilee, right on the border with Jordan, at one o'clock, in time for lunch: real bread, salad, boiled eggs and fruit, the usual kibbutz picnic food. Hammat Gader is principally a natural hot spring which has been used for thousands of years. It was colonised by the Romans who built a theatre on the site along with a bath complex around the steaming hot water. At the time of our visit there were several pools in which you could immerse yourself, ranging in temperature from twenty-eight degrees centigrade to the hottest at fifty-two degrees. The smell was incredible. These were sulphur springs, so the air was thick with the pungent smell of rotten eggs, which was dense and heavy in the steamy atmosphere. I enjoyed the sensation of bathing in the hot water, and some took advantage of also being smothered in the supposedly cleansing mud, in a similar way to that at the Dead Sea.

I took a shower and dressed. I sat by the steaming pools and smoked a Camel. There was an interesting view along the border with Jordan, and it was occasionally marked by the presence of active watch-towers and rolls of barbed-wire. By mid afternoon we all clambered back aboard the bus for the drive home. We passed through Tiberias and along the western shores of the Sea of Galilee, climbing back up towards Kiryat Shmona. We arrived back at the kibbutz at six o'clock when it was still light. The sun finally plunged behind the Naftali Hills at six-thirty, just as we walked into the dining-room.

UNDER GROUND…OVER GROUND

Despite my ear still causing me problems, I worked an extra eight hour shift on the conveyor in order to earn myself three free days. My ear was checked again in the clinic by my surrogate mother. She gave me some ear drops and yet more antibiotics. There was a very gradual improvement from then on, and by the end of that week it had all but cleared up. After five weeks spent mainly working the conveyor, the work list dictated my return to the zipper. I worked with Laura and Sue, along with Jenny on the tear-drop machine. We became a very efficient little team, able to despatch no less than eight racks of boots in a single shift.

On the first Friday after *Pesach*, Ezra returned to Dafna. He was in high spirits and was happy with his new posting in the Sinai. He was lean and tanned as everyone seemed to be when they spent any time down there. He wouldn't tell us exactly where he was based, or what he was doing, but spoke at length about the peace treaty with Egypt. We guessed he was involved somehow in the forthcoming Israeli withdrawal. He was only home for a couple of days, so I took the opportunity of asking him to sign the back of my diary before he left. He wrote more than half a page of Hebrew and drew a cartoon figure smoking a pipe, similar to *Popeye*. Out of his pipe came the English words: '*Don't wash too much dishes*!' He then added: '*KIBBUTZ DAFNA*' with the 'Z' the wrong way around. It was still a lot better than any attempt I could make at writing Hebrew. The next day he returned to his unit. I never saw Ezra again.

This was also the day when at three o'clock in the afternoon, Chris and Barclay walked into our room after finishing work, stating they had something for me. I'd already checked the day's post so I had no idea what they could have in their hands, until they came close enough for me to recognise Chrissie's handwriting on a letter addressed to me. My heart skipped a beat as I snatched it from Chris's hand and climbed up onto the *miklat* outside our room to read it in peace. This was the first letter I'd received from her in almost three weeks since she'd left Dafna. I was thrilled and excited to see it and opened it carefully, extremely anxious to know how she was getting on, and where she was. She'd started her tour of Europe in Istanbul and was now in Greece, having been 'island hopping' in the Aegean for two weeks. Apparently Sarah had met a Turkish lad in Istanbul and was quite struck by him. So much so that Chrissie had carried on her travels alone. I found this more than a little ironic! Her next stop was Venice. Of course I couldn't write back but I wrote a letter of reply in a page of my diary, which has forever remained un-sent.

I reacquainted myself with Sick Mick and his dog, Blackie. I often sat in his room smoking as much of his Old Holborn as I could, along with Ian Anarchist. We listened to the 'Voice of Peace' and the BBC of course. I also spent some time with Alan, who worked the *refit* with John. He had managed to obtain a room similar to 17a, on his own at the bottom of volunteers' row. We talked about the Air Force, the future, and the rock band, Genesis. We listened to their new album, a taped copy of which he'd brought with him from home, *And then there were three....*Sadly guitarist Steve Hackett had left the band, and though this first album without him was quite good, in my humble opinion they were never the same again. Alan and I had some interesting and civilised conversations and I enjoyed his company.

The evenings were becoming warm and the paraffin heaters were almost redundant, other than for making toast, as they had been when I first arrived. On 23rd April six huge candles were lit in the dining-room for 'Holocaust Memorial Day', and they were left burning all night as an act of remembrance. Films were shown in the dining-room about the Holocaust, or *Shoah*. I briefly saw some of the images when I passed the dining-room on my way to work a night shift on the zipper. Grainy black and white film of Allied soldiers with cloths held over their faces driving huge mechanical excavators, shovelling great mounds of naked skeletal corpses into mass graves.

The next day I walked up the river path to the Banniass on my own. Everywhere was incredibly overgrown and a wonderful mass of beautiful wild flowers. There was thick new growth from the bamboo plants and reeds at the water's edge, and I almost missed a tank which was lying upside down in the river, at the foot of a particularly steep-sided section of the path. It was rusty and empty but otherwise in one piece, complete with all its tracks intact, as though it had fallen into the water, rather than being blown down there in battle. It was known locally as The Syrian Tank but it was not easy to distinguish what sort of tank it was. I sat on its upturned iron carcass in my cut-off denim shorts with my feet hanging over the edge in the clear water. I lit a Nelson and the cool damp air was utterly still as my cigarette smoke spiralled upwards, broken occasionally by some near-perfect and very forceful smoke rings. It was thirty-three degrees centigrade that day, ninety degrees Fahrenheit. The waterfall was wonderful, as usual. I dipped my head under the surface to cool down, before walking back down the path towards Dafna.

That night I worked the zipper with Val and Cindy in a stiflingly hot factory. I then had a quick change, to work a day shift the next day starting at ten in the morning.

Thursday 26th April started the same as any other. Sue and Laura were working on the zipper with me again, and we were fully established in our highly efficient routine when Gidon the factory manager wandered past us muttering *miklat* over and over. Then to my surprise I heard the conveyor shut down. It wasn't until that moment, when the machinery came to a stop, that I heard the kibbutz air raid siren blaring away. Gidon came up to us and told us to go to the *miklat* behind the factory. The girls had not experienced an air raid before, so were extremely nervous and abandoned their posts immediately. Gidon searched around the factory for anyone else to inform, but by then it was clear there was a raid as the siren was resounding loudly across the whole kibbutz. I called into the canteen and quickly made myself a coffee and took a handful of biscuits with me. I'm not about to say I was brave or stupid enough to ignore advice and not bother with the *miklat*, because I wasn't. I went down there with everyone else. It's just that perhaps I didn't run quite as fast as some others.

There were not many people in the factory *miklat*, and I probably appeared a little odd strolling down the concrete steps with a Turkish coffee in one hand and a cigarette in the other, like Noel Coward about to play the piano. I reached the bottom of the steps to find most people were chattering loudly. There was quite a convivial atmosphere. We wondered if it was a genuine alert. Then we felt several dull but powerful thuds in the earth from somewhere not far away. The atmosphere in the *miklat* changed immediately. Everyone was quiet and listened for the next thud. I guessed the detonations were thankfully not in the immediate vicinity of any of the kibbutz buildings. I was actually gaining an ability to assess the proximity of exploding munitions. It was only a few months ago when the nearest I'd come to such a thing was seeing and hearing fireworks at a bonfire party. Gidon was the last inside the miklat, and stood next to the steel door at the top of the steps looking attentively at his beloved factory. The ground shuddered again a few more times, but luckily seemed further away than ever. Fifteen minutes later we heard the 'all clear' siren and emerged from the shelter. We walked back into the factory, and carried on.

When I arrived in the dining-room for lunch I saw Ian was busily removing plates and cutlery at the dishwasher. While I was eating my salad with other volunteers, the sirens started again. Everyone began to leave the dining-room. I made sure Ian knew about it, so I shouted at him through the gap from the dining-room to turn off the machine, which he did. He could then hear the siren and we both headed out the back towards the dining-room *miklat*. It was huge but full to bursting. There were no children in there with us, as they had all been taken into the nursery shelters before the first raid. As usual they would now stay down there all day. So we alternately sat on the bench seats, and stood around, waiting. We were at least twenty feet underground, with thick concrete above us. We stared at the white-washed walls, listening for the explosions. Ian told me again how much better The Clash were than Pink Floyd. Perry and Raquel were down there too, and they asked me about Chrissie. I told them I'd received a second letter, from Venice, and that she was fine. These were safe, random conversations while we hid together in a bomb shelter during an air raid.

We climbed out after half an hour. The air was just beginning to become a little stale, so it was a relief to be out in the open and on the surface again. I finished my meal and wandered back across to the factory. I resumed my post at the zipper. The girls were understandably worried, so I tried to reassure them. I told them of the chances of being struck directly, and I hoped I was right. Just as we were settled back into full production, within an hour Gidon told us yet again to shut everything down and return to the factory *miklat*. Dutifully we descended the concrete steps again but this time it was all getting a little bit boring. I don't think Gidon and some other *kibbutzniks* even bothered. I don't blame them. But we *did* hear some more noises which sounded suspiciously like *Katyusha* rockets hitting the ground and exploding somewhere nearby.

Twenty minutes later we were allowed back into the factory. For the rest of the shift until four o'clock the zipper was faulty and temperamental, and we couldn't achieve our best as a result. The conveyor took some time to resume its usual efficiency too. It seemed the machines didn't appreciate repeated shutdowns. There were no other air raids that day. At dinner we found out several *Katyushas* had landed in Dafna's top fields among the cotton plants, but thankfully no-one had been hurt. It didn't even get a mention on the news, either on the radio or television. We were obviously not important enough. My diary entry for that day was a reflection of this, and started with the line:

'*Katyushas hit Dafna's cotton fields during several alerts today – had to go in the shelters a lot. Otherwise nothing unusual.*'

DOPE

Just as my ear cleared up I realised I'd caught a nasty cold from somewhere. It was as though someone was trying very hard to keep me feeling miserable. So I trotted off back to the clinic to see my surrogate mother. She seemed both surprised and happy to see me. She took my temperature, frowned and muttered something in Hebrew. She then gave me some tablets called Coldex, which I gratefully accepted, and which turned out to be brilliant.

I took a trip into Kiryat Shmona with Chris and we enjoyed several pint glasses of beer at Yuval's bar. I noticed quite a few large white army trucks parked in the town, all of which had two huge letters on all sides painted in light blue: 'U.N.' It seemed they were part of a force called 'UNIFIL', the 'United Nations Interim Force In Lebanon'. They were Norwegian peacekeeping troops in blue berets collecting provisions in the town before driving their bright white vehicles up into the hills.

It was Friday night again. Barclay and I raided the *moadon*, returning to our room with four large jugs of gin punch. Five minutes later our room was full of people taking advantage of our hospitality. I'm not sure how they found out we'd acquired all the punch. It must have been the old kibbutz bush telegraph again. At nine o'clock we all rolled into the *moadon*. I danced with Greek Nick for quite some time, mainly at his insistence. I wasn't sure who was the most inebriated, but he seemed to be in a far worse condition than me. Nick was brilliant fun. If I was to make a modern comparison to anyone, I would say he was very similar in some ways to '*Borat*', Sasha Baron Cohen's hilarious fictional character. Nick tried to teach me Greek dancing in the manner of *Zorba the Greek*, but his efforts were utterly wasted on me.

I then heard there was a party somewhere down on volunteers' row, so I set off to see what I could find. I was a little drunk by this time, but not too bad, as I didn't really like the gin punch, so didn't drink much of it. When I saw the door of room 17a I was gripped by a very powerful wave of nostalgia. I opened the door without knocking and inside disturbed a German couple who were understandably surprised at the intrusion and asked me what I wanted. I said nothing to them directly, but slid the door shut and wandered off, mumbling something along the lines of 'I used to live there...' or similar. I found the room where there was indeed a party, but that was not where I ended up. Just a couple of doors further down I heard Pink Floyd's *Dark Side of the Moon* drifting from one of the rooms and decided to investigate.

Just as I reached the door Sick Mick walked past me with Blackie on a lead: "I wouldn't go in there Biggles. You'll be flying without wings if you do!" and walked off, laughing, talking to his dog.

I pushed at the door and it opened easily. The room was dimly lit by a cluster of small candles on a table next to one of the beds. Hot wax had gathered thickly around the base of the candles and it had pooled together and then cooled, like lava from a volcano. I'd seen the two occupants before, but I'd no idea where they worked, or even their names. I knew they'd been volunteers on the kibbutz for several weeks but I'd not yet seen them in work clothes of any sort. They were both American and from New York or so I guessed, as their accent was the same as Perry's. They were lying almost horizontal on their beds, with just their heads propped up on pillows against the wall.

"Hey dude, come on in, man!" one of them said, as I stepped into the gloom through a fog of smoke. I realised this thick smoke had the same odour as that which had filled the air in Henry's Bar in Eilat, that night of our kibbutz trip. It was a very rich, sweet, distinctive smell.

One of them sat up slightly and began fiddling with a

pack of cigarettes. It slipped from his grasp and dropped onto the bed. He started giggling.

The other one laughed and said: "Hey man, you're totally wasted…" and lay back on the bed, shaking his head slightly. The first one picked up some cigarette papers, pulled three from the packet and started to join them together, after dragging each one slowly across his tongue. He then started to disassemble a cigarette and sprinkle the tobacco onto the elongated cigarette paper as it lay on the bed between his legs.

I shut the door behind me, and carefully sat on one of the beds. I then leaned against the wall. The alarm clocks from the Pink Floyd track *Time* came on loudly, sharply piercing the smoky atmosphere. One of my hosts picked up what appeared to be a lump of yellowy light-brown earth the size of my thumbnail. He held it briefly over the tall flame of his 'Zippo' lighter, and then started crumbling an edge of it into the long cigarette, spreading small lumps of it evenly across its length. I guessed immediately what was happening. Another cigarette was broken open and the contents sprinkled over the top, before he carefully tore a small piece of card from the corner of the Rizla packet, rolled it up to form a tiny tube, and placed it gently into one end of the cigarette. The whole thing was undertaken very delicately and with reverential precision, like defusing a bomb or mending a priceless wristwatch. The cigarette was carefully lifted with two hands and rolled very gently, thin at the cardboard end, but almost half an inch thick or more at the other. Finally he stroked the full length of it tenderly with his tongue, like a grateful child licking an ice cream on a hot day. He twisted the thick end and sealed it.

He glanced at it admiringly for a moment, holding it in one hand. He then said: "Oh yeah…" smiling, as his eyes widened in anticipation. The rocket ship to another dimension was ready for ignition.

This was to be my first ever encounter with illegal drugs. I'd been in the Air Cadets throughout my teens and had just not mixed with anyone my age who took part in this type of thing. I'd been living a life protected and removed from this aspect of youth culture, and my isolation had continued in Israel right up until that point. I've no doubt, on reflection, that a lot of my friends on the kibbutz had been smoking cannabis, including Chrissie. This was certainly the case in places like Eilat. But I had been excluded as much through my own actions and attitude as anything else. I'd been approached on more than one occasion when in Kiryat Shmona by some shady and furtive individuals, who would appear from the shadows, step up close to me, and mutter in my ear: "You smoke hash?"

To which I would usually reply with an absurd and very pompous: "Of course not, I'm British!" before brushing them aside and storming off. I doubt the local drug dealers had ever heard such a reply, and I must have left them rather bewildered and probably doubting the future of their own chosen career path. So perhaps on this occasion I should have politely stood up and left the room. But I didn't.

Clouds of thick white, sweet-smelling smoke billowed from the 'joint' as it was lit, and I could smell the petrol from the lighter as the flame burned. As soon as it was well established, the joint was passed in my direction first. I took hold of the five inch monster and held it between my lips. I took a long drag. It was quite sweet tasting and not at all unpleasant. I took several hefty pulls on it, inhaling the hot smoke deeply, before passing it back. Both my hosts now sat up and were a little more attentive. They passed the joint back and forth between them for a few minutes before sending it my way again. I noticed while smoking the joint they would retain the smoke in the lungs for much longer than usual, as though they were holding their breath. So I tried this too.

I felt no different at all, or so I thought, as I sat there chuffing away on the joint as though it was an after dinner Christmas cigar. Until, that is, a few minutes later. We were still listening to *Dark Side of the Moon*, when the track *Us and Them* came on. As I was sitting there, leaning against the wall, something of a sensory revelation swept over me. I realised I'd never heard saxophone playing quite like that ever before. Suddenly the music seemed to be the greatest sound I had ever heard. It floated around me and filled the room, and I felt as though the notes were actually *inside* my head, magically tickling my brain as they flooded in through my ears. I heard a piano being played in such a beautiful way that I was completely mesmerised.

Very gradually my limbs began to feel incredibly heavy. The mere act of sitting upright felt extremely tiring and uncomfortable. The joint was passed around again and again until it diminished to no more than a half an inch in length. The music began to slow, and the three of us were quiet, listening to the four genius musicians that were Pink Floyd.

"Wow." I managed to utter between tracks, intending to make reference to the music. I crawled down onto the bed. I had to make myself horizontal at any cost; there was just *too* much effort involved in staying anywhere near upright.

"Yeah, great stuff eh? We don't get this type of hash much back home. So that's why..." said one of them, pausing, as though he'd been suddenly caught in a daydream.

"That's why we like to get so fuckin' bombed now, man!" my other host said. For some reason this statement was funny in the extreme, and I laughed almost to the point of incontinence. All three of us did. I laughed until my jaw ached and tears rolled down my face.

I lay on the bed for what seemed hours, frequently laughing out loud at intervals, quite at random. *Dark Side of the Moon* ended, and when it did, I realised I was almost overcome by a powerful, raging thirst. I needed a drink as soon as possible. The inside of my mouth felt as dry as desert sand, and my tongue seemed huge and erroneous. I thought that if I didn't drink something I would almost certainly shrivel up and die, right there and then.

"Thanks guys," I said to my hosts, as I struggled off the bed, trying to stand upright. I noticed one of them had started the whole process of rolling another joint again, so I needed to make my exit.

"Hey, any time, catch you later, man!" the other replied, as

I aimed myself towards the door. I stepped outside into the clear night air. I immediately saw a vast panorama of a brilliant, star-filled night sky above. I tried to walk as soberly as I possibly could, on legs which felt strangely numb and spongy, as though I was walking through thick porridge. I slowly walked up volunteers' row in the direction of the party. Simply placing one foot in front of the other seemed to take a huge amount of concentration and coordination. I don't remember whose party it was, probably one of the many new volunteers. The room was brightly lit and full of people, and there was a gathering outside the open door. Someone shouted my name and handed me a Goldstar beer, pulling the cap off for me as they did so. I stood outside and took a sip. It was cold, fizzy, *full* of flavour, and wonderful. It must have been the tastiest beer ever made. I stood at the door among a crowd of others, clutching my beer tightly, trying very hard not to look too obvious. I was busy minding my own business, when a *kibbutznik* came up to me from nowhere and whispered directly into my ear:

"Kiryat Shmona?" he said to me, in a questioning, accusatory tone. I didn't know who he was, but I knew he lived on the kibbutz. He was short and very dark-skinned, and looked like a hunch-back. He sounded serious, but also a little comical, like Michael Palin's character in the Monty Python sketch, *The Spanish Inquisition.* He looked at me briefly, before walking away and mingling with the crowd, occasionally staring back at me. At first I found him mildly amusing. Then I panicked. How on earth does he know what I've been doing? *Does* he know what I've been doing? Is he going to ring the police? Is he a cop himself? What the hell's going on? I was suddenly in a very paranoid and agoraphobic state, and started looking around at other people's faces to see if they were looking at me. I thought a lot of them were, and not only that, some of them seemed to be laughing! I felt very uncomfortable, so I had to leave.

I walked around the corner, trying my best to appear calm, and started to walk back to our room. In the darkness between the buildings the night sky was even more amazing.

249

A huge full moon was reflecting a brilliant white light from the rooftops and the grass. I tried to walk with my head back at forty-five degrees in order to catch a better look at the moon and stars. I strode along, carefully, with my neck straining and head back, looking up at the heavens. I completely forgot why I'd just left the party.

A hundred yards seemed like a mile, and back in our room I lay on my bed. There was no-one else in the room. Everything started to spin. I shut my eyes and it spun even more. I then realised I was incredibly hungry. I didn't want to stand up due to the sheer effort involved, and the fact that I was worried the room seemed to be moving around me. But I was just too hungry to do nothing. Eating something, *anything,* became an absolute priority, and the thought of eating food completely filled my mind to the exclusion of absolutely everything else. I sat up and managed to stand. I crossed the floor with some very careful, measured steps, to the kitchen.

I opened the fridge door and found an ancient uncut loaf of bread sitting all alone on a shelf. I lifted it reverently from the fridge and placed it on the work surface. It was as hard as concrete and the size and shape of a rugby ball. I carefully tried to cut a slice from it with a very blunt knife, but quickly realised I was not even making an impression on it. For a few seconds I stabbed at it with the knife, and it jumped around on the work surface as though it had legs and was trying to escape from me. I then gave up chasing it around and decided on a more subtle approach. I picked it up and broke it in half with both hands, like Samson, in a very manly fashion. I then cut a huge lump from inside the loaf and spread greasy margarine all over it. I added some strawberry jam, a lot of which dropped onto the floor. I reached down, scooped it all up, and dabbed it carefully back onto the lump of bread. I stood at the fridge admiring my creation for a moment before taking a bite. It was a culinary masterpiece. What a great way to eat bread, I thought, no need to slice it, just rip it apart and cover the thing in whatever you want! I bit huge chunks from it, and it was heavenly. Every single wonderful mouthful simply burst with flavour and I'd never tasted anything as good as that ever before.

I sat back down on my bed still chewing. The room started to spin again. I reached across to the table and found a cassette of *Seconds Out,* the live Genesis concert, and slotted it into the tape machine. I turned all the lights off. The track *Supper's Ready* came on, and I was slowly lowered into a void somewhere in another world.

At some point in that twenty-two minute epic of a song, and long before Phil Collins pronounced *A New Jerusalem*, I fell asleep.

THE END

Near the End

In the morning I woke up with a clear head and no hangover. This was very unusual for a Saturday morning on the kibbutz. My fingers were incredibly greasy and my bed seemed full of crumbs. A hollow loaf was on the floor near my bed, and our resident ants were feasting on a large blob of jam that had been trodden into the floor tiles.

Breakfast in the dining-room tasted particularly good. I ate three huge bowls of delicious semolina. I had a bad cough which I assumed was part of my cold, but of course may well have been connected to the previous night. Though still warm, it was extremely windy, and broken branches from many trees were scattered across the roads and paths all over the kibbutz. At noon the sun appeared, and the wind dropped. I spent the next three hours sunbathing and reading while sitting on top of the *miklat* near our room. The skin on my face became very hot and red. It felt uncomfortably tight and dry, as though stretched and shrink-wrapped over my cheekbones.

In the afternoon I walked with a group of mainly new volunteers to the She'ar Yashuv cinema. Among them was another Graham, who was utterly unlike the Graham I knew from Birmingham. This Graham was from London. He was openly gay, very funny, and good company. He was also as camp as a row of pink tents. He was sometimes known as 'London Graham' but inevitably in those very politically incorrect times, he was more often referred to as 'Queer Graham', or even 'Nancy Graham'. I suppose he had to be distinguished from the other one, so at the time this epithet seemed appropriate. He was quite outrageous though, and outwardly at least, the only gay on the kibbutz. San Francisco Mary came with us to the cinema. She was sometimes referred to as 'Chinese Mary', though I doubt she was aware of this. After Chrissie left Dafna I talked to her quite often. She was very patient, as she seemed to tolerate quite a lot of my drunken ramblings on Friday nights.

As usual we didn't know what the film was going to be until we'd paid our five *lira* at the door. There was usually a hand-made poster outside but it was always in Hebrew, with no clue in English as to what it might be. Sometimes the person taking the money would try their best to provide a translation of the title into English from its literal Hebrew. This was usually wildly off the mark and often hilarious. On this occasion it was *The Wind and the Lion*, with Sean Connery and Candice Bergen. I'd seen it before, months ago on Dafna, not long after my arrival. I was happy to see it again. The woman at She'ar Yashuv described it as: *The Lion with Wind,* which was close, but not quite accurate. I viewed the whole story in a slightly different way this time. I came to the conclusion that Sean Connery's bloodthirsty character would be far more likely to rape Candice Bergen and then slit her throat. He would then probably kill both the children and dump all their bodies in the desert.

Sunday April 29th 1979 was my last working day on Kibbutz Dafna. I worked a morning shift on the zipper, starting at four o'clock as usual. I had accrued no less than seven 'free days', so my last week was to be one of leisure. There was no ceremony when I turned the zipper off at ten o'clock, no fanfare or handshakes from anyone. I didn't really expect any. It was an important personal event for me, but not for anyone else. The next shift arrived and the work continued. I wandered into the factory canteen and sat alone with my Turkish coffee and biscuits. I could hear all the very familiar noises from the factory; the hissing, banging, and clattering of machinery. The music from the Israeli radio station bounced around the inside of the building, echoing off the blackened walls, adding to the general cacophony.

Much of the last of my money, 250 *lira,* had been spent on my ticket for the forthcoming Elton John concert. This sounds a lot, but it worked out at roughly £7, and was about the right price for a concert in 1979. I'd seen the British band Camel at the Sheffield City Hall the year before for only £2.25, less than the price of a vinyl LP record at the time. My impecunious condition during my last week would therefore prevent me from disappearing for a few days on a final tour of the country, so I stayed local. I sat in the sunshine on top of the *miklat* near our room and finished reading Leon Uris's *Exodus.* I then started reading an old and very tatty copy of James Clavell's *King Rat,* which I could identify with if only very slightly, while living on the kibbutz. The smooth, hard surface of the angular and utilitarian *miklat* was warm and hospitable to the touch in the strong sun, and I settled onto it with my book every day like a contented and indolent pub cat.

Every morning the sky was now clear and cloudless. Summer asserted itself with relentless authority causing each day to be hot and dry, with temperatures over ninety degrees Fahrenheit, or the high thirties in centigrade. Each evening and night became warm and sultry too. This utterly linear and predictable weather would last well into the autumn, with little variation. It was so very different to the British weather I had grown up with. The many winding pathways and meandering narrow streets of the kibbutz were now as familiar to me as some well-trodden streets of home. In so many ways of course Dafna had become my home.

Life in a small room with four other men was as interesting and annoying as ever. John frequently bought ingredients from the kibbutz shop as usual, and treated the rest of us to the results of his wonderful culinary experiments. One afternoon he made orange custard in our kitchen area, the whole process of preparation for which needed protection from the legions of determined ants in our room. Barclay was happy to step in as ant pest controller. He killed them mercilessly in huge numbers with a rolled up newspaper, thereby preventing them from dropping into the custard.

Chris enjoyed a similar role to Barclay, but his expertise lay in cockroach destruction. Some quite large, dark brown ones that could run extremely fast, often tried to set up home in the shower and needed chasing away or killing. They would often disappear like lightning down the plughole in the shower tray to avoid extermination. Graham lay on his bed breaking wind and belching simultaneously, which he was extremely proficient at. Luckily all the doors and windows were wide open so any noxious gasses escaped very quickly.

Graham continued to be absent from our room for a good deal of the time when visiting and staying overnight with Kim. Chris was away two or three nights a week at El Rom in the Golan, staying with Raquel. She would also visit Chris in our room frequently when he was not at El Rom. There wasn't a day that passed without them seeing each other. They would sit together on Chris's bed until the early hours chatting in whispers, obviously deep in conversation. Chris seemed to be able to whisper very well but we could hear Raquel repeating the word: '*Ma?*' meaning 'what?' over and over, and: '*Lama?*' meaning 'why?' They were clearly quite intense and very fond of one another. Barclay's relationship with Doris was going strong, and so was John's with Denis. I was in receipt of an occasional letter from Chrissie from different parts of Europe, and I savoured each one. She was getting closer to England.

For the first time in my life my hair was now long enough to touch my shoulders. It had been eight months since I'd had it cut. I felt extremely self-conscious about it, even though compared to some it was still quite short. To me it seemed impossibly long and incongruous as I stared back at my reflection. My face was tanned and lined from the sun, as was much of the rest of my body, and I felt lean and fit. I was the same person, and yet somehow different. John commented that I had changed but was unable or unwilling to be specific.

On the evening of 30th April at eight o'clock, while most of us were still in the dining-room, the air raid siren started wailing. On this occasion no-one ran for the doors to the dining-room *miklat*, but stood up at the table where they were, and bowed their heads in silence. There followed a formal two minute silence for all those who had lost their lives fighting for the creation of, and in defence of, The State of Israel.

At the beginning of May there were some welcome changes regarding the welfare of the kibbutz volunteers. We were given a pay rise! Currently the 'pay' was 240 *lira* per month, and fifty coupons per week for use in the kibbutz shop. This was increased to 320 *lira* per month, and five packets of cigarettes of your choice if you smoked. Alternatively, if you were a non-smoker, then you would receive 520 *lira* a month in cash. Each volunteer was also to receive a kilo of fruit every week, in addition to the usual food on offer in the dining room. The food was not the best in the world, but there was plenty of it. No-one should ever go hungry. There was always bread available in an unlocked room adjacent to the kitchens, which also contained an electric slicing machine that could turn an uncut loaf into sliced bread in an instant. I realised our pay rise was not wholly the result of kibbutz generosity alone, but mainly the product of rampant inflation in Israel at the time. Prices were rising in the kibbutz shop and in the real world of Kiryat Shmona very rapidly, to the extent that price tags had to be increased on the goods almost on a daily basis.

THE END

Three momentous events happened on Wednesday May 3rd 1979 on Kibbutz Dafna. Firstly, everyone was given the day off because it was Israel's Independence Day. This was great for me, as I was off work anyway of course, so it meant I would then have some company. Secondly it was officially deemed to be summer in the Upper Galilee, so the kibbutz swimming pool was uncovered and filled with water after being closed all winter. Thirdly, Phil returned to Dafna from England as he said he would when he left, just before Christmas.

After much hype and excitement about Dafna's pool, and despite the fact it was almost a hundred degrees in the shade, we were not yet allowed in the water until it had been thoroughly cleaned and treated. In frustration, a group of us decided to walk up the river path to the Banniass for a swim. It had actually been Gary's idea, as he'd called in our room at eight thirty that morning stating he and Claudie intended going up there.

Breakfast in the dining-room was sugar puffs and eggs. Now that summer had arrived there was sadly no more semolina. After breakfast I set off with Gary and Claudie, Wolfie and Ian Anarchist, up the overgrown river path. We stopped occasionally for a drink and cigarette as we walked. Wolfie and Ian had not yet seen the Syrian tank, so we spent a few minutes sitting on the rusty upturned hull before carrying on. We finally arrived at the waterfall just as the day was becoming very hot. Gary and I jumped in the water almost simultaneously, and we swam together in the deepest part of the pool at the foot of the waterfall. It was very cold but lovely and refreshing. The water took my breath away and I climbed out after only a few minutes to sit on a rock. Gary hauled himself from the water and joined me. Claudie and

Wolfie jumped in and splashed about, laughing at Ian, who was standing waist deep at one end of the pool, his top half warm and dry, edging himself slowly deeper into the cold. Claudie splashed him and shouted in her very sexy French accent: "Come on in Ian, it's very nice you know!"

"Ja! It's better to jump in quick!" Wolfie shouted, laughing.

Gary threw his head back in one practised movement, and his long wet black hair slapped onto the top of his back and shoulders. He looked at me with one of his knowing smiles and fumbled about in the pocket of his shirt before offering me a Nelson.

"What are you going to do when you get home, Jonathan?" he asked, teasingly, almost as though he knew full well what the answer was going to be.

"No idea, Gaz," I replied, staring up at the waterfall. The falling water and the rocks looked powerful and resplendent. Blue sky was occasionally visible though gaps in the trees above us, and great thick shafts of golden sunlight fell onto the water, glinting on the surface like a thousand sparkling diamonds. Gary and I sat on the wet rocks, smoking. Our cigarette smoke rose straight above us in the calm, undisturbed coolness by the water. I had no idea what I was going to do. Before I arrived on Dafna my life was virtually planned out for me. I would join the Air Force and fly aeroplanes. That was it. Now I wasn't so sure. I'd met so many people from all around the world, and heard so many interesting stories. I wanted to see some of the places they talked about. I didn't feel ready for the strictures of a military life. I'd tasted freedom and it was wonderful.

My last Friday night *Shabbat* meal in Israel was a fancy dress costume occasion, a 'May Ball'. No-one in our room felt inclined to wear a costume of any sort. Everyone seemed to get very drunk as usual though. I drank quite a lot but curiously didn't seem to reach the same level of inebriation. My mind was preoccupied, constantly filled with thoughts of the future and what was to happen to me. The kibbutz had been a formative experience and an utterly intoxicating one. I was beginning to doubt whether I would ever be completely free of it.

On my last full day, John told us over our sugar puffs at breakfast that he had free use of a tractor for a couple of hours. This was an irresistible invitation. I knew he often had access to a tractor because he was trustworthy, and needed one when working with the cows. Kim, Graham, Chris and I then walked with him over to the *refit* and climbed onto the back of the machine. John drove us three kilometres out the back gates to Kibbutz Dan. I discussed the rock band Genesis with Kim, who I discovered was also a fan. Much to John's disgust I stated I'd decided to cut my hair, at least a little, before going home. From what I can remember, I think Kim trimmed it for me that night. We had a swim in a deep part of the river before clambering back on board and returning to Dafna. Our own pool was finally open, so we jumped straight in. Phil was there, so I asked him to take a photo of me, as I was the very first in the pool.

That afternoon I decided to wander the volunteers' quarters with my diary soliciting autographs. Sadly I couldn't find some people I wanted to see. Some were reluctant to sign my book, and others flatly refused. But I gathered a few anyway.

Appropriately I found John first, and he wrote:

'Words of wisdom here, women are dangerous, I know, so be always on your guard and try to forget them for two minutes a day and maybe you will last a bit longer. All the best and keep that head up! John. *** YORKSHIRE!!***'

I asked Graham for an autograph and he wrote:

'To Biggles and Chrissie. Hope you get married soon and have lots of little Biggles. All the breast, Gray.'

Chris wrote:

'Biggles, have a good time with everything you do in the future. Me and wee Nort will see you again somewhere and we'll check out some more foreign women. Take it easy me old mucker, Chris.'

His girlfriend Raquel was in our room at the time and

scribbled some Hebrew, but unfortunately I am unable to read it or transcribe it here. Kim walked in and she wrote:

'Am I wrong to believe in the City of Gold that lies in the deep distance – welcome home. Good luck and best wishes in all that you do in the future. Make sure Trick of the Tail is the first L.P. you play when you get home or you won't be a true Genesis fan, alright! Phil Collins rules okay! Lots of love, nice to have known ya! Kim.'

I wandered up volunteers' row and found Marianne. She wrote four lines in German. I recognised some words such as *'Supertramp'*, *'Chrissie'* and *'Volunteer'*, but otherwise I have no clue as to what she put. The same happened with Doris, Barclay's girlfriend; being Swiss she wrote five lines in German of which I recognised only one word: *'Conveyor'*.

I found Perry and in capital letters he wrote:

'SHALOM! I HOPE AND WISH YOU A GOOD AND LONG NICE LIFE. IN THIS LIFE WE ARE ALL LIVING TODAY, IT'S HARD AND VERY MUCH A DIFFICULT THING TO BE STRONG, ALSO TO SURVIVE. THE BEST THING FOR ALL OF US TO DO IS TO 'KEEP ON TRUCKING'. GOOD LUCK WITH SINCERITY ALWAYS. PERRY. 5-5-79.'

Perry's Argentinean girlfriend Raquel then wrote nine lines in Spanish, and the only words I recognised were *'Volunteer'*, *'Chrissie'* and *'Israel'*.

Sadly I couldn't find Sick Mick, and Claudie was out somewhere but I found Gary:

'Well Biggles, I hope your hair changes and your character does not. Enjoy your pint in England for me; with luck we'll see you soon. Gary & Claudie. May the Floyd Rule, and bollocks to Ian and the Clash!'

I had to find Ian Anarchist to see if he wanted to counter Gary's entry about The Clash, and he wrote:

'Biggles. The Clash – best rock 'n' roll band of the 70's! May 18 year olds inherit the earth! The revolution shall come! Walsall will stay in the third division!'

I knocked on a few more doors and found San Francisco Mary, who wrote:

'*Remember M, Remember E, put them together and remember ME! Here's mud in the eye! PS. Try and stay 40% sober. Lots of love and kisses love Mary xxxxxxx.*'

Then I found London Graham who was tearing his room apart having just lost his cigarettes:

'*Biggles. The other day I woke up all slack and tingly, wet and slimy. I thought it was you but my candle had melted! But seriously now, any time you are around, you don't have to be invited, please slip, I mean drop in. Lots of love, and be a good girl, Graham.*'

At the bottom end of volunteers' row I tapped on Alan's door and he invited me in. He simply wrote:

'*Make it into the RAF. It's better than picking apples! Alan.*'

The last autograph in my diary was Phil's. I don't think he remembered writing in it before, unofficially, and defacing the top of each page with 'Shit' and 'Bollocks', and so I shouldn't have let him loose on it again, but I did:

'*To Chrissie, big tits Biggles. Hope your leg is better after 4 years in a German P.O.W. camp. His Royal Highness Lt. Col. Philip 1st, King of Dafna, MP, RC, VC, DCM, MBE, CBE etc.*'

Collecting these few autographs took most of the afternoon and early evening. I saw the sun descend behind the Naftali Hills for the last time, just as *Twilight Time* came on *The Voice of Peace*. I actually started to feel uneasy about leaving Dafna. I felt the same emotions then as I had when I first arrived. I felt strange feelings of uncertainty for what lay ahead and a fear of the unknown, just as I had when I stood alone at the gates of the kibbutz six months before. Life on Dafna was solid and predictable, it was safe (at least when not in an air raid!) and constant. It was home from home and would always be there like a guaranteed eternal sanctuary. I didn't need to look for a job or a career, or worry about where my next meal was going to come from. I had friends, companionship, even love if I wanted it.

Friendships made on the kibbutz were real and unpretentious. Amid the harsh prosaic reality of daily kibbutz life, personalities and attitudes were more important than the size of your house, the type of car you drive, how many figures you had in the bank or your family background. All these were irrelevant. We were all stripped bare and exposed for who we really were. This was entirely unique in a modern world where money and material possessions seemed paramount.

HOME

The kibbutz bus left Dafna just after lunch at two o'clock. Unlike everyone else I had my back pack and all my possessions with me. I would guess there were about fifteen of us volunteers who were going to see Elton John, along with about the same number of *kibbutzniks*. As soon as the bus started out of the gates the bottles of vodka punch were passed discreetly around. We drove past Kiryat Shmona bus station where I'd seen Chrissie leave weeks ago. It seemed years since I'd seen her and even her image in the photograph I kept in my wallet began to seem a little distant. I'd almost forgotten what it was like to hear her call my name, though San Francisco Mary did a pretty good job, as her accent was just about the same.

It was hot inside the bus, and as usual the radio was virtually inaudible. We could hear more than the usual amount of Elton John however, and the Israeli disc jockey frequently mentioned his name. I guess it was not every day someone of his stature played in Tel Aviv.

We passed Rosh Pina and Tiberias. I never did get to swim in the Sea of Galilee. We drove up through the Galilee Hills, through the Yizreel Valley and on to Hadera on the Mediterranean coast. The road at this point was wonderful, and the sea looked fantastic. We passed Netanya and arrived in Tel Aviv just before six o'clock. The bus pulled up in the very busy car park of the Mann Auditorium off Dizengoff Street, right in the centre of Tel Aviv. We climbed out of the bus a little worse for wear already, and we made our way to the main entrance. A *falafel* stand nearby caught our attention immediately. We strolled over to it and ordered one each. Tel Aviv was very busy with traffic, buses and a burgeoning nightlife. Dizengoff Street was the first really trendy, cosmopolitan street in Tel Aviv, and was alive with bars and restaurants even then. I bought my last beer in Israel and drank it just before we entered the auditorium.

Elton John was brilliant. He was alone on the stage with an enormous grand piano, while Ray Cooper helped in the background with the percussion, using an array of drums and other instruments. They were on stage for almost three hours and played all the hits. I held up a lit match along with everyone else in the three-thousand-seat concert hall during *Candle in the Wind* and thought of Chrissie when Elton played my favourite: *Your Song*. There was a huge amount of applause for a fantastic performance and yet more applause when he ended with *Crocodile Rock*.

We filed out at just after eleven o'clock. I said goodbye to John, Chris, Barclay, Graham and Kim, Gary and Claudie and Ian. Some of the new volunteers came with me to the airport, to stay the night, so I caught a number twelve bus to the Central Bus Station with Robert (from London), London Graham, Chris (from London), Mary, and Michelle. At the bus station an El Al bus was waiting so we jumped straight on board. We were at the airport twenty minutes later. We found a quiet space in a secluded part of the departure check-in area and spread out our sleeping bags. We talked for a while and each bought a coffee just before the shop closed at midnight. I slept from one o'clock until five o'clock.

The sun was bright and warm at six o'clock in the morning when the others left. They were heading back into the city to spend a day on the beach. I stood outside the departure building in the early morning sun watching the El Al bus as it disappeared into the distance. My last connection with Kibbutz Dafna had gone. For the first time in months I felt truly alone. Even when Chrissie had left I didn't feel quite as solitary as I did at that moment. It was as though my family had abandoned me at the airport.

The Israeli sky was as gorgeous and blue as ever, as it had been that first morning when I sat leaning against the wall outside. I took out my now very tatty copy of *A Postillion Struck by Lightning*, the only book I wanted to keep, and re-

read some of it. I wondered where the last six months had gone.

I checked in my rucksack at the El Al counter after it was thoroughly searched, then obtained my boarding card. I casually exchanged greetings and brief pleasantries in Hebrew with the airline staff. I just had enough money left to pay the 210 *lira* departure tax. At one o'clock the ageing El Al Boeing 707 took off very smoothly from Ben Gurion airport. Just before three o'clock, and when we were well established into the flight, a meal was served. Chicken, peas, fruit juice, and tea with no milk, followed by some cake and biscuits. It all tasted wonderful. I slept for most of the flight after the meal. When I woke up we were over the Austrian Alps, and then France. The aircraft landed with a clean, gentle bump on the ground at Gatwick airport near London at five o'clock, UK time, Monday 7th May. There was no cheering inside the aircraft.

It was fifty degrees Fahrenheit when I arrived back in England, precisely half the number I'd just left. Even though most of the trees still didn't have their new leaves the countryside was incredibly green, though it looked very wet and cold. The streets were clean and orderly and there was no summer dust in the air or on the trees. Houses were in neat rows, and all the people were wearing thick coats and carrying shopping bags and umbrellas instead of kit-bags and machine-guns. Everyone was also driving on the left hand side of the road. There were no soldiers lingering on street corners hitch-hiking, and the atmosphere was cool, bleak and dismal.

My parents picked me up from the airport in their new pale blue Vauxhall Chevette hatchback. They somehow both looked smaller and much older, even in six months. I talked endlessly about Israel, and there's no doubt I must have sounded as though I worked for the Israeli Tourist Board. The three hour journey up the rainy and wet M1 motorway to Sheffield passed very quickly.

When I finally walked into my home, everything appeared smaller but wonderfully rich and luxurious with beautiful ornaments everywhere, and thick, spongy carpet underfoot. I was living in a palace! Huge comfortable chairs were in the living room and there was a *colour* television, and a fridge full of lovely food! Then of course, I had my own private bedroom!

I rang Dave, my best friend, and told him of my arrival. I had a wonderful hot bath, which was my first in six months, if you don't count the one at Hammat Gader hot springs. I put on some different clean clothes for the first time in months. Then I had a huge, amazing meal of roast beef and Yorkshire pudding which I struggled to finish, before stepping out of the house.

I walked the three quarters of a mile to my local pub, The Hare and Hounds. Dave was already there when I walked in. To my horror while I was away, a Space Invaders machine, which looked like a large and very ugly glass-topped coffee table, had been brought into the pub and plonked in the corner where we usually sat. It was the first of many such unwelcome changes. Dave sprang to his feet and shook my hand.

"Sit down, I'll get you a pint," he said, as I sat in our usual spot. I looked disdainfully at the new machine in front of me, which constantly and very rudely flickered and bleeped away to itself. Dave walked over with two pints of pale brown Stones Bitter, and stood them carefully on the glass surface of the awful new table. He sat down and looked at me with a wry smile. He then said:

"Well, what was it like?"

EPILOGUE

I was glad to be home, of course. But this was when the haunting started. I frequently imagined I saw *kibbutzniks* from Dafna walking and driving around the streets of Sheffield in occasional glimpses of passing faces, which for an instant looked familiar. A second look confirmed the olive-skinned man with black curly hair driving past me in a white van was *not* actually Ishi from the factory or Yisrael on his way to collect newspapers from Kiryat Shmona. I was painfully aware I was unlikely to bump into Chris and Graham in the bar of my local pub, and when I felt quietly sociable I couldn't just call in on Sick Mick or Alan for a chat. If I became ill I had to find a doctor. I couldn't simply stroll into the clinic to see my matronly nurse. Life for me had become as gentle and slow moving as a trickling stream, but now it had returned to being a very wide and fast flowing river. Someone had suddenly pressed the 'fast forward' button on the pace of life and I had to make a choice between jumping back in, and looking for a way around.

Four days after arriving home I took a job in a local hotel. It was a chaotic establishment that was in every way similar to *Fawlty Towers*. I was expected to do everything except cook the meals. I served behind the bar, took the food orders, and served the wine and the meals (sadly spilling a lot of it on the customers). I worked a twelve hour day, six days a week for £35. I flew aeroplanes when I could afford to, which was quite infrequently. One highlight was converting onto the four-seat Cessna 172 from the two-seat Cessna 152. I flew over the Derbyshire Dams pretending I was piloting a Lancaster bomber, shouting: 'Lower...lower...lower...bomb gone!' before applying full throttle and climbing away.

On Tuesday 3rd July I resigned from my job at the hotel. The next day, in a state of febrile excitement, I collected Chrissie from my local railway station. Gary and Claudie had returned to the UK and they also visited my parents' house for a weekend while Chrissie was there, along with Ian Anarchist and Mary from Southampton. We had a small 'Dafna Reunion'. Chrissie and I spent a wonderful three weeks together in England before she finally flew home. We remained in touch, and I was to meet her again years later in Adelaide while hitch-hiking around Australia.

I visited Gary and Claudie in Birmingham, and when they returned home I went to see Chris and Graham too. Chris didn't stay very long in England though. He returned to Israel and married Raquel. The last I heard about them was that they were very happy and living in Haifa with their children.

Phil now lives in South Africa with his family. He says he has no recollection of defacing every page of my diary! Tim runs a pub in Yorkshire, and I'm in touch with him, as I am with Phil, via Kibbutz Dafna's *Facebook* page.

Soon after arriving home I wrote to John at his parents' address in Menston near Ilkley, West Yorkshire. Gary told me he had left Dafna and had returned to the UK. Strangely, no-one had heard from him. I was keen to find out what he was up to, and maybe arrange to meet him somewhere. A few days after writing, I received a reply in the form of a brief and clearly very painful letter from his mother. John had been killed while riding his motor-cycle on one of the many winding roads of his beloved Yorkshire. He had apparently left his side-stand down and it had caused the machine to lose grip on a bend not far from his home. He was travelling so fast he must have died instantly when he collided with oncoming traffic. This was devastating news.

On 1st August I spent a wonderful but fruitless ten days hitch-hiking around France. When I returned home I worked night shifts in a supermarket stacking shelves for £36 a week. Then on October 1st 1979 I moved into my own rented room in a tall old town house in Grantham, Lincolnshire, and started work in a job which was perhaps intended to become my life long career: bank clerk. At the end of my first crushingly boring week I bought some Camels, a bottle of Smirnoff vodka, some oranges, and a world map. I realised I was not destined for a career in banking. Most nights I would sit in the nearest pub to where I lived, The Spotted Cow, and drool over my beautiful map, reading all the romantic and exciting place names, listing the fabulous cities I wanted to visit, and things I wanted to see. I began to plan another trip.

Finally, on one very foggy, dark and cold November morning in 1980, I arrived at London's Heathrow airport. I had a rucksack, a change of clothing, a paperback book, a pen, a sketchpad and a diary. In my pocket with my passport was a ticket to Tel Aviv. I wanted to return to that lifestyle I had tasted so briefly on Dafna. I missed it and longed for it like a peremptory but irresistible and alluring mistress. I was no longer a kibbutz virgin. I knew how good the life could be. She was a demanding mistress and I wanted to submit myself to her again. She was in my blood and in my soul. The kibbutz was my adventure and I wanted more of it.

ACKNOWLEDGEMENTS

I'd like to thank Jeremy Thompson and his team at Matador, including Amy Cooke and Sarah Taylor, for helping to get this book into print, and for putting up with my many emails. You've been wonderful and very patient!

I'd like to thank the residents of Kibbutz Dafna in Northern Israel for accommodating me all those years ago. I'm not sure the *kibbutzniks* of Israel fully realised the powerful influence kibbutz life had on the minds of the 400,000 or so volunteers from across the world who passed through the gates of their many *kibbutzim*. This book is a modest attempt at acknowledging this fact, along with my sincere gratitude, which is so often left unsaid. Israel remains under constant attack to this day. I hope there will soon come a time when a lasting peace prevails.

Thanks also to my fellow volunteers named in the book. I've referred to most of them by their real first names. I often joked about writing this book as I sat scribbling away in my diary, so now here it is! We really did have a marvellous time. I hope this book has reminded some people of their own experiences of kibbutz life and rekindled some fond memories.

I'd like to say a big thank you to my wife, Alyson, and my boys, Nick and Jonny. Without a stable family life behind me I doubt I would have been able to sit in my study for months at a time 'like a mad professor' tapping away on the computer.

Finally, thanks to my parents, Betty and Dennis, for their constant encouragement and support. It means more than you probably realise.